ADAPTATION: STUDYING FILM AND LITERATURE

ADAPTATION : STUDYING FILM AND LITERATURE

John M. Desmond

Dutchess Community College

Peter Hawkes

East Stroudsburg University of Pennsylvania

Boston   Burr Ridge, IL   Dubuque, IA   Madison, WI   New York   San Francisco   St. Louis
Bangkok   Bogotá   Caracas   Kuala Lumpur   Lisbon   London   Madrid   Mexico City
Milan   Montreal   New Delhi   Santiago   Seoul   Singapore   Sydney   Taipei   Toronto

The McGraw·Hill Companies

ADAPTATION: STUDYING FILM AND LITERATURE
Published by McGraw-Hill, an imprint of The McGraw-Hill Companies, Inc., 1221 Avenue of the
Americas, New York, NY 10020. Copyright © 2006. All rights reserved. No part of this publication
may be reproduced or distributed in any form or by any means, or stored in a database or
retrieval system, without the prior written consent of The McGraw-Hill Companies, Inc., including, but not limited to, in any network or other electronic storage or transmission, or broadcast for
distance learning.

This book is printed on acid-free paper.

1 2 3 4 5 6 7 8 9 0 DOC / DOC 0 9 8 7 6 5

ISBN 0-07-282204-X

Editor in Chief: Emily Barrosse
Publisher: Lyn Uhl
Senior Sponsoring Editor: Melody Marcus
Executive Marketing Manager: Suzanna Ellison
Developmental Editor: Chris Narozny
Editorial Assistant: Beth Ebenstein
Senior Production Editor: Brett Coker
Manuscript Editor: Sheryl Rose
Design Manager: Kim Menning
Text Designer: Linda M. Robertson
Cover Designer: Yvo Riezebos
Art Editor: Ayelet Arbel
Photo Researcher: Natalia Peschiera
Senior Production Supervisor: Tandra Jorgensen
Lead Media Producer: Shannon Gattens

Composition: 10/12 Palatino by Precision Graphics
Printing: 45# New Era Matte by RR Donnelley, Crawfordsville

Cover photo: © Courtesy Everett Collection/Everett Collection.

Credits: The credits section for this book begins on page C-1 and is considered an extension of the
copyright page.

Library of Congress Cataloging-in-Publication Data

Desmond, John M.
    Adaptation: studying film and literature / John M. Desmond, Peter Hawkes.
    p. cm.
    Includes bibliographical references and index.
    ISBN 0-07-282204-X
    1. Film adaptations. 2. Film criticism. 3. Motion pictures and literature. I. Hawkes, Peter
(Peter Joseph) II. Title.

PN1997.85.D38 2005
791.43′6—dc22

                                                2004059288

The Internet addresses listed in the text were accurate at the time of publication. The inclusion of a
Web site does not indicate an endorsement by the authors or McGraw-Hill, and McGraw-Hill
does not guarantee the accuracy of the information presented at these sites.

www.mhhe.com

ACKNOWLEDGMENTS

The authors would like to thank the late Lowell Butler for desktop publishing our book proposal and Ron Crovisier, Tom Trinchera, and Chris Craig of the Dutchess Community Library and Patricia Jersey of Kemp Library for their assistance in locating articles and books. We would also like to thank East Stroudsburg University's Instructional Resources Staff, especially Frank Kutch and Luis Vidal, as well as Ian Ackroyd-Kelly and Diana Cardwell for their support. Finally, we would like to thank the following reviewers for their thoughtful suggestions: Fredric Dolezal, University of Georgia; Lisa Honaker, Richard Stockton College of NJ; Bill McBride, Illinois State University; Joanna E. Rapf, University of Oklahoma; Hugh Ruppersburg, University of Georgia; Paul Sorrentino, Virginia Tech; and Kenneth Womack, Penn State Altoona.

For my family, Karen, Robert, and Mark, for their patience
and support.
John M. Desmond

For my wife Colleen and my children Harry and Helen, for their
encouragement and support, and in memory of Joseph Carafice,
an aspiring filmmaker whose life was cut short.
Peter Hawkes

CONTENTS

INTRODUCTION

WHY STUDY FILM?

One argument is that film is worth study because it is an art form. It deserves our attention just as music, dance, poetry, painting, and other art forms do. The study of film may reveal the coherence of its elements; uncover human creativity; explain how it expresses beauty, passion, and ideas; or show how it conveys a deeper knowledge of the human condition.

Another argument for studying film is that it offers a reflection on the world around us. Films can both embody and reflect the problems, anxieties, and values of the society that produced them. For example, a war film like *We Were Soldiers* (2002) can reflect on the futility of American battle tactics used in Vietnamese jungles. An allied argument sees film as symptomatic of modern society. Film is a commodity that is dependent on the machine (both the camera and the projector). It is mass produced, mass distributed, mass marketed, and mass consumed. At the levels of production and distribution, film reflects what urbanized, industrialized, capitalist society is like.

Others believe that film should be studied because it is an ideological apparatus that invisibly infiltrates everyday life. Study of mainstream cinema may reveal how it represents gender, class, or race; how it normalizes heterosexuality; how it legitimizes patriarchal values or other forms of thought and feeling promoted by the prevailing ideology.

Whether one believes film has intrinsic value as an art form or as a cultural artifact that holds promise for social or ideological analysis, many believe that film has become the dominant art form in our time. Since it occupies such an important place in our society, film deserves study.[1]

WHAT IS FILM ADAPTATION?

Film **adaptation** is the transfer of a printed text in a literary genre to film. Adaptations may be made from novels, short stories, novellas, plays, nonfiction books, essays, graphic novels, or narrative poems. Even when the adapter attempts to

---

[1]This discussion is indebted to an essay by Richard Dyer.

transfer the original story to film as closely as possible, film is another medium with its own conventions, artistic values, and techniques, and so the original story is transformed into a different work of art. Adaptation, then, is an *interpretation,* involving at least one person's reading of a text, choices about what elements to transfer, and decisions about how to actualize these elements in a medium of image and sound. The comparison of text to film reveals what is distinctive to each form while making clear the different interpretations of the story.

The study of adaptations may sound like a narrow focus within film studies, but it is not. One reason is that there have been so many adaptations made over a century of film history. In any given year, about one-third of all commercial films produced in the United States started as published texts. Film adaptations deserve study not only because of their quantity but also because of their quality. One measure of quality is that the majority of films nominated for Academy Awards in the category of best picture are adaptations. Another measure is the large number of prominent film directors who have made adaptations. And still another indication (although some might dispute it) is that most of the all-time top-grossing films are adaptations.

THE FIDELITY ISSUE

There is another reason adaptation studies have been regarded as narrowly focused. Put simply, the field has been preoccupied with the fidelity issue. The main question asked about adaptations by reviewers and critics alike has been to what degree the film is *faithful* to the text. The practitioners of this approach tend to judge a film's merit based on whether the adaptation realizes successfully the essential narrative elements and core meanings of the printed text. Critics using the fidelity approach often ignore its problems. How is it possible to identify the core meanings of a text when we know literary texts are capable of supporting an indefinite number of interpretations? How can critics make useful judgments about fidelity when there is no agreed-upon method to compare text and film and no standard measure as to how much of the text must be transferred in order for the film to be judged faithful? How can critics assume that fidelity is a measure of cinematic merit when so many close adaptations have resulted in less than memorable movies?

CLASSIFYING ADAPTATIONS

Still, if a film is based on a text, comparisons between the two are inevitable, and certainly this textbook encourages you to make comparisons. However, we use *fidelity* not as an evaluative term that measures the merit of films, but as a descriptive term that allows discussion of the relationship between two companion works. To begin the description of the relationship between text and film, we ask you to compare the two in detail and then to classify the adaptation as a *close, loose,* or *intermediate* interpretation. A film is a close adaptation when most story elements in the literary text are kept in the film and few elements are dropped or added. A film is a loose interpretation when most story elements are dropped and the literary text is used as a point of departure. A film is an intermediate adaptation when it neither conforms exactly nor departs entirely from the literary text but stays in the middle of the sliding scale between close and loose.

There are other such classifications. Michael Klein and Gillian Parker describe three different approaches to adaptation: (1) an adaptation that literally translates "the text into the language of film" [close]; (2) an adaptation that "retains the core of the structure of the narrative while significantly reinterpreting . . . the source text" [intermediate]; and (3) an adaptation "that regards the source merely as raw material, as simply the occasion for an original work" [loose] (9–10).

These and other classification systems move away from relying on fidelity as the single criterion of merit by acknowledging that filmmakers use literary sources in different ways. Identifying the type of adaptation, intended or achieved, should be a part of any critical judgment of the film. The key thing to remember about fidelity is that it is not a useful evaluative term, but it is a useful descriptive term in that it helps to clarify a general relationship between a text and its film adaptation.

ADVANCED INQUIRIES

After you have read a text and viewed the film adaptation, we ask you to note which narrative details are kept, dropped, and added and then to decide whether the film is a close, loose, or intermediate interpretation. However, that determination is not the end point but the starting point—a springboard to launch you into more advanced inquiries. Once you identify the type of interpretation, the next step is to look back at the changes the adapter made, the alternatives available to him or her at the time, and the consequences of the choices made. Asking questions about the adapter's choices will lead you to the wide variety of concerns addressed by contemporary film studies. For example, what technological alternatives were available to the film adapter at this point in **film history?** How did economic or market considerations affect the casting? What impact did film stars have on the filmmaker's choices? What effect did industrial production practices (such as studio audience analysis) have on the adaptation? What role did the Production Code (or some other form of censorship) play? Which narrative elements from the text were easy to transfer to film and which were difficult? How did the literary genre narrow down or open up choices for the filmmaker? How did the adaptation relate to the filmic style of its period? What was the dominant ideology operating in the film? Why was this text—or this kind of text—chosen to be adapted during this period of history? What kinds of sense did differentiated audiences make of the film? In other words, what are some of the technical, narrative, stylistic, historical, and spectatorial contexts that are important in understanding the differences between text and adaptation?

Of course, addressing all the questions raised by contemporary film studies is beyond the scope of any one text. Therefore, we encourage you to focus primarily on a detailed analysis of text and film, and then to move on to whatever larger contexts seem most relevant.

SOME LIMITATIONS

The American Film Institute Catalog lists more than 45,000 feature-length films made in America or financed by American producers from 1893 to 1970. Clearly, no person can expect to see more than a fraction of the films produced here or elsewhere. Therefore, applying a purely inductive method to the study of film adaptation, which would mean viewing all adaptations in all periods in all film-producing societies, would be humanly impossible. Of necessity, we proceed deductively, making generalizations based on the adaptations we have seen and studied. Since our generalizations are based on a limited number of films, they invite refinement, contradiction, and elaboration as you study other adaptations. Bear in mind that adaptation study is an ongoing inquiry.

The textbook has other limits. Film adaptations have been produced for more than a hundred years, and adaptation is a practice found in the more than three dozen film-producing countries. Since film adaptation encompasses such a wide historical and international field, some lines have to be drawn. We choose to discuss mainly modern and contemporary American and British adaptations. This means we do not address such areas as Soviet Social Realism, Italian Neo-Realism, and French New Wave. Since our interest is in narrative cinema, we do not talk about avant-garde films or special types of documentary (such as the newsreel, the travelogue, or the educational film), although occasionally we do discuss TV.

The chapters use many films to explain the problems of adapting a literary genre or to explain the conventions of a film type. These examples are not meant to outline a course but are intended for illustration. At the end of Chapters 5–10 we suggest other adapted films to be studied. The textbook is intended to work with a host of possible film choices made by the course instructor.

Film and literature are compelling contemporary topics. We believe this textbook offers a useful way to explore them.

WORKS CITED

Dyer, Richard. "Introduction to Film Studies." *Film Studies: Critical Approaches.* Ed. John Hill and Pamela Church Gibson. Oxford: Oxford University Press, 2000. 1–8.

Klein, Michael, and Gillian Parker, eds. *The English Novel and the Movies.* New York: Frederick Ungar, 1981.

1 CINEMA'S TURN TO NARRATIVE

Cinema is primarily a storytelling medium, but it wasn't always that way.

Early Cinema History

Historians commonly focus on four areas in recounting the story of early cinema: (1) the technological development of the machines that made cinema possible; (2) film producers' growing awareness of how to use the camera and editing; (3) the changing conditions of film production, distribution, and exhibition; and (4) the shifting responses and demands of spectators as they grew more sophisticated at watching movies. All four areas—technology, filmmaking, the industry, and the audience—played roles in early cinema's shift from realistic scenes and staged performances to a primarily narrative medium.

The advent of cinema in the late nineteenth century was preceded by almost a century of discoveries, collaborations, and rivalries among artists, inventors, and entrepreneurs. The inventions associated with cinematography were developed simultaneously in different countries (primarily in the United States, France, England, and Germany), so there are conflicting claims about who invented cinema. A convenient way to enter the discussion is to begin with the invention of two essential machines: a camera capable of recording motion and a projector capable of showing moving images to an audience.

Although there were important antecedents, many historians agree that the first motion-picture system was developed in the laboratory of the inventor and entrepreneur Thomas Alva Edison. In 1887, Edison had invented the phonograph and wanted a companion apparatus—something that would record and reproduce moving pictures to accompany recorded music. For this purpose, he hired William K. L. Dickson, who did much of the work in inventing the camera. Dickson and Edison spent a fruitless year trying to develop a recording machine modeled on the cylinder, the basis for Edison's phonograph. In 1889, on a trip to Paris, Edison saw Étienne-Jules Marey's camera, which used paper film and a roll mechanism to take a series of photographs at a high speed. Upon Edison's return, Dickson acquired some flexible celluloid film perfected by George Eastman, but work on a new kind of recording device was delayed by other projects. By 1891, Dickson had constructed a motion picture camera called a *Kinetograph,* which was a huge, unwieldy, battery-powered machine that weighed about 500 pounds. Dickson's contributions lay in narrowing the Eastman film by cutting it into one-inch strips (or approximately 35mm, the standard today) and then perforating the film with four holes on each side of a frame so a series of sprockets could advance the photographic film past the camera lens. In order to allow people to see the recorded images, Dickson developed a viewing box, called a *Kinetoscope,* which had a peephole device that created the illusion of moving pictures. The significant limitation of the Kinetoscope was that only one person at a time could view the moving images.

Edison turned to other projects, and so it was entrepreneurs Norman Raff and Frank Gammon who, hearing of the camera, instigated a partnership that led to the marketing of the Kinetoscope. Films were needed for public exhibition, so Dickson took on the job of producing them. Since daylight was often insufficient, the world's first film studio, called the Black Maria, was built at Edison's laboratories in West Orange, New Jersey, in 1893. This shack-like structure had a roof that opened to admit light, a circular track that allowed the whole building to rotate to catch maximal sunlight, and tarpaper walls to act as background for scenes. The earliest movies were short—only 20 seconds long—corresponding to 50 feet of film, the greatest length a Kinetoscope could hold. Scenes showed staged performances, including vaudeville routines, animal acts, athletic displays by acrobats and strongmen, and artistic displays by

The Black Maria, Edison's film studio, located in West Orange, New Jersey, where some of the first American films were shot with a Kinetoscope beginning in 1893.

singers and dancers. Since the 500-pound camera could not be moved easily, each film consisted of a single, unedited, stationary, usually long shot of whatever motion was performed before the camera lens. Edison and his partners offered entrepreneurs the opportunity to buy the Kinetoscope and the Black Maria films for commercial viewing. On April 14, 1894, a Kinetoscope parlor opened in New York City, and its popularity soon led to others being opened across the United States and abroad.

During this period, Edison decided not to move beyond the Kinetoscope to a projection system that would throw large images on a screen for group viewing. In 1891, when he applied for a United States patent to protect the Kinetograph and the Kinetoscope, he decided not to take out an international patent. This meant that inventors in Europe could study and make use of the Edison/Dickson machines for their own designs.

A Kinetoscope exhibitor in France asked Auguste and Louis Lumière, manufacturers of photographic equipment in Lyons, to make films that were cheaper than Edison's. The brothers studied Edison's device and by 1894 invented a system called the Cinématographe. Its main component was a hand-cranked camera, so lightweight and portable that films could be made on location. More important, the camera linked to equipment that projected moving images on a screen for group viewing.

Most film historians mark the beginning of modern cinema on December 28, 1895, when the Lumière brothers used the Cinématographe to show a program of ten silent films at the Grand Café in Paris. This was the first time in history that continuous moving images were projected on a screen for public viewing by a paying audience. Each film consisted of a single unedited shot lasting only one or two minutes. The Lumière brothers captured scenes of everyday life: workers exiting a factory, a train coming into a station, a baby feeding, and laborers knocking down a wall. The films were what the Lumières called *actualités* or documentary views. The significant point is that the Lumière *actualités* were *not* narratives.

Hearing about the Lumières' success, Edison became interested in developing a projector. In 1895, Major Woodville Latham invented the Latham loop. Previously, film from 50 to 100 feet long was likely to break because the take-up reel would jerk, splitting or tearing the film. By placing a loop in the filmstrip that would absorb the jerking action, a much longer piece of film could be projected. In that same year, Thomas Armat and Charles Frances Jenkins developed a projector called the Phantascope that had an intermittent motion device parallel to a camera's. In 1896, the Edison Company bought rights to the Phantascope and marketed it as the Vitascope under Edison's name, even though he had no part in inventing it. This prototype for the modern projector was used in public for the first time on April 23, 1896, at Koster and Bial's Music Hall in New York City. Edison's Vitascope films looked like the Kinetoscope films, but soon after the Bial exhibition, Edison became less dependent on films shot at the Black Maria and sent men with portable cameras to shoot on location. The subjects of these films included street scenes, railway trains, a fire engine, a waterfall, and other outdoor scenes.

There are several reasons why in the mid-1890s the films of Edison, the Lumière brothers, and other filmmakers were primarily nonnarrative in nature, consisting of reproductions of realistic scenes or of staged theatrical performances. The most immediate is that nineteenth-century technology limited the length of a film to the point where it was difficult to tell a story. Early films were short because a film lasting longer than a minute or two would break in most projectors. Since it is difficult to tell a complex story in such a short stretch, the evolution of narrative cinema was tied to the development of projection technology.

Another limit on cinematic storytelling in the mid-1890s was that filmmakers had a primitive understanding of the new medium. It simply did not occur to them to move beyond recording a real or staged event. But even if it had, they did not yet know how to move the camera to tell a story. Whether the camera was as heavy as the 500-pound Kinetoscope or as light as the 16-pound Cinématographe, it was set up as a stationary device. There was only one shot, one point of view, and one scene. It was difficult to tell a story with a beginning, middle, and end using one short scene and a single, motionless, usually long shot to frame the action.

Furthermore, audiences regarded films differently than we do today. At this point in history, film was a novelty, a curiosity, a technological miracle. Viewers were excited by the mere existence of moving pictures. To view a train barreling into a station was utterly astonishing. It wasn't until the novelty wore off that viewers demanded something more sophisticated.

Perhaps a more important difference between early audiences and today's is that the earliest viewers saw films as motion-animated photographs within a frame. Each scene was viewed as a self-contained unit. It was only with the development of multiscene movies and continuity editing that viewers learned to make connections between one scene and the next and to view multiple incomplete scenes as adding up to a story.

This is not to say that there were not early examples of embryonic narratives. Many film historians claim an early Lumière short *Le Jardinier et le petit espiègle* (1895) (later entitled *Arroseur Arrosé* or "The Waterer Watered") anticipates narrative cinema. This one- to two-minute, single-shot film adapted a well-known newspaper cartoon. In it, a gardener waters his lawn with a hose. A boy steps on the hose, deliberately shutting off the water supply. When the man looks closely at the nozzle to see what is wrong, the boy steps off the hose, causing the man to squirt himself in the face. Realizing the trick, the man runs after the boy and spanks him.

One of the filmmakers given credit for introducing a storytelling dimension to film in the period between 1895 and 1900 is George Méliès, a former magician, who produced films that astonished audiences with their special effects. Méliès, unlike Edison, the Lumières, and other early film producers, came from an entertainment background, and so adapting theatrical conventions to the new medium was natural for him. When Méliès first began making films in 1896, he shot everyday scenes, travelogues, and magic tricks, but soon he experimented with film in ways that took him outside the domain of documentary views and staged performances. One technique was stop-motion photography, a procedure in which the camera is stopped during a shot, a change is made in the scene, and then the camera resumes shooting. In this way, Méliès was able to make an object or a human disappear, move, multiply, or be replaced. In *The Vanishing Lady* (1896), for example, a seated woman is replaced by a skeleton.

Méliès soon began filming a series of theater-like scenes he called "tableaux." A scene was shot, the camera stopped, and then an entirely *new* scene was shot from the same angle. He developed transition devices to connect the scenes: the fade-in, fade-out, and several kinds of dissolve. Méliès' first multiscene film was *The Dreyfus Affair* (1899), based on contemporary events. However, *A Trip to the Moon* (1902), an adaptation of Jules Verne's *From the Earth to the Moon* and H. G. Wells's *First Men in the Moon,* became his most popular and influential film. This 14-minute, 825-feet-long film contains 30 separate scenes. The 30 tableaux are connected by a transition device called the lap dissolve in which the first scene slowly fades out and the next scene slowly fades in with some overlap between the two scenes. The most famous tableau is an animation scene of a rocket hitting the "man in the moon." Events in *A Trip* are

One of George Méliès' special effects: a rocket hitting the "Man in the Moon" right in the eye in *A Trip to the Moon* (1902).

presented in a sequence, but, as some critics point out, a story is a series of *causally related* events. In that sense, *A Trip* is more a theatrical spectacle than a narration.

In the period between 1895 and 1903, cinema was not primarily a story-telling medium. Certainly, there were some narrative films; however, until around 1904 early cinema saw storytelling as a subordinate task. The development in early silent film, then, was from a cinema of everyday life and of staged entertainments to, by 1908, a cinema that clearly focused on the development of characters and stories (Gunning 6).

Audiences, Production, and Distribution

We have looked briefly at how the possibilities of cinematic narration in the mid-1890s were limited by the state of film technology, film producers' primitive understanding of the medium, and spectators' viewing habits. But *why* was there a shift sometime after the turn of the century from the coexistence of different cinematic entertainments—*actualités*, comic vaudeville acts, theatrical pieces, topical historical events, short travelogues, sporting events, and early stories—to a medium that was primarily narrative? What decisively tipped the balance in favor of cinema as storytelling?

Robert C. Allen explains that one answer to the question is public interest. Early multiscene films that established continuity among shots, such as Edwin S. Porter's *Life of an American Fireman* (1903) and *The Great Train Robbery* (1903), were highly popular with audiences. *The Great Train Robbery,* which lasts about

Robbers hold their guns on the conductor in one of the scenes from the multiscene *The Great Train Robbery* (1903), one of the first narrative films.

twelve minutes, consists of fourteen shots that, although incomplete scenes in themselves, are linked in time and space and arranged in narrative order. Audiences liked the dramatic suspense and excitement of Porter's realistic narratives. And that popular demand for narrative was communicated by exhibitors to film producers.

Allen also claims that the needs of the growing film industry shifted production toward narrative. After Edison's Vitascope exhibition in 1896 at Koster and Bial's, the Vitascope was not available for sale, but rights to its use were sold to exhibitors. Exhibitors bought film prints outright from Edison and other film producers and showed them as traveling exhibitions. Exhibitions were irregularly scheduled and took place at a variety of temporary sites: vaudeville halls, storefronts, music halls, bars, amusement parks, and even churches. But soon film exhibition in this country became most commonly associated with vaudeville where a program of about ten films was considered a complete act.

For a period, itinerant exhibitors moving from place to place coexisted with permanent vaudeville halls. The traveling showmen had an economic advantage over the theaters. The itinerant exhibitor could show the same program of about ten films to new audiences. The permanent theaters, however, had fixed local audiences. To keep viewers coming, the theaters had to purchase new films in order to vary their programs. To solve this problem, a new middleman system evolved whereby distributors bought prints from producers and rented them to exhibitors, allowing permanent theaters to vary their programs with less cost because they no longer had to buy prints outright.

One consequence of the new rental system was the movement of film exhibition from vaudeville theaters, where they constituted only a part of the performance, to storefront operations called nickelodeons that were devoted solely to film exhibition. Nickelodeons derived their name from the original 5-cent price of admission. They sprang up in large numbers across the country, increasing from a few in 1904 to almost ten thousand over the next four years. By 1910, the nickelodeons drew huge crowds, "attracting some twenty-six million Americans every week, a little less than 20 per cent of the national population" (Merritt 86). During the nickelodeon boom, production companies multiplied their weekly output of film footage but still could not keep up with demand.

Under pressure for new films, producers came to realize that narrative films had several advantages over nonfiction films. Filmmakers intent on documenting a topical or sporting event had to wait until the event happened and then bear the cost of transporting men and equipment to the location, possibly during uncertain weather. Furthermore, events of great popular interest—elections, battles, tornadoes and floods—did not happen on a weekly schedule. With fictional films, production companies could avoid the delay, uncertainty, and expense of location shooting. Stories could be written and filmed as needed—producers didn't have to wait for anything, and they could shoot locales owned by the studios. It was simply cheaper and more convenient to make narrative films than documentary films. According to copyright records, by 1908, 96 percent of all films were either comic or dramatic narratives (Allen 212). Thus, in the early days of cinema, public enthusiasm and the needs of an emerging commercial industry provided the impetus for film to become a predominately narrative medium.

Why Adapt a Text?

If by 1908 cinema had reoriented itself to the task of storytelling, with its future set as a narrative art form, how does adaptation relate to this historical development?

First of all, when film production companies needed material to meet the growing demand for narrative movies, one alternative was to turn to short stories, novels, and plays. Here were ready-made scenes, plots, and characters. It was easier to adapt existing stories and plays than to invent new scenarios. Furthermore, authors of literary texts did not have to be paid for film rights since copyright laws at the time did not cover motion pictures.

Another reason for adaptation in the early period of cinema was to borrow literature's prestige for the new art form. Nickelodeons were mainly concentrated in manufacturing cities with large populations of blue-collar workers and immigrants. Men and women working long hours in the factories found film viewing a relatively inexpensive form of pleasure and escape, and silent films were popular with immigrants because they posed no language problems. One contemporary survey reveals that "in 1911, 78 per cent of the New York [City] audience consisted of members 'from the working class' " (Merritt 87). Early on, nickelodeon owners sought to attract the middle class to their theaters. One way was by encouraging producers to make films that would appeal to middle-class women and children. Adaptation of classic literary works was a marketing device that exhibitors used to draw the middle class. Adapting such prestigious writers as Shakespeare, Zola, Tolstoy, Hugo, Dante, Dumas, and Dickens became a way to achieve a kind of legitimacy for filmgoing.

A third reason for adaptation comes from the notion that the purpose of motion pictures is to teach the masses about their literary heritage. In this view, film is a pedagogical medium useful for introducing literary masterpieces to contemporary audiences. The pedagogical view is more commonly held in England, where generations of film producers have adapted the Great Books. There have been so many British adaptations of Shakespeare that at times they are regarded as a separate category in adaptation studies. Other frequently adapted British authors include Charles Dickens, Jane Austen, the Brontë sisters, Thomas Hardy, Joseph Conrad, Virginia Woolf, D. H. Lawrence, and E. M. Forster. Director James Ivory, producer Ismail Merchant, and screenwriter Ruth Prawer Jhabvala have made successful careers by regularly adapting canonical works. And both the BBC and PBS reflect the pedagogical view when they adapt literary classics and then issue online study guides.

But the most common reason that commercial filmmakers adapt a printed text is that they believe the film will make money. Today a film from a major Hollywood studio costs an average of a hundred million dollars to produce and market. The rising cost of the Hollywood movie is likely to continue. A-list actors such as Tom Cruise and Julia Roberts are paid ever-increasing sums because studios know box-office hits are usually star-driven. Likewise, some directors are being rewarded with huge salaries and a percentage of gross profits. Peter Jackson, director of *The Lord of the Rings* trilogy (2001–2003), received $20 million and 20 percent of the gross receipts for his remake of *King Kong* (2005). In movies such as *The Matrix Reloaded* and *Terminator 3: Rise of the Machines* (2003), special effects are as expensive as stars, with better effects needed each year to attract viewers. Marketing spending has also ballooned because of increasingly expensive TV advertising.

Ticket prices have risen as well, but domestic receipts rarely cover movie costs. Today studios know the bulk of a film's revenue will come from worldwide release, DVDs, videocassettes, network and cable TV, soundtrack albums, video games, and commercial tie-ins.

Despite new revenue sources, filmmaking remains a big gamble. Hollywood executives know they cannot pretest the market before they make a movie and they know that they produce far more disasters than hit films. How can they predict which project will make back its initial investment and then some? With budgets dauntingly high, executives tend to green-light projects that minimize risk, such as prequels, sequels, remakes, special-effects extravaganzas, and adaptations.

Film companies know that literary texts, whether classics from the Western canon or popular literature likely never to enter the canon, are good candidates for filmmaking because their stories have already proven to be enjoyable to many people. A story's popularity comes in two ways: It can be popular over time to many generations—a literary classic; or, it can be widely popular to a contemporary audience—a best seller. The popularity of either kind of text is likely to translate into a box office success, or at least that's the basic assumption.

The classic story has proved it can hold audience appeal over time, and the marketing of the film will benefit from name recognition of the author, title, or story. Think of the many adaptations made of Shakespeare's plays or Dickens's novels. Similarly, the bestseller is "pre-kissed," meaning it has a wide audience already and one that is likely to follow the story into the theater. Recent examples of bestsellers that have drawn huge film audiences include J. K. Rowling's *Harry Potter* series and J. R. R. Tolkien's trilogy *The Lord of the Rings*. One thinks also of best-selling novels like John Grisham's *The Firm*, Michael Crichton's *Jurassic Park*, Tom Clancy's *The Hunt for Red October*, and Robert James Waller's *The Bridges of Madison County*. Today, whether the work is a classic story or a best seller, it most likely reaches the screen because studio executives believe it is a safe bet to make money.

A less common reason for adaptation, but one worth mentioning, is that a powerful person (say, a producer, star, or director) becomes committed to a text. For example, Oprah Winfrey was the leading force behind the adaptation of Toni Morrison's *Beloved*. Soon after the novel was published, Winfrey acquired the film rights. She hired at least three screenwriters over the next ten years to adapt the story, and, after it was finally made in 1998, ceaselessly promoted it. Steven Spielberg optioned Thomas Keneally's novel *Schindler's List*, developed the project over a decade, and then directed the film *Schindler's List* (1993), which allowed him to make a personal, public, and artistic statement about the Holocaust and genocide in general. Mel Gibson spent $30 million of his own money and used his Hollywood influence and connections to make *The Passion of the Christ* (2004), a film that shows the last twelve hours of Jesus' life, based on incidents from the four Gospels. " 'There was no way this movie wasn't going to happen,' " Gibson said. " 'I just know that I was compelled to (make it)' " (Cava 1).

Cinema's early turn to narrative and its sustained use of literary texts for more than a hundred years have given the opportunity to adapt to countless

The controversial adaptation *The Passion of the Christ* (2004) made it to the screen because of Mel Gibson's personal commitment.

directors, screenwriters, producers, and studios. Filmmakers will continue to make adaptations for various and overlapping reasons, but never without encountering difficulty in negotiating the differences between the two art forms. Some of these differences will be discussed in Chapter 3.

WORKS CITED

ALLEN, ROBERT C. *Vaudeville and Film 1895–1915: A Study in Media Interaction.* New York: Arno Press, 1980.

CAVA, MARCO R. DELLA. "Gibson Personalizes 'Passion of the Christ.' " *USA Today* 20–22 Feb. 2004: 1+.

GUNNING, TOM. *D. W. Griffith and the Origins of American Cinema: The Early Years at Biograph.* Chicago: University of Illinois Press, 1991.

MERRITT, RUSSELL. "Nickelodeon Theaters, 1905–14: Building an Audience for the Movies." *The American Film Industry.* Ed. Tino Balio. Madison: University of Wisconsin Press, 1985. 83–102.

2 LITERARY AND FILM TERMS

Cinema's turn to narrative was not inevitable. Cinema could have developed into a documentary form or some kind of non-narrative sound and image entertainment. But in the twenty-first century, most films tell stories. Because films are primarily fictional narratives, they require an understanding of terms traditionally associated with literature. Of course, films use images and sound in ways that go far beyond verbal language, so the student needs to understand the basic terms and techniques of filmmaking as well. Without such terms, it would be hard to describe how film adaptation works, just as it would be hard to describe how a computer works without a technical vocabulary. The important terms are defined in this chapter and at the end of the book in the glossary. Keep in mind that literary and film critics have developed far more elaborate definitions than the ones introduced here.

Literary Terms

Because screenwriters often reorder the events in a story to be adapted, it is useful to keep in mind a distinction between **story** and **plot**. The *story* is a succession of events involving characters told in chronological order. But *plot* refers to the selection and arrangement of events so that they are interdependent and causally related and their outcome, given the characters and initial situation, seems inevitable. The story's happenings, then, are raw material. Plot selects the happenings, puts them in some sequential order (not necessarily chronological), and establishes causality.

In *Aspects of the Novel*, E. M. Forster gives a now famous example of this distinction between story and plot. According to Forster, to say that "the king died and the queen died" is to tell a story because the two events are not logically related. But to say that "the king died and then the queen died of grief" is to establish a plot. The added three words explain that an event happened and that it had a consequence. The causal link converts story into plot.

Plot is a structural device that enables the author and screenwriter to maintain causal links while presenting events outside the constraints of chronological order. For example, an author or adapter need not start at the beginning of the story but can begin *in medias res* (in the middle of things) and then flash back to show past events that led up to the present, or flash forward to indicate future consequences. A screenwriter may also decide to rearrange events so that the source's ending becomes the film's beginning. For example, *The Ice Storm* (1997), directed by Ang Lee, begins with the ending of Rick Moody's novel of the same name and then backs up to the period before the deadly ice storm. These changes in chronological order are often made to elicit emotional reactions such as surprise or suspense or an impending sense of doom.

Plot is usually divided into three parts following Aristotle's *The Poetics:* a beginning, a middle, and an end. Some critics use Gustav Freytag's expanded definition of Aristotle's tripartite structure: **exposition, rising action, climax, falling action,** and **catastrophe.** (The last event is also called **resolution** or **dénouement**). The exposition or introduction establishes the place and time of the action, introduces the character or characters, gives any necessary background information, and establishes the mood or tone of the story. The rising action introduces a conflict, or complication, that intensifies the original situation and moves towards a major turning point or climax. The downward or falling action shows events going from bad to worse, leading to some final reversal of fortune for the protagonist.

There are other forms of plot one can identify that are not dominated by cause and effect. A **nontraditional plot** may present events in nonlinear sequence, use coincidence rather than causality to link events, and leave the resolution indeterminate or open-ended. William S. Burroughs's novel *Naked Lunch* is an example of nonlinear narration.

Some stories consist of a series of episodes that are loosely related by the presence of a hero, a specific location, a theme, or a historical event. An example of an **episodic plot** is Henry Fielding's eighteenth-century novel *The History of Tom Jones, a Foundling.* The first section of the novel is set at the country home of Tom's guardian Squire Allworthy; the middle chapters describe a complicated set of adventures that takes place on the roads to London; and the final third of the novel is set in London. What ties together the settings and scenes is the presence of the title hero.

Plots are sometimes distinguished by their mood and outcome. **Comic plots** usually end with a happy event such as the marriage in Shakespeare's *As You Like It,* whereas **tragic plots** may end with the protagonist's isolation and death as in Shakespeare's *Macbeth.* **Subplots** are minor or subordinate actions often used to contribute interest and action to the main plot.

Some critics identify character rather than plot as the defining feature of narrative. In this view, plot is a framework of actions that focuses attention on character. The character's desires, motives, or goals lead to action. However, when someone claims a story is more character-driven than plot-driven, keep in mind that character and action are often so intertwined that it is difficult to distinguish between the two. In sophisticated narratives, action grows out of character and character grows out of action.

Character is a personality on paper or film. In literary fiction, characters are often described both *outwardly* and *inwardly.* We come to know one through what he or she does, says, and looks like, or through the opinions and reactions of others. We may also get to know a character inwardly through an omniscient author's presentation of the character's thoughts and feelings or through a narrator's direct commentary. In film, however, characters are usually portrayed *outwardly only*—through their appearance, dress, speech, expressions, gestures, and movements, or through the reactions and comments of other characters. Filmmakers use camera movement and angles, lighting, color contrasts, editing, and other devices to reveal character. But unless a device such as a voiceover is used, we don't know *exactly* what the character is thinking nor do we hear a narrator's direct comments on the character's inner life.

Forster distinguishes between flat and round characters. A **flat character** is a one-dimensional type, known by a single idea or quality; in contrast, a **round character** possesses the multidimensional qualities of actual people. Characters can also be divided into **static characters,** who do not change, and **developing characters,** who do. The terms suggest that both literary and screen characters can be distinguished by their complexity and depth. Many are single-trait characters who exist on the surface; others are defined by a number of traits and suggest inner states of thought and feeling that sometimes are in conflict. For example, in Dashiell Hammett's *The Maltese Falcon,* Sam Spade's partner Miles Archer is a flat character distinguished by his sexual interest in a female client and his greed for money, but Spade is much more layered: he is a tough, cynical detective who displays a number of inner conflicts, such as his dislike for his partner but his loyalty to him after Miles is killed.

When a specific character seems to be the focus of the story, he or she is called a **protagonist.** Hester Prynne is the protagonist in Nathaniel Hawthorne's *The Scarlet Letter,* and Othello is the protagonist in Shakespeare's *Othello.* If the protagonist is in a major conflict with another character, that character is called the **antagonist.** An example is Iago, who, resentful at being passed over for promotion, makes Othello jealous in order to undermine him.

Setting is the geographical place, the historical time, and the social milieu in which the characters live and act. It includes the cultural and historical conditions that provide an intellectual and emotional context for the characters' thoughts and beliefs. Charles Dickens's *A Christmas Carol* is set in early nineteenth-century London, among the middle and lower classes, and Mark Twain's *The Adventures of Huckleberry Finn* is set in Hannibal, Missouri, and along the Mississippi River during the antebellum South, among several classes of river-town folk.

Point of view refers to the vantage point from which a narrative is presented. To decide on point of view, ask, "Who is telling the story?" and "Are we told the inner thoughts and feelings of the characters?" Literary works sometimes combine points of view, but the most common are the **first person** and the **third person.** In first-person narration, the narrator refers to himself or herself as "I" and is a major or minor character, or merely a witness of events. "Call me Ishmael," the famous first line of Herman Melville's novel *Moby-Dick,* signals to the reader that events will be filtered through Ishmael's eyes.

Third-person narration uses the pronouns "he," "she," and "they" to tell the story. This point of view has two important subdivisions: (1) the **omniscient** or all-knowing narrator and (2) the **third-person limited** or **limited-omniscient** narrator. The omniscient narrator has complete knowledge of the inner and outer lives of all of the characters and is able to move freely from one to another. This narrator may also choose to comment directly on the characters or their actions. Omniscient narrators are often subdivided into **intrusive—** those who make judgments on characters or actions as they are presented—or **unintrusive** or **impersonal**—those who introduce characters or events neutrally without evaluation.

Third-person limited or limited-omniscient narration presents the story as it is seen, thought, felt, or remembered by one or more characters. Often, the author restricts knowledge to what a single character knows and perceives and does not go into the minds of other characters. Many famous novels have used the omniscient point of view—for example, Gustave Flaubert's *Madame Bovary,* Thomas Hardy's *Tess of the d'Urbervilles,* and Leo Tolstoy's *War and Peace.* Other literary works have used the more restrictive limited-omniscient narration, such as Stephen Crane's *The Red Badge of Courage,* Melville's "Benito Cereno," Henry James's *The Ambassadors,* and James Joyce's "The Dead."

There is also the **objective or dramatic** point of view, which uses the third person and is limited to recounting what characters say or do. The objective narrative does not relate what characters think or feel nor comment directly on their actions. The story is told almost completely through dialogue. Ernest Hemingway's short stories "Hills Like White Elephants" and "The Killers" are examples of the objective point of view.

Determining point of view helps in understanding a story. For the first-person narration, ask, "Who is the narrator? How does his or her personality shape the story? Is the narrator accurate or is the reader expected to see the narrator as untrustworthy and discount his or her interpretations of events?" For the omniscient point of view, ask, "Does the author use the omniscient point of view for its flexibility in shifting point of view or for its ability to reveal maximal information about the inner lives of all of the characters in a work?" For the limited omniscient, ask, "Does the author choose this point of view because there is information the author wants to withhold from the reader in order to achieve an artistic effect such as mystery or suspense?"

Like literary works, films narrate stories from a certain perspective, and recognizing a film's point of view can be important in interpreting its meaning. The most common points of view in film parallel those in literature: first person, omniscient, and limited omniscient. However, it is difficult to apply the literary definitions of point of view directly to film because the two forms express point of view differently and because literature and film have different capacities for conveying perspective. Therefore, many critics talk about analogies or parallels between literary and cinematic points of view.

In a literary work, the first-person point of view is made clear through the narrator's sustained use of "I." For example, in J. D. Salinger's novel *The Catcher in the Rye,* readers are constantly reminded that events are filtered through the single consciousness of Holden Caulfield by his distinctive teenage "voice." To replicate first-person narration, a film adapter often uses (1) the narrator's voice in a **voiceover**—an offscreen voice that supplies background or commentary on screen images—and (2) visual strategies to identify the camera with the narrator's perspective. For example, many adaptations are based on first-person retrospective narratives in which a character in the present recalls events from the past. To suggest this point of view, a film may begin with a narrative frame that briefly introduces the narrator in the present before he or she becomes a participant in the story's *past* events. The transition from present to past usually is handled by a voiceover and a **dissolve**—the end of one shot superimposed on the beginning of another. The beginning of *Double Indemnity* (1944) shows an office scene in which the narrator, insurance salesman Walter Neff, speaking into a Dictaphone, confesses a murder he committed "for money and for a woman." "It all began last May," he says, as the office dissolves into a exterior scene showing Neff driving up to that woman's house "to check," his voiceover explains, "about an auto renewal." The voiceover and the office scene return throughout the movie to remind the audience of point of view until the end when past events catch up to Neff's present, and he is shown slumped in his office chair, wounded and bleeding, talking directly to the claims officer investigating the case. The use of the narrative frame, voiceover, and dissolve help to establish and sustain the film's first-person narration.

Another common strategy in narrated films is to use a series of shots to tie the camera to the narrator's field of vision. Point-of-view shots may show the narrator looking at something offscreen, followed by a shot of the space toward which the character is looking (using the narrator's visual perspective), and then a shot of the narrator's reaction to what is seen. Although the camera's positions in the first and third shots are not identical with the narrator's physical position, the shots, taken together, suggest that events are seen through his or her eyes.

In narrated films, the knowledge the audience is given may be restricted to what the narrator knows or could know. This can be done by having the camera show only scenes the narrator is involved in and not showing scenes where the narrator is not included or those the narrator could not know about. Through these and other strategies, viewers are led to see that the story depends on the narrator's perspective and that the events are shaped by this character's values and attitudes. However, in film, the first-person point of view is hard to sustain. Even when reminded by voiceovers, viewers forget that the events are filtered through a character because the camera shows them as if they were unfolding directly before the viewers' eyes.

The most common point of view used in films is some form of third-person narration. Third-person omniscient narration tells the story from multiple perspectives signaled by frequent shifts in camera position. The camera moves freely from one character to another, from one place to another, and from one angle to another without identifying itself with any one character's point of view. Omniscient narration need not restrict the audience's knowledge as in first-person and limited-omniscient narration. In fact, sometimes the audience is given more knowledge of a situation than the characters in the scene, which is often the case in horror and suspense films. For example, in *Jaws* (1975), directed by Steven Spielberg, theme music by John Williams is used to signal the approach of a shark, letting the audience know of the danger before the vulnerable swimmer does. The omniscient perspective knows all and can decide to withhold details or give them to the audience, but whatever information is given does not need to come through any single character.

Filmmakers sometimes use the third-person, limited-omniscient point of view, where the camera shows events mainly from the perspective of one or two characters. For example, *Rear Window* (1954), directed by Alfred Hitchcock, concerns Jeff, a magazine photographer, who breaks his leg and is confined to a wheelchair in his New York City apartment. While he recuperates, Jeff views his apartment neighbors out his "rear window," which looks out on a courtyard, through the telephoto lens of his camera. Most camera angles are shot from Jeff's apartment, so the audience is mainly restricted to his point of view.

Of course, with this point of view, the camera may still act at times as an omniscient narrator by offering information outside the view of the main characters.

Most films tell stories using thousands of shots from different angles. These films repeatedly shift among the three main points of view to achieve different aesthetic effects. The questions to ask are, "What point of view is being used in this series of shots?" and, when the perspective shifts, "Why did the director decide to change the point of view in this sequence?"

Another important literary figure useful for film analysis is the symbol. A **symbol** is something in a text or in a film that represents something else, often an idea or an attitude. Symbols can be objects, persons, places, or events. For example, an American flag is a physical object, usually made of cloth, but it stands for an entire nation. The symbol is not simply verbal. It is some element represented as physically present in a work of art but that nonetheless signifies something beyond its literal meaning.

Symbols derive their associations from long tradition or acquire their meanings from their use in a specific work of art. For example, through long association, a crossroads traditionally means a decision, a rose represents love, and spring and winter suggest birth and death. But authors and filmmakers can go beyond the use of these universal symbols to create their own by stipulating a link between a specific thing, person, place, or event and a general idea. For example, Hawthorne's use of the scarlet "A" makes it stand, at least initially, for adultery; Hemingway's use of rain in *A Farewell to Arms* associates it with death; and Orson Welles's use of the sled "Rosebud" in *Citizen Kane* (1941) associates it with Kane's lost childhood.

The main idea, or the central generalization, implied or stated in a work is called the **theme.** For example, the subject of a mystery may be homicide, but the theme or "message" may be that crime never pays or that everyone must respect limits. The dominating idea or generalization is made tangible through its depiction in character, action, and imagery. Most complex works have a number of themes, and when making statements about them, care must be taken to present supporting evidence. Some recent critics question whether a work contains an identifiable theme or set of themes and stress instead the indeterminacy of texts.

Film Terms

The following terms describe basic elements used in telling a story cinematically. The terms refer to four main areas of film: (1) mise-en-scène, (2) camerawork, (3) editing, and (4) sound.

Mise-en-Scène

Mise-en-scène refers to all elements placed before the camera. These elements include sets, costumes, lighting, makeup, props, placement of objects and people, and the actors' gestures and movements.

Alan Ladd as the title character in *Shane* (1953) dressed in buckskins, a costume suggesting the time and place of action as the American West of the nineteenth century.

Sets are real or artificially constructed places used as background for actions. They are the physical space shown by the camera in which the actors move. For example, the detective office in *The Maltese Falcon* (1941) was artificially constructed on a sound stage at Warner Bros. Studios; however, the Big Blackfoot River, portrayed in *A River Runs Through It* (1992), was shot on location on five different rivers in Montana. Although sets in films often appear natural or accidental, they are carefully selected and controlled by set designers who, in conjunction with the director, cinematographer, and others, wish to achieve certain visual effects in telling a story.

Costuming is the clothing worn by actors. The clothes can be contemporary or historical, suggest the time and place of the action, indicate a character's social status, and contribute to the color scheme of the film. For example, Alan Ladd as the title character in *Shane* (1953) dresses in a light-colored buckskin shirt and pants, suggesting the frontier period of the film and his social distinction from the denim-clad farmers he defends.

Left: Nicole Kidman, a glamorous star, arriving at the Critics' Choice Awards, January 17, 2003, in Beverly Hills, California. Right: Virginia Woolf, the British novelist, crtitic, and essayist, ca. 1936.

Lighting is the illumination of actors and sets in the production of a film. A cinematographer decides whether the light is natural or artificial, the direction it should take, and its intensity. Lighting can direct attention toward major areas of interest such as an actor's face. An example is the light flaring up from the just-struck match that illuminates the sinister visage of Perry Smith as played by Robert Blake in *In Cold Blood* (1967).

Lighting also can help create mood and atmosphere through its design. The major types are high- and low-key lighting. With **high-key lighting,** a scene is brightly lit and shadows kept at a minimum. High-key lighting generally creates a buoyant and joyful mood and is often used in comedies and musicals such as *South Pacific* (1958), *My Fair Lady* (1964), and *The Sound of Music* (1965). With **low-key lighting,** a scene is dimly lit and there is a good deal of shadow. Low-key lighting creates a darker, harsher, and more somber mood and is often used in mystery, horror, drama, and science fiction films such as *The Big Sleep* (1946), *Alien* (1979), *Apocalypse Now* (1979), and *Blade Runner* (1982).

Makeup emphasizes the mobile—and thus meaningful and representative— elements of an actor's face. The cosmetics enhance or change an actor's natural appearance in a way appropriate to the role he or she is playing. An example of a challenging assignment was the use of a prosthetic nose and makeup to

Nicole Kidman, made up as Virginia Woolf in *The Hours* (2003), illustrates how an actor's natural appearance might be altered to suit the role he or she is playing.

transform the glamorous Nicole Kidman into the plain-looking character of author Virginia Woolf in *The Hours* (2002).

Props are any items employed on a set or in a scene. These objects can be a stationary part of the set such as a table or a chair, or moveable items like a book or a vase. The selection, placement, and movement of props can reinforce the realism or authenticity of the setting and add meaning to a film. For example, the childhood objects placed in the opening montage of *To Kill a Mockingbird* (1962) may suggest to viewers that the story will concern childhood experiences and even a child's point of view.

Camerawork

The **shot** is the basic unit of film. The shot is a single, continuous run of the camera that records an uninterrupted action that viewers see on the screen. Shots are generally divided into four types according to how much of the human figure is shown: long shot, medium shot, close-up, and extreme close-up. The three most important shots to be able to identify are the **long shot,** which shows the full human figure of a character or characters within an environment; the **medium shot,** which shows a character or characters from the knees up within part of the setting; and the **close-up,** which shows the full head and shoulders of a character or an object in detail. For example, in *Quiz Show* (1994), a long shot shows the set of the game show *Twenty-One* with the two contestants standing inside their separate, soundproof booths and the game-show host standing at a podium just below them, thus establishing the configuration of the three principal characters in the scene. Later in the scene, a close-up shot of one of the contestants deciding on an answer to a question shows the real (or, as revealed even later in the film, pretend) anguish on the contestant's face.

Camera angle is the camera's position in relation to the subject being photographed. There are three main angles: the **high angle,** in which the camera looks down on the subject; the **straight-on** or **eye-level angle,** in which the camera looks straight ahead at the subject; and the **low angle,** in which the camera looks up at the subject. Within the context of the film, camera angles may add meaning to the subject being filmed. For example, a high-angle shot may diminish a character and make him or her seem helpless and vulnerable. A low-angle shot may make a figure seem towering and powerful. A straight-angle shot usually suggests neutrality toward the subject. In *All the President's Men* (1976), a high-angle shot of Carl Bernstein and Bob Woodward sitting at a desk and searching through withdrawal slips from the Library of Congress diminishes the two men within the enormous space of the room and minimizes their significance as reporters from the *Washington Post* who seek answers to the Watergate affair. Later in the film, Woodward and a male friend of his with close contacts within the Nixon administration, whom Woodward nicknames "Deep Throat," meet in a parking garage late at night. The low-angle shots of the two men talking conspiracy increase their physical stature and enlarge the significance of their illuminating discussions.

Camera movement refers to any motion of the camera that changes the camera's perspective on its subject. Common camera movements include tilting, panning, tracking, and crane shots. A **tilt shot** involves the camera moving upward or downward, thereby scanning the scene vertically while remaining fixed on a tripod or mount. For example, a tilt shot may follow a person ascending or descending a flight of stairs. In *Double Indemnity,* after Walter Neff has killed Mr. Dietrichson, he returns to his apartment by climbing the back stairway, so as not to be seen. The camera tilts upward as it follows Neff's surreptitious climb toward apparent freedom. A **pan shot** moves left or right, scanning the scene horizontally yet remaining in a fixed position. For example, a pan shot may follow a person crossing a room or a street. In the credits shot of *The Killers* (1946), after the last title card has been displayed, the two would-be killers approach the camera; it pans left to follow their movement to a closed gas station where their intended victim works, pans right as they move away from the station and look across the street at a diner, and pans even further to the right as they walk toward the diner and their planned ambush of their victim. A **tracking shot** moves forward, backward, or laterally, moving toward, away, with, or around the subject. The camera is not in a fixed position but travels on a track or dolly following a moving subject, such as a person walking down a sidewalk. At other times, the subject remains fixed, and the camera tracks toward, away, or around the subject. In *The Swimmer* (1968), Ned Merrill races a horse along a pasture fence and holds his own with the animal, much to his smiling satisfaction. The camera also holds its own as it tracks the two of them, the sprinting Merrill and the loping horse. A **crane shot** occurs when the camera is mounted high on a crane and moves in any direction, often with an ascending or descending motion. The crane shot offers a bird's-eye view of the action. The high-angle shot of Bernstein and Woodward in the Library of Congress, mentioned before, begins as a conventional camera placement for a high angle, but then the camera ascends through a series of dissolves to become a crane shot from the top of the room's very tall ceiling, thus minimizing the two reporters to mere specks in the vast room.

Editing

Editing refers to the twofold job of choosing the best camera shots taken and then joining these shots together to build a scene, a sequence, and ultimately a completed movie. These joins, or transitions, can take the form of a **fade-in,** in which the beginning of a shot goes gradually from dark to light, usually signaling the beginning of a scene; a **fade-out,** in which the end of a shot goes gradually from light to dark, usually signaling the end of a scene; a dissolve, in which the end of one shot is for a moment superimposed with the beginning of the next shot, usually suggesting a close cinematic and/or narrative connection between two scenes; a **wipe,** in which the end of one shot appears to be pushed aside by the beginning of the next shot, also suggesting a close cinematic and/or narrative connection between two scenes or two shots within scenes; a **cut,** in which the end of one shot is simply spliced to the beginning of the shot that immediately replaces it on the screen, used either between scenes or between shots within scenes; and a **jump cut,** in which one shot is replaced abruptly with another shot that is mismatched in a way that calls attention to the cut and jars the viewer.

Within a scene, whatever transition device the film editor uses creates a relationship of continuity or discontinuity between two shots in terms of their photographic elements. If the two shots are similar, then the film editor has created a **graphic match** between the two shots; if the two shots are different, the film editor has created a graphic variance.

When the matches are assembled in such a way as to relate a story clearly, concisely, and with unity and cohesion, the film editor in conjunction with the director has created continuity within the film. Various strategies of editing contribute to **continuity editing.** Among these strategies are **crosscutting,** which uses alternating shots of at least two strands of action happening in different places at the same time; **establishing shots,** which show in long shots and extreme long shots the characters and the objects in spatial relation to one another within the setting; **eyeline matches,** in which a character in one shot is shown looking in a direction and in the next shot the space toward which the character is looking is shown; **match on action,** in which one shot of an action is replaced by another shot of the same action in the same moment but from a different focal view, so there appears to be no interruption to the action; and **shot/reverse shot,** in which at least two shots joined together show first one character and then another character talking to each another.

An example of continuity editing occurs in the fight scene between the Maclean brothers in *A River Runs Through It,* which we discuss in detail in Chapter 3. An establishing shot shows the brothers in their family kitchen, Norman sitting at the table ready to eat a sandwich and Paul entering and beginning to advise his older brother on how to make a better sandwich. Once the fight over fixing the sandwich begins, eyeline-match shots show each brother angrily confronting his offscreen adversary and sizing up the next opportunity to throw a punch. Match-on-action shots show the successful punches landing and driving each brother either against a kitchen wall or against the kitchen sink. Crosscutting shots alternate between the battling brothers and their mother's entrance into the kitchen from another door, her alarm at their fighting, and her rush to stop it by mistakenly getting between them. Shot/reverse shots show the brothers' furious reactions and name calling after their mother slips and falls down on the floor between them. A reestablishing shot shows their mother getting up without their assistance and quietly leaving while the brothers stare at each other without saying another word or throwing one more punch.

Opposed to continuity editing is **disjunctive editing,** which emphasizes the cut from one shot to another. The variances among shots can be in terms of space, time, or visual patterns, and the goals may be to disturb the viewer or to interrupt or undercut the story's verisimilitude. After the conclusion of the scene described in the previous paragraph, at the end of the shot showing Mrs. Maclean leaving her kitchen and her two boys staring at one another, there is a cut to a downward tilted, extreme long shot that shows the brothers and their father fly-fishing together. The variances between the two shots are in terms of space, time, and visual pattern. The viewer is transported from the cramped kitchen/boxing arena in the early morning to the spacious, sunny outdoors where, according to the voiceover narrated by the elderly Norman, the brothers have gone back to being gracious to one another as their faith prompted them to behave. The goal of this disjunctive editing is to interrupt the antagonism between the brothers and to suggest a sudden and steadfast reconciliation between them, expressed through their common love of fly-fishing and respect for religious teaching.

The term **montage** can be used in a general sense to indicate any kind of editing, but it has come to refer to an editing technique that juxtaposes dissimilar shots, calls attention to their discontinuity, and thus leads the viewer to make conscious connections among the images. The assemblage of contrasting and conflicting images achieves a significance that goes beyond the meaning implicit in any of the individual shots.

The opening sequence of *A River Runs Through It* is an example of a montage. This series of juxtaposed, dissimilar shots, filmed by Philippe Rousselot, is made up of fourteen still, black-and-white, mostly archival photographs of life in Montana during the time period in which the film is set. Each shot is straight on, runs from between four and eight seconds, tracks forward in order to carry the viewer nearer to observe the detail in the characteristically extreme long-shot photographs, and then dissolves into the next still life.

The first two shots are of still photographs featuring, in a formal pose, Norman and Paul as children by themselves, and then, in another formal pose, Norman and Paul, again as children, accompanied by their parents. These two photographs are followed by a series of photographs presenting Montana life in the first quarter of the twentieth century. These are comprised of a river flowing through a countryside, a dirt street running through a town, another dirt street, a horse and wagon on a dirt street running through a settlement, a settlement located at the bottom of a mountain range, a bunch of loggers posed around a pile of logs, another bunch of loggers standing in a camp, a church standing near a bridge spanning a river, people posed in a field, more people standing in front of a city hall whose façade is covered with huge U.S. flags, a woman with two boys standing on a tree-lined street, and, lastly, another church. Taken together, these contrasting and conflicting images suggest this film is the story of a small family living in a place that is a civic- and religious-minded community whose way of living is intimately joined to nature.

Sound

There are four types of **sound** heard in films: speech, music, sound effects, and silence. **Speech** is **dialogue,** or character discourse, spoken by the actors onscreen or spoken by the actors offscreen, as in voiceover narration. Sometimes a character is seen alone on screen but is not speaking, while the voice of the character is heard on the sound track thinking about something, as in the black-and-white sequences in *Memento* (2001). Dialogue conveys background information; expresses the thoughts and feelings of the characters about actions, the behavior of other characters, or features of the setting; and distinguishes each character by language idiom.

Music refers to the score composed to establish structural patterns throughout a scene, a sequence, or the entire film, and to evoke emotional reactions in the audience. Structural patterns assist in establishing the atmosphere of a setting; they supply background for an otherwise mundane scene of unexciting visual content, or to fulfill an industry strategy of having music in every scene from start to finish; they provide continuity, or smooth transitions and flow, from shot to shot and scene to scene; and they underscore the climax and conclusion of scenes. The score influences the audience's emotional reactions to the action and characters in a particular scene, a sequence, or the entire film. In

Rashômon (1950), music phrases are linked to major characters in the film for viewer identification and emotional association.

Sound effects are noises made by people and objects situated within the scene shown. These consist of **ambient sound,** or background noises in a scene, such as people opening or closing a door, water running in a stream, or automobile horns blaring in city traffic. Ambient sound also consists of noises made by people or objects performing significant actions such as someone crying or laughing, a gun firing, or a bridge collapsing. Sound effects can be used for comic purposes. For example, in *The Simpsons'* adaptation of Edgar Allan Poe's "The Raven" (1989), Homer, the speaker of the poem, says:

> Back into the chamber turning, all my soul within me burning
> Soon again I heard a tapping something louder than before.
> Surely, said I, surely that is something at my window lattice;
> Let me see, then, what thereat is, and this mystery explore. (31–34)

The "tapping something louder than before" is represented in the film as a loud banging whose force shakes the frame and disturbs the delicate assonance in the Scholar's lines.

The total absence of sound in a scene is called a **dead track.** The absence breaks the expected sound pattern of dialogue, music, and effects established in the film up to that point; surprises the audience; makes the audience concentrate on the image; and creates anxiety and anticipation in the audience as it waits for sound to resume. That resumption may be in the form of an unforeseen, startling noise.

In *Dracula* (1931), directed by Tod Browning, Renfield, who has fainted, is approached by three of Dracula's wives in an apartment within Dracula's castle. Dracula himself appears in the window, waves them off, and then approaches Renfield for the first drink of his blood. This brief scene is silent from the time Renfield feels the room is stuffy, goes to the window to open it, is accosted by a bat (which does squeal for a moment), and faints, until the fade-out with Dracula bending over Renfield's limp body. The first shot of the next scene shows a storm-tossed sailing ship with the sound of whistling wind on the sound track. The sudden absence of sound in the fainting scene interrupts the pattern established up to then, surprises the viewer, and makes the viewer concentrate on the bizarrely costumed, emaciated figures of the wives. It also heightens Dracula's suddenly hostile behavior toward Renfield, whom up until now he has treated with businesslike courtesy.

Sound is either **diegetic** or **nondiegetic.** Diegetic sound is produced within a screen space. For example, characters talk, make noise, or play a musical instrument in a room. Nondiegetic sound does not occur within the screen space. An offstage voiceover and music score are examples. One way to distinguish between diegetic and nondiegetic sound is to ask whether the characters *and* the audience are meant to hear the sounds (diegetic) or whether the sounds are intended *solely* for the audience (nondiegetic). In the example of camera tracking from *The Swimmer,* mentioned earlier, Ned Merrill and the horse he is racing do not hear the music we hear on the sound track, yet the rousing music expresses an excitement about their race that the man and the horse might actually be feeling; thus, the nondiegetic music helps the viewer to experience the emotions of the characters on screen.

Literature and film share many terms. Analysis of both forms involves talking about character, setting, action, theme, and symbolism. But film requires its own special vocabulary to describe how images and sounds tell stories. Both sets of terms will be useful in the following chapters where we explore the ways filmmakers adapt literature to film.

3 FILM ADAPTATION

The Case of Apples and Oranges

Take your favorite novel and imagine making it into a film. Keep as close to the book as possible. Assume you have a fine director, talented actors, a good screenplay, cutting-edge equipment, and a production crew of thousands. Make the movie. Have you succeeded in producing a *truly faithful* adaptation? Our view is that you have not (and cannot) because *strict fidelity* is impossible. An adaptation is different and original because it is a work in another medium. Literature and film are apples and oranges.

Unfixed to Fixed

One explanation for the difference between literature and film is that the text's verbal language and the film's pictorial and aural languages have distinct qualities that prohibit the exact replication of a text on screen. No matter how concrete and specific an author's diction, his or her verbal language is ultimately unfixed and unspecified. On the other hand, pictorial and aural languages are fixed and specified.

Take the following sentence:

> *A tree stood in front of the house where I used to live.*

The author of the sentence chose not to include details that would answer questions such as: What kind of tree? How tall? How far from the house? What kind of house? In what season? The reader fills in the answers to these questions with stored mental images.

But to shoot this setting, a filmmaker would have to photograph a tree of a certain species, with a definite height, at a specific distance from a particular kind of house, during an actual season of the year. In addition, the filmmaker would have to photograph the tree at a certain distance from the camera, at a definite angle, in a particular focus, with a specific lens, possibly with a filter. The unfixed language of the literary text will become fixed in exact screen images chosen by the filmmaker, and so the viewer may see a departure from the mental images conjured when he or she first read the passage.

Let's look at the shift from unfixed to fixed languages in the physical description of a character. Below Dashiell Hammett describes the protagonist in *The Maltese Falcon.* In a moment, we will discuss how filmmakers translated this description.

> Samuel Spade's jaw was long and bony, his chin a jutting v under the more flexible v of his mouth. His nostrils curved back to make another, smaller v. His yellow-grey eyes were horizontal. The v *motif* was picked up again by thickish brows rising outward from twin creases above a hooked nose, and his pale brown hair grew down—from high flat temples—in a point on his forehead. He looked rather pleasantly like a blond satan. (3)

Despite Hammett's plain writing style, his concrete and specific diction, and his reference to the particular facial details of Spade, his language is unfixed and unspecified enough that we naturally form our own mental pictures of "a blond satan."

Humphrey Bogart, who plays Sam Spade in John Huston's *The Maltese Falcon* (1941), does not fit the description. Although Bogart has bushy (read "thickish") eyebrows, he has dark (not blond) hair, penetrating (rather than "horizontal") eyes, and a craggy face with not a "v *motif*" in sight.

We may wish that Spade were played by another actor who more closely resembles our mental pictures of Spade, or that elaborate makeup was used to bring Bogart closer to Hammett's description of the character. But the point is that some actor had to play Spade, and no matter who had been chosen, there would still be a gap between the nonspecific literary language that produced images in our heads and the specific facial looks of the actor used.

Humphrey Bogart as Sam Spade in *The Maltese Falcon* (1941), looking nothing like a "blond satan" and without a "v *motif*" in sight.

An exaggerated way of saying this is that filmmakers have difficulty adapting literature closely *not* because literature is too specific but because, at least in representing the physical world, it is too vague. One could also argue the opposite—that language's "vagueness" makes texts easier to adapt because it gives filmmakers the freedom to make specific choices while maintaining the features of the story.

Single to Multitracks

Another way to talk about the difference between literature and film is offered by critic Robert Stam, who suggests that a text is a single-track medium and film a **multitrack medium.**

The printed text communicates information through a single track—words. It is true that words are multidimensional. They have sounds and carry denotative and connotative, or literal and figurative, meanings. But film uses more than just words to communicate. Here is a list of film's five tracks:

1. theatrical performance (live or animated)
2. words (spoken and written)
3. music
4. sound effects (noise and silence)
5. photographic images (moving and still) (Stam 56)

Let's apply this explanation to an adapted text. The scene printed below comes from Norman Maclean's memoir *A River Runs Through It*. Later, we'll describe how screenwriter Richard Friedenberg adapted this scene in *A River Runs Through It* (1992), directed by Robert Redford. In both literary passage and film sequence, Norman and Paul, two teenage brothers, engage in a fist-fight that is interrupted by their mother.

> I suppose it was evitable that my brother and I would get into one big fight which also would be the last one. When it came, given our theories about street fighting, it was like the Battle Hymn, terrible and swift. There are parts of it I did not see. I did not see our mother walk between us to try to stop us. She was short and wore glasses and, even with them on, did not have good vision. She had never seen a fight before or had any notion of how bad you can get hurt by becoming mixed up in one. Evidently, she just walked between her sons. The first thing I saw of her was the gray top of her head, the hair tied in a big knot with a big comb in it; but what was most noticeable was that her head was so close to Paul I couldn't get a good punch at him. Then I didn't see her any more.
>
> The fight seemed suddenly to stop itself. She was lying on the floor between us. Then we both began to cry and fight in a rage, each one shouting, "You son of a bitch, you knocked my mother down."
>
> She got off the floor, and blind without her glasses, staggered in circles between us, saying without recognizing which one she was addressing, "No, it wasn't you. I just slipped and fell."
>
> So this was the only time we ever fought. (8)

The passage summarizes the action but leaves the reader without many details, such as when and where the fight took place or even how the round was going before the boys' mother was knocked down. But when Friedenberg and others decide to adapt this scene, they have to answer these and other questions if they are to translate the passage into theatrical performance, words, sound effects, and photographic images (there is no music used in the scene)—four of the five tracks film uses to communicate information.

As we observed, Maclean never says when or where the fight takes place, but the filmmakers have to set the theatrical performance somewhere and at some time. They choose the cramped confines of the Maclean kitchen to serve as a makeshift arena. The kitchen needs to be lit, and so a muted lighting is chosen that suggests morning sunlight shining in through a kitchen window to the right and out of the frame. That light becomes diffused through the rest of the room and casts a gloomy pall over most of it, perhaps suggesting that the boys' fight is a depressing and melancholy affair.

Maclean never mentions the characters' clothing, so informal period wear is chosen for the brothers and a starched white blouse for their mother, which is intensified by a bright direct ray of sunlight when she enters her kitchen and notices her boys fighting. Except for the mother's hair comb and glasses, Maclean mentions no physical objects. The film most notably adds a sardine sandwich as the immediate cause of the fight and the mother's laundry basket, the family kitchen table, cabinets, and other furniture and objects needed to suggest a kitchen.

Maclean says the fight was "like the Battle Hymn, terrible and swift." Nothing in that brief, vague description prepares us for the specific images of the fight produced by Philippe Rousselot's camera work: level, straight-on, mostly medium close-ups of Norman and Paul that draw us into their fight and let us see their facial contortions of effort and pain.

The speed of Maclean's "terrible and swift" fight is suggested by the quick pace and fluid editing—the rapid cuts between shots that show punches and reactions to punches, and the camera's panning as it follows the brothers violently shoving each other across the few feet of open kitchen.

Described nowhere in the text are the *diegetic* sounds—the sounds that could be expected to occur within the screen space—that need to be added to the sequence. In the film version, we hear fists hitting faces, cups and dishes being knocked over and breaking, the legs of a wooden table sliding across a wooden floor, and the grunts of effort and pain bursting from the battling brothers.

The two lines of dialogue are kept, and some lines are added. Mother screams at her boys to stop fighting. They do not stop. At this point, neither brother seems to be winning. After their mother falls, both Paul and Norman shout accusations and call each other "bastard" and "son of a bitch." Finally, after getting up off the floor, Mother has the last word—or words. She insists first loudly and then softly that she just slipped.

Maclean's text follows Norman's point of view through the fight: "The first thing I saw of her was the gray top of her head." But in the film scene, the camera uses the omniscient point of view. This is clear at the end of the fight when a high-angle long shot shows the three characters standing in the kitchen, everyone silent. Mother picks up her glasses, reminds the boys once again in a whisper that she slipped, and walks away. In a close-up, the brothers stare at one another and cry. We are clearly standing outside Norman's first-person point of view. Because of this selection of point of view, the viewer, of course, never learns about Mother's naiveté concerning fistfights that Norman reports directly to the reader in the novella.

The screenwriter, director, cinematographer, production designer, set decorator, costume designer, film editor, actors, and others supply substance to the fight scene in Maclean's text by using not only words but also theatrical performances, sound effects, and images. The filmmakers necessarily supplement this literary scene in translating it from one to four tracks, but in doing so they make the film scene into something different from the text. Whether or not you accept the notion that adaptation involves moving a text from one to five tracks, the explanation underlines the point that literature and film—even when using the same basic story elements—make meaning differently.

The Maclean brothers' fight broken up by their mother in the Maclean kitchen in *A River Runs Through It* (1992).

Story and Discourse

If literature and film are so different, how is it possible to translate a narrative from one medium to another? Here's one answer. Some contemporary theorists claim that a narrative has two parts: a story and a **discourse.** The story is the content—the chain of events, the characters, and the setting. Adapters, we assume, focus their attention first on the story to be transposed to film. But the story is realized in something larger—a discourse. According to Seymour Chatman, discourse is "the expression, the means by which the content is communicated. In simple terms, the story is the *what* in a narrative that is depicted, discourse the *how*" (19).

The first job of the adapter is to identify the "what" of the narrative. Screen-writer Linda Seger, for example, advises would-be adapters to find the story-line. But once the adapter identifies the storyline, she or he must translate it to another medium. The assumption here is that stories are "structures indepen-dent of any medium"(Chatman 20) and that these independent structures are transposable from one discourse to another.

For the transposition to be successful, it is important that the adapter understand the story as well as the means of expression of both discourses. Another way of saying this is that the adapter needs to be aware of the conventions of the literary story as well as of cinema itself. **Conventions** are accepted methods and practices in a specific form that are understood by the artist and the audience. If the adapter doesn't take into account the conventions of each form, the conventions of the antecedent form will stubbornly cling to the adaptation and make it seem uncinematic. Here's one general example. A central element of most short stories and novels is dialogue. Dialogue communicates the thoughts and feelings of one character to another, but it also can be used to convey other information such as how the characters are positioned or what is happening in their immediate environment. When dialogue is carried from a literary text to a film adaptation, it has to be rewritten to fit the conventions of film. Film uses images more than words to convey meanings; if the dialogue is not pared down to the essential (for example, eliminating what is obvious because the scene is shown), then the film will appear tedious and talky.

Adapters have made this transposition from textual to screen conventions from the earliest days of filmmaking. For almost as long, some reviewers have evaluated the merits of those adaptations on the basis of their "faithfulness" or **fidelity** to the anterior text. We discuss a number of problems with this approach below.

Is It Faithful or Not?

Some film reviewers judge an adaptation on whether it carries over the essential story elements and core meanings of the literary text. This approach raises several important questions. How is it possible to identify the core meanings of a story when we know literary texts are capable of supporting an indefinite number of interpretations? If we leave aside the problem of identifying what is essential in a text, we are still left with the difficulty of judging the degree to which the essential has been transposed. How can reviewers make useful judgments about fidelity when there is no agreed-upon method to compare text and film? Most large-circulation reviewers preview films in private screening rooms, where there is no opportunity to make the point-by-point comparison of details that we recommend. Moreover, there is no standard measure as to how much of the "essential" text must be transferred in order for the film to be judged faithful. Perhaps this explains why sometimes an adaptation can receive one review saying it is faithful and another claiming it is not.

A related problem has to do with the language commonly used to deliver a judgment about an adaptation's fidelity to a text. You can find this **language of fidelity** in many of the newspaper or magazine reviews of the latest film adaptation now playing at your local theater. The reviewer claims the adaptation is "faithful" or "unfaithful" and that this degree of faithfulness is either good or bad. The problem with this language is that it tends to imply that the book is better than the movie.

For the most part, the language of fidelity uses neutral-sounding terms that are buried metaphors or, more technically, *personifications*. **Personification** means giving the attributes of a human being to an animal, an object, or a concept. When a reviewer says an adaptation is "faithful," he or she personifies the film by attributing to it the human quality of loyalty. It is equivalent to saying the adaptation is loyal to a text like a trusted lieutenant or a faithful spouse. The reviewer who says the adaptation is "unfaithful" claims that the film betrays the text like a traitor betrays his or her country.

There are other metaphors that belong to the language of fidelity, and each term carries with it a negative moral overtone.

> *Infidelity* resonates with overtones of Victorian prudishness; *betrayal* evokes ethical perfidy; *deformation* implies aesthetic disgust; *violation* calls to mind sexual violence; *vulgarization* conjures up class degradation; and *desecration* intimates a kind of sacrilege toward the "sacred word." (Stam 54)

The language of fidelity, then, is a language of buried metaphors that inappropriately draws the adaptation into the human moral dimension. In such language, the literature and film are not equals. The text is never judged as being faithless to its film adaptation; rather, it is the adaptation, and only the adaptation, that is capable of being "unfaithful" to the text.

Besides implying something humanly moral about adaptations, the language of fidelity suggests a hierarchy. When a reviewer says a film is faithful to a text, she or he calls attention to a time sequence. The text may be true to itself, but the adaptation must be true to something other than itself, something that came before, something anterior. In this sequence, the literature comes first as "source"; the film comes later as derivation. The literature is regarded as the "original" (a supreme value in art); the film is regarded as a "copy." Although the literary work was created first, that fact is no guarantee that the text is superior to its film adaptation. For example, James M. Cain's novella *Double Indemnity*—the "original"—is a lesser work of art than Billy Wilder's "copy" of the same title. Although the film keeps almost all of the characters and a good deal of the plot, it replaces the book's unlikely characterization of the central female character, stilted dialogue, and convoluted conclusion with more believable characterization, humorous and vivid dialogue, and a straightforward ending.

Richard Schickel reports a conversation in which Cain agrees that Wilder's film improves upon his story:

> "It's the only picture I ever saw made from my books that had things in it I wish I had thought of. Wilder's ending was much better than my ending, and his device of letting the guy tell the story by taking out the office dictating machine—I would have done it if I had thought of it." (65)

Walter Neff (Fred MacMurray) using the Dictaphone, an addition of a narrative element to the adaptation of *Double Indemnity* (1944).

About his own novella, Cain explains: "My story was done very slapdash and very quick—I had to have money" (66).

James Naremore offers a list of films that exceed their literary sources: "Murnau's *Sunrise*, Welles's *The Magnificent Ambersons*, Ophül's *Letter from an Unknown Woman*, Ford's *The Man Who Shot Liberty Valance*, and Hitchcock's *Psycho*" (7). The fact that the text comes first is no guarantee that it is aesthetically superior to its film adaptation.

Finally, one might ask how reviewers can assume that fidelity is a measure of cinematic merit when so many close adaptations have resulted in less than memorable movies. An adaptation is not a better film because it is a close interpretation as opposed to an intermediate or loose one. In fact, some people argue that fidelity to a text is a surefire way to make a bad film. For example, Nicolas Roeg and Francis Ford Coppola both adapted Joseph Conrad's 1902 novel *Heart of Darkness.* But no critic has said Roeg's relatively close 1994 adaptation, set in Africa in the 1890s, is a superior work to Coppola's loose rendering of the novel in *Apocalypse Now* (1979), set in Vietnam during the 1960s. Fidelity, then, should not be used as a value term to judge the merit of films. Instead, it should be used as a descriptive term that leads to a much more interesting discussion about the complicated relationship between text and film.

Status of Literature versus Film

Becoming aware of the loaded language of fidelity is not enough. You also need to become aware of the way Western culture values literary art over film art. Stam argues that this view is derived from a number of historical attitudes:

> *seniority,* the assumption that older arts are necessarily better arts; *iconophobia,* the culturally rooted prejudice (traceable to the Judaic-Muslim-Protestant prohibitions on "graven image" and to the Platonic and Neoplatonic depreciation of the world of phenomenal appearance) that visual arts are necessarily inferior to the verbal arts; and *logophilia,* the converse valorization, characteristic of the "religions of the book," of the "sacred word" of holy texts. (58)

In other words, our culture grants superiority to literature because it is an older, more established art form than film and because words are given priority over images. So when talking about adaptations, keep in mind that there are prejudices inscribed in critical language and in our cultural attitudes that assume literature is superior to film.

Close, Loose, and Intermediate

In the introduction, we used the words "close," "loose," and "intermediate" to define a general relationship between a text and its film adaptation. The words measure whether an adaptation stays close to its literary counterpart, departs from it, or stays somewhere in between. We use these words in place of the language of fidelity.

Like the language of fidelity, these words carry their own implications. "Close" has many positive connotations. For example, there are the expressions "close friend," "close to my heart," and "up close and personal." Occasionally, the term might have slightly negative connotations—such as in the expression "close quarters" (positive, though, when you are with someone you want to be with) or in the expressions "close call" or "close play" (both of which are positive if you like the result). On the other hand, the term "loose" generally has negative connotations, as in the expressions "loose morals," "a loose animal," "a killer on the loose," and even "a loose connection." Only occasionally does "loose" not connote excess freedom or a problematic situation, as in the expressions "set loose" (which can be negative) and "footloose and fancy free" (normally used jokingly or as exaggeration). Notice—in contrast to these terms—how neutral and barren of connotation "intermediate" sounds. Despite their implications, these terms seem more neutral than the language of fidelity, commonly used in newspaper and magazine reviews. Keep in mind that the purpose of classification is not to evaluate an adaptation but to make an initial, approximate description of the relationship between a text and its adaptation. That description can be dispensed with once a more nuanced definition of the relationship is achieved.

A film is a **close adaptation** when most of the narrative elements in the literary text are kept in the film, few elements are dropped, and not many elements are added. For example, *Harry Potter and the Sorcerer's Stone* (2001), directed by Chris Columbus, is a close adaptation partly because J. K. Rowling, the best-selling author of the Harry Potter series, knew that she had a loyal readership, and so in selling the film rights, she stipulated that the film stay close to the Potter text, even insisting on her approval of the director and actors.

A film is a **loose adaptation** when most of the story elements in the literary text are dropped from the film and most elements in the film are substituted or added. A loose adaptation uses the literary text as a point of departure. *To Have and Have Not* (1944), directed by Howard Hawks, is an example of a loose adaptation of Hemingway's novel because the film keeps just the title and the main character's name. Similarly, Christopher Nolan uses the basic premise of his brother Jonathan's short story but invents a whole new story for *Memento* (2001).

A film is an **intermediate adaptation** when it is in the fluid middle of the sliding scale between close and loose. Some elements of the story are kept in the film, other elements are dropped, and still more elements are added. An intermediate adaptation neither conforms exactly nor departs entirely. *What's Eating Gilbert Grape* (1993), directed by Lasse Hallström and adapted from Peter Hedges's novel, is an example of an intermediate adaptation because the film keeps most of the plot, characters, and settings but drops several minor characters and subplots.

Again, while it is difficult to avoid the language of fidelity commonly used to characterize the relationship between a text and an adaptation, it is possible to become aware of the implications of that critical language. As a substitute, we recommend the use of "close," "loose," and "intermediate" even though they carry their own connotations and are general terms that will not apply evenly to every sequence in an adaptation.

The Auteur

In talking about adaptations, it seems natural enough to talk about the author of the text and the director of the film as equivalent. Each produced a comparable work of art. For example, someone might say that *The Maltese Falcon* is director John Huston's interpretation of Dashiell Hammett's book on the screen. People who know about film production will object. They would say the adaptation is not Huston's interpretation; it is a collective interpretation. One can identify the author of a book, but one cannot identify the author of a film.

Their objection is based on the observation that it is not the director alone who decides what will be in a film. The screenwriter, production designer, actors, cinematographer, production recorder, film editor, and others contribute as well. So whose film is it, anyway? Were the realities of film production betrayed by the statement that *The Maltese Falcon* is "Huston's interpretation . . . on the screen"?

In the 1950s, the French director and film critic François Truffaut offered an answer to the question of film authorship in *Cahiers du cinéma,* a famous French film journal still publishing today. Truffaut called the director an *auteur* or author in French, hence, the **auteur** theory. Truffaut emphasized the director as the main creative force behind a film, who imprints the material with his or her own unique personal style, vision, and thematic preoccupations. Not all directors are equal; some are merely competent. Truffaut praised such directors as D. W. Griffith, Howard Hawks, John Ford, Samuel Fuller, and Alfred Hitchcock because he claimed that their vision and style constituted the controlling force behind the thematic and stylistic elements of their films. But there are problems with equating the role of the author with the role of the director. The main problem with the auteur theory is that it deemphasizes film as a collective enterprise.

In answering the question, "Who is the author of a film?" David Bordwell and Kristin Thompson maintain that

> [t]he question of authorship becomes difficult to answer only when asked about large-scale production, particularly in the studio mode.
>
> Studio film production assigns tasks to so many individuals that it is often difficult to determine who controls or decides what. Is the producer the author? In the prime years of the Hollywood system, the producer might have had nothing to do with shooting. The writer? The writer's script might be completely transformed in shooting and editing. So is this situation like collective production, with group authorship? No, because there is a hierarchy in which a few main players make the big decisions. . . .
>
> Most people who study cinema regard the director as the film's "author." Although the writer prepares the script, later phases of production can modify it beyond recognition. And although the producer monitors the entire process, he or she seldom controls moment-by-moment activity on the set. It is the director who makes the crucial decisions about performance, staging, lighting, framing, cutting, and sound. On the whole, the director has more control over how a movie looks and sounds. (40–41)

We agree with Bordwell and Thompson that film's collaborative nature makes it difficult, without research and even then, to determine who contributed what.

Moreover, it has become the convention for critics to identify a film by title, date, and director, thereby giving more credit to the director than to anyone else. We follow this convention in the book because it is awkward to identify even the main contributors to a film production. However, where relevant to the discussion, we mention individual contributors, especially the *screenwriter* who structures and shapes the adaptation.

Intertextuality

In our discussion, we usually focus on one printed text and one film adaptation. But in doing so, we don't mean to suggest that these two works exist in isolation or only in relationship to each other. Our view is that texts and films come out of other texts and other films. **Intertextuality** is the term used to suggest that texts refer to or cite other works. Film adaptations are by definition intertextual since they refer to an antecedent text. However, any adaptation has additional relationships with other works. For example, the adaptation may have relationships with previous forms of the literary text and with different film adaptations of the same source. An adapter of Shakespeare's *King Lear* may choose to look at three different variants of the play and fourteen previous film adaptations. And someone adapting Richard Connell's "The Most Dangerous Game" may choose to view at least seven previous film adaptations of that short story. This collection of remakes constitutes another anterior "text" that may be as important to the adapter as the original printed text.

Acknowledging intertextuality is one thing, but actually exploring all the important intertextual relations a film has—the ones that may influence a "reading"—is difficult to accomplish. To make our discussions manageable, we have decided in most cases to leave aside commentary on other forms of intertextuality that may be relevant to text and film. The emphasis in this textbook will be on *hypertextuality,* what Gérard Genette defines as any relationship uniting one text to an earlier text or, in this case, uniting a film to its anterior literary text (5).

A Method of Comparison

In the next chapter, we ask you to read a text carefully, to view its film adaptation closely, and to note down what narrative elements have been **kept, dropped,** and **added.** We emphasize "carefully," "closely," and "note down," so you will not casually scan a text, watch a film, and trust to your memory alone. Instead, you will methodically and thoroughly record your detailed observations.

We then ask you to compare your individual list with other students' lists. Group discussion allows members to come to a consensus on story elements kept, dropped, and added. After group reports, a teacher-guided discussion may expand and refine the lists further, providing the class with a fairly accurate inventory of narrative elements.

Next give special attention to *changes* made between the text and the film and discuss whether those changes were made for practical or interpretative reasons. Research of articles and books written about the literary text and the film adapted from it, and about literature and film in general, may confirm your decisions.

Finally, decide whether the film is a close, loose, or intermediate adaptation of the literary text. The decision should be based on your collective comparison of the text and film and not on individual impressions of the two films made in the studio of your mind. Next, try to move beyond this statement of proximity to a statement about the filmmaker's interpretation of the text.

This method promotes a community of observers who, by sharing observations and opinions, build a consensus that is critically attentive to the text, the film, and the relationship between the two.

Once again, there are many things to be mindful of when disussing film adaptations. Remember that the auteur concept is a misleading idea but a useful fiction for discussion purposes. Beware of the language of fidelity that appears neutral but carries unfortunate implications. And try to move beyond the issue of fidelity by using it as a springboard to more advanced questions about adaptations.

TOPICS FOR DISCUSSION

1. Take a descriptive sentence from any literary text, or make one up. For example, "The dog slept in the shade between two trees." On a piece of paper or transparency, draw the scene. Indicate the camera distance, angle, and movement, lighting, mise-en-scène, and other cinematic elements. Compare your version to other students' drawings. What do the various versions say about the possibilities of faithful adaptation?

2. Some critics judge an adaptation's merit based on whether the film realizes successfully the essential narrative elements and core meanings of the literary text. In your view, how much of a text must be carried over for the film to be judged faithful?

3. Take a descriptive passage from a literary text that has been adapted into a film. Read the passage and then view the corresponding scene or sequence from the film. How do the filmmakers translate the verbal passage into a live or animated theatrical performance, with words, music, sound effects, and photographic

images, the five tracks film uses to communicate information?

4. The fact that the text has seniority is no guarantee that it is aesthetically superior to its film adaptation. Take a film adaptation that seems to be aesthetically superior to the literature upon which it is based. What narrative and/or cinematic elements of the film contribute to its superiority?

5. Take a passage from a literary text that has been adapted into not just one film but also into a remake of that film. An example could be a passage from the novella *The Strange Case of Dr. Jekyll and Mr. Hyde,* by Robert Louis Stevenson, and any number of films adapted from the novella, including *Dr. Jekyll and Mr. Hyde* (1931), *Dr. Jekyll and Mr. Hyde* (1941), *Jekyll and Hyde* (1990), and *Mary Reilly* (1996). How do the various filmmakers translate the passage in different ways yet still employ the five tracks film uses to communicate information? How does the later film refer to or cite the earlier film?

■■■ **WORKS CITED**

BORDWELL, DAVID, AND KRISTIN THOMPSON. *Film Art: An Introduction.* 7th ed. New York: McGraw-Hill, 2004.

CAIN, JAMES M. *Double Indemnity.* 1936. *Three of a Kind.* New York: Knopf, 1943. 215–327.

CHATMAN, SEYMOUR. *Story and Discourse: Narrative Structure in Fiction and Film.* Ithaca: Cornell University Press, 1978.

Double Indemnity. Dir. Billy Wilder. Perf. Fred MacMurray, Barbara Stanwyck, and Edward G. Robinson. Paramount, 1944.

GENETTE, GÉRARD. *Palimpsests: Literature in the Second Degree.* Trans. Channa Newman and Claude Doubinsky. Lincoln: University of Nebraska Press, 1997.

HAMMETT, DASHIELL. *The Maltese Falcon.* New York: Vintage, 1992.

MACLEAN, NORMAN. *A River Runs Through It and Other Stories.* Chicago: The University of Chicago Press, 1976. 1–104.

Maltese Falcon, The. Dir. John Huston. Perf. Humphrey Bogart and Mary Astor. Warner Bros., 1941.

NAREMORE, JAMES, ED. *Film Adaptation.* New Brunswick: Rutgers University Press, 2000.

REDFORD, ROBERT. Introduction. *A River Runs Through It: Bringing a Classic to the Screen.* By Richard Friedenberg. Livingston, Montana: Clark City Press, 1992. 1–2.

River Runs Through It, A. Dir. Robert Redford. Perf. Craig Sheffer, Brad Pitt, Tom Skerritt, and Emily Lloyd. Columbia, 1992.

SCHICKEL, RICHARD. *Double Indemnity.* London: British Film Institute, 1992.

STAM, ROBERT. "Beyond Fidelity: The Dialogics of Adaptation." *Film Adaptation*. Ed. James Naremore. New Brunswick: Rutgers University Press, 2000. 54–76.

TRUFFAUT, FRANÇOIS. "A Certain Tendency of the French Cinema [1954]." Reprinted in *Movies and Methods*. Ed. Bill Nichols. Vol. 1. Berkeley: University of California Press, 1976. 224–37.

4 A METHOD FOR STUDYING FILM ADAPTATION

In the lobby of a cineplex, after a showing of *Harry Potter and the Prisoner of Azkaban* (2004), you may hear exiting viewers say: "I liked the book better than the movie." It's a casual remark and a common one, perhaps because it makes the speaker sound literate and astute. But remarks are not criticism, to paraphrase a remark Gertrude Stein made to Ernest Hemingway. Serious students of adaptation move beyond casual comments to a close comparison of text and film—a comparison that is informed by an understanding of film as an art form, a business, a technology, and a shaper and reflector of social values.

Chapter 3 explained a comparative method for studying adaptations. Now, this chapter asks you to apply the method to a specific adaptation. You need to do the following:

1. Read carefully the first chapter of the private-detective novel *The Maltese Falcon*, written by Dashiell Hammett.
2. Analyze the chapter for its elements of narrative.

3. View closely the corresponding opening sequence from *The Maltese Falcon*, directed by John Huston.

4. Analyze the sequence to determine what elements of narrative Huston chooses to keep, drop, or add and what film elements Huston chooses to use.

5. Focus on what elements are changed—i.e., substituted, dropped, or added (including cinematic elements).

6. Propose a reason for each change. Filmmaking is deliberate, not accidental, and changes can indicate an adapter's practical considerations in making the film, his or her interpretative insights into the literary text, or outside factors. At this point, research on both the literary text and the film may be necessary. This research may carry you into considerations of biographical, historical, industrial, and production contexts. Even so, you may not find a reason for every change and may find it necessary to suggest a plausible reason for a change based on your own observations of both the literary text and the adaptation and on your general knowledge of literature and film.

7. Focus on the practical and then the interpretative choices made in order to examine the relationship between the first chapter of the text and the opening sequence of the film.

8. Based on your comparison, decide whether the adaptation is close, loose, or intermediate. Does the film conform to the text, use it as a point of departure, or situate itself somewhere in between?

9. Use your decision as a step toward making a more nuanced statement of the relationship between the first chapter of the text and the opening sequence of the film.

Hammett's "Spade and Archer" is reprinted below. As you read, keep in mind the elements of narrative defined in Chapter 2: plot, character, setting, point of view, and theme.

▪ ▪ ▪

"SPADE AND ARCHER"

CHAPTER 1 OF THE MALTESE FALCON (1930),

by Dashiell Hammett

Samuel Spade's jaw was long and bony, his chin a jutting v under the more flexible v of his mouth. His nostrils curved back to make another, smaller, v. His yellow-grey eyes were horizontal. The v *motif* was picked up again by thickish brows rising outward from twin creases above a hooked nose, and his pale brown hair grew down—from high flat temples—in a point on his forehead. He looked rather pleasantly like a blond satan.

He said to Effie Perine: "Yes, sweetheart?"

She was a lanky sunburned girl whose tan dress of thin woolen stuff clung to her with an effect of dampness. Her eyes were brown and playful in a shiny boyish face. She finished shutting the door behind her, leaned against it, and said: "There's a girl wants to see you. Her name's Wonderly."

"A customer?"

"I guess so. You'll want to see her anyway: she's a knockout."

"Shoo her in, darling," said Spade. "Shoo her in."

Effie Perine opened the door again, following it back into the outer office, standing with a hand on the knob while saying: "Will you come in, Miss Wonderly?"

A voice said, "Thank you," so softly that only the purest articulation made the words intelligible, and a young woman came through the doorway. She advanced slowly, with tentative steps, looking at Spade with cobalt-blue eyes that were both shy and probing.

She was tall and pliantly slender, without angularity anywhere. Her body was erect and high-breasted, her legs long, her hands and feet narrow. She wore two shades of blue that had been selected because of her eyes. The hair curling from under her blue hat was darkly red, her full lips more brightly red. White teeth glistened in the crescent her timid smile made.

Spade rose bowing and indicating with a thick-fingered hand the oaken armchair beside his desk. He was quite six feet tall. The steep rounded slope of his shoulders made his body seem almost conical—no broader than it was thick—and kept his freshly pressed grey coat from fitting very well.

Miss Wonderly murmured, "Thank you," softly as before and sat down on the edge of the chair's wooden seat.

Spade sank into his swivel-chair, made a quarter-turn to face her, smiled politely. He smiled without separating his lips. All the v's in his face grew longer.

The tappity-tap-tap and the thin bell and muffled whir of Effie Perine's typewriting came through the closed door. Somewhere in a neighboring office a power-driven machine vibrated dully. On Spade's desk a limp cigarette smoldered in a brass tray filled with the remains of limp cigarettes. Ragged grey flakes of cigarette-ash dotted the yellow top of the desk and the green blotter and the papers that were there. A buff-curtained window, eight or ten inches open, let in from the court a current of air faintly scented with ammonia. The ashes on the desk twitched and crawled in the current.

Miss Wonderly watched the grey flakes twitch and crawl. Her eyes were uneasy. She sat on the very edge of the chair. Her feet were flat on the floor, as if she were about to rise. Her hands in dark gloves clasped a flat dark handbag in her lap.

Spade rocked back in his chair and asked: "Now what can I do for you, Miss Wonderly?"

She caught her breath and looked at him. She swallowed and said hurriedly: "Could you—? I thought—I—that is—" Then she tortured her lower lip with glistening teeth and said nothing. Only her dark eyes spoke now, pleading.

Spade smiled and nodded as if he understood her, but pleasantly, as if nothing serious were involved. He said: "Suppose you tell me about it, from the beginning, and then we'll know what needs doing. Better begin as far back as you can."

"That was in New York."

"Yes."

"I don't know where she met him. I mean I don't know where in New York. She's five years younger than I—only seventeen—and we didn't have the same friends. I don't suppose we've ever been as close as sisters should be. Mama and Papa are in Europe. It would kill them. I've got to get her back before they come home."

"Yes," he said.

"They're coming home the first of the month."

Spade's eyes brightened. "Then we've two weeks," he said.

"I didn't know what she had done until her letter came. I was frantic." Her lips trembled. Her hands mashed the dark handbag in her lap. "I was too afraid she had done something like this to go to the police, and the fear that something had happened to her kept urging me to go. There wasn't anyone I could go to for advice. I didn't know what to do. What could I do?"

"Nothing, of course," Spade said, "but then her letter came?"

"Yes, and I sent her a telegram asking her to come home. I sent it to General Delivery here. That was the only address she gave me. I waited a whole week, but no answer came, not another word from her. And Mama and Papa's return was drawing nearer and nearer. So I came to San Francisco to get her. I wrote her I was coming. I shouldn't have done that, should I?"

"Maybe not. It's not always easy to know what to do. You haven't found her?"

"No, I haven't. I wrote her that I would go to the St. Mark, and I begged her to come and let me talk to her even if she didn't intend to go home with me. But she didn't come. I waited three days, and she didn't come, didn't even send me a message of any sort."

Spade nodded his blond satan's head, frowned sympathetically, and tightened his lips together.

"It was horrible," Miss Wonderly said, trying to smile. "I couldn't sit there like that—waiting—not knowing what had happened to her, what might be happening to her." She stopped trying to smile. She shuddered. "The only address I had was General Delivery. I wrote her another letter, and yesterday afternoon I went to the Post Office. I stayed there until after dark, but I didn't see her. I went there again this morning, and still didn't see Corinne, but I saw Floyd Thursby."

Spade nodded again. His frown went away. In its place came a look of sharp attentiveness.

"He wouldn't tell me where Corinne was," she went on, hopelessly. "He wouldn't tell me anything, except that she was well and happy. But how can I believe that? That is what he would tell me anyhow, isn't it?"

"Sure," Spade agreed. "But it might be true."

"I hope it is. I do hope it is," she exclaimed. "But I can't go back home like this, without having seen her, without even having talked to her on the phone. He wouldn't take me to her. He said she didn't want to see me. I can't believe that. He promised to tell her he had seen me, and to bring her to see me—if she would come—this evening at the hotel. He said he knew she wouldn't. He promised to come himself if she wouldn't. He—"

She broke off with a startled hand to her mouth as the door opened.

The man who had opened the door came in a step, said, "Oh, excuse me!" hastily took his brown hat from his head, and backed out.

"It's all right, Miles," Spade told him. "Come in. Miss Wonderly, this is Mr. Archer, my partner."

Miles Archer came into the office again, shutting the door behind him, ducking his head and smiling at Miss Wonderly, making a vaguely polite gesture with the hat in his hand. He was of medium height, solidly built, wide in the shoulders, thick in the neck, with a jovial heavy-jawed red face and some grey in his close trimmed hair. He was apparently as many years past forty as Spade was past thirty.

Spade said: "Miss Wonderly's sister ran away from New York with a fellow named Floyd Thursby. They're here. Miss Wonderly has seen Thursby and has a date with him tonight. Maybe he'll bring the sister with him. The chances are he won't. Miss Wonderly wants us to find the sister and get her away from him and back home." He looked at Miss Wonderly. "Right?"

"Yes," she said indistinctly. The embarrassment that had gradually been driven away by Spade's ingratiating smiles and nods and assurances was pinkening her face again. She looked at the bag in her lap and picked nervously at it with a gloved finger.

Spade winked at his partner.

Miles Archer came forward to stand at a corner of the desk. While the girl looked at her bag he looked at her. His little brown eyes ran their bold appraising gaze from her lowered face to her feet and up to her face again. Then he looked at Spade and made a silent whistling mouth of appreciation.

Spade lifted two fingers from the arm of his chair in a brief warning gesture and said:

"We shouldn't have any trouble with it. It's simply a matter of having a man at the hotel this evening to shadow him away when he leaves, and shadow him until he leads us to your sister. If she comes with him, and you persuade her to return with you, so much the better. Otherwise—if she doesn't want to leave him after we've found her—well, we'll find a way of managing that."

Archer said: "Yeh." His voice was heavy, coarse.

Miss Wonderly looked up at Spade, quickly, puckering her forehead between her eyebrows.

"Oh, but you must be careful!" Her voice shook a little, and her lips shaped the words with nervous jerkiness. "I'm deathly afraid of him, of what he might do. She's so young and his bringing her here from New York is such a serious—Mightn't he—mightn't he do—something to her?"

Spade smiled and patted the arms of his chair.

"Just leave that to us," he said. "We'll know how to handle him."

"But mightn't he?" she insisted.

"There's always a chance." Spade nodded judicially. "But you can trust us to take care of that."

"I do trust you," she said earnestly, "but I want you to know that he's a dangerous man. I honestly don't think he'd stop at anything. I don't believe he'd hesitate to—to kill Corinne if he thought it would save him. Mightn't he do that?"

"You didn't threaten him, did you?"

"I told him that all I wanted was to get her home before Mama and Papa came so they'd never know what she had done. I promised him I'd never say a word to them about it if he helped me, but if he didn't Papa would certainly see that he was punished. I—I don't suppose he believed me, altogether."

"Can he cover up by marrying her?" Archer asked.

The girl blushed and replied in a confused voice: "He has a wife and three children in England. Corinne wrote me that, to explain why she had gone off with him."

"They usually do," Spade said, "though not always in England." He leaned forward to reach for pencil and pad of paper. "What does he look like?"

"Oh, he's thirty-five years old, perhaps, and as tall as you, and either naturally dark or quite sunburned. His hair is dark too, and he has thick eyebrows. He talks in a rather loud, blustery way and has a nervous, irritable manner. He gives the impression of being—of violence."

Spade, scribbling on the pad, asked without looking up: "What color eyes?"

"They're blue-grey and watery, though not in a weak way. And—oh, yes—he has a marked cleft in his chin."

"Thin, medium, or heavy build?"

"Quite athletic. He's broad-shouldered and carries himself erect, has what could be called a decidedly military carriage. He was wearing a light grey suit and a grey hat when I saw him this morning."

"What does he do for a living?" Spade asked as he laid down his pencil.

"I don't know," she said. "I haven't the slightest idea."

"What time is he coming to see you?"

"After eight o'clock."

"All right, Miss Wonderly, we'll have a man there. It'll help if—"

"Mr. Spade, could either you or Mr. Archer?" She made an appealing gesture with both hands. "Could either of you look after it personally? I don't mean that the man you'd send wouldn't be capable, but—oh!—I'm so afraid of what might happen to Corinne. I'm afraid of him. Could you? I'd be—I'd expect to be charged more, of course." She opened her handbag with nervous fingers and put two hundred-dollar bills on Spade's desk. "Would that be enough?"

"Yeh," Archer said, "and I'll look after it myself."

Miss Wonderly stood up, impulsively holding a hand out to him.

"Thank you! Thank you!" she exclaimed, and then gave Spade her hand, repeating: "Thank you!"

"Not at all," Spade said over it. "Glad to. It'll help some if you either meet Thursby downstairs or let yourself be seen in the lobby with him at some time."

"I will," she promised, and thanked the partners again.

"And don't look for me," Archer cautioned her. "I'll see you all right."

Spade went to the corridor-door with Miss Wonderly. When he returned to his desk Archer nodded at the hundred-dollar bills there, growled complacently, "They're right enough," picked one up, folded it, and tucked it into a vest-pocket. "And they had brothers in her bag."

> Spade pocketed the other bill before he sat down. Then he said: "Well, don't dynamite her too much. What do you think of her?"
>
> "Sweet! And you telling me not to dynamite her." Archer guffawed suddenly without merriment. "Maybe you saw her first, Sam, but I spoke first." He put his hands in his trousers-pockets and teetered on his heels.
>
> "You'll play hell with her, you will." Spade grinned wolfishly, showing the edges of teeth far back in his jaw. "You've got brains, yes you have." He began to make a cigarette. (3–10)

Analysis of Narrative Elements of "Spade and Archer," Chapter 1 of THE MALTESE FALCON (1930)

Plot

Since "Spade and Archer" is the first chapter of *The Maltese Falcon*, the main aspect of plot that applies to it is *exposition*. Exposition recounts existing or past events essential to appreciate plot development, introduces characters, establishes setting, and sometimes suggests the initial conflict. The recounting of past events begins with the "facts" that Miss Wonderly tells Sam Spade about her missing sister Corinne and that he, in turn, summarizes for Miles Archer.

Characters

Hammett mentions six characters in the first chapter: Sam Spade (the detective), Effie Perine (the secretary), Miss Wonderly (the client), Miles Archer (the partner), Corinne (Wonderly's sister), and Floyd Thursby (Corinne's supposed companion). Hammett categorizes them by physical type: in brief, Spade is a "blond satan"; Perine is "a lanky sunburned girl"; Wonderly is, according to Perine, "a knockout"; Archer is "medium and solid"; and Thursby gives Wonderly "the impression of violence." Corinne is not described. Their relationships are also briefly indicated. Spade is a friendly boss, and Perine is a helpful employee. Spade and his client Wonderly are polite and businesslike toward one another. Wonderly is worried about Corinne and frightened of Thursby. Spade and Archer are unperturbed by Wonderly's description of an intimidating Thursby. Archer is civil toward Spade and Wonderly while she is in the office, but after she leaves, he frankly declares to Spade his lust for her and her money. Archer also boasts to his partner of his one-upmanship of Spade. Spade ironically expresses his disapproval of Archer's predatory plans.

Jerome Cowan as Miles Archer, Mary Astor as Miss Wonderly, and Humphrey Bogart as Sam Spade not looking exactly like Hammett's description of how the characters dress and look in *The Maltese Falcon* (1941).

It is important to recall that the elements of narrative, such as plot and character, do not exist in isolation but work together. William Luhr points out that Spade's summary of Wonderly's facts to Archer reveals Spade's character.

> When [Wonderly] first comes to [Spade], she gives him a complicated story. He says little; he watches. When Archer arrives, however, Spade fires off an elaborate and detailed summary of what has been said, showing that he has missed nothing, retained everything, and plotted out a course of action. (168)

By simplifying and organizing Wonderly's story, Spade not only informs Archer, but also reminds readers of her problem and indicates his ability to understand that problem and formulate a plan of action to solve it, certainly a positive quality in a detective.

Setting

The setting of "Spade and Archer" is the detectives' San Francisco office during working hours. San Francisco plays no role in the first chapter of the novel

Miles Archer inspecting Miss Wonderly's money in *The Maltese Falcon*.

except that it is mentioned as the city in which the action is set. The office is a functional backdrop, a place of noises that indicate work and of window breezes that unsettle things, such as the ashes on the surface of Spade's desk. Neither the general descriptions of the office furniture and equipment nor of the characters' business clothes and hairstyle specifically suggest the 1920s, the period in which Hammett set the novel.

Point of View

"Spade and Archer" is narrated in the past tense, using the limited-omniscient *point of view* throughout the chapter. The story is told in the third person with the action confined to what would be seen and heard by Spade. The narrator neither explains to us what any of the characters thought and felt, nor what the narrator thinks and feels about them, but only reports how they looked and what they said and did.

Writing Style

Hammett's writing style in "Spade and Archer" is plain. Because the purpose of the first chapter is to establish one of the settings, introduce some of the characters, and set the plot in motion, the writing in the chapter consists primarily of informative dialogue with some orienting description and narration. Accordingly, the language in the dialogue, description, and narration is mostly clear, concise, concrete, and specific, somewhere between formal and informal. The words and sentences do not call attention to themselves.

Theme

First chapters can introduce topics that will be developed into themes over the course of the novel. The last exchange between Spade and Archer suggests the themes of unbridled greed, predatory sexuality, and one-upmanship. These themes are developed later in the novel, not only in relation to Spade and Archer but also in connection with Wonderly and her circle of companions.

Opening Sequence of THE MALTESE FALCON (1941), Directed by John Huston

After reading "Spade and Archer," view just the opening sequence of *The Maltese Falcon*. A **sequence** is a fairly large section of a film featuring a whole action and, in this case, consists of the first six minutes of the film or approximately thirty-three shots. The sequence begins with the Warner Bros. crest logo and ends with a shadow cast on the office floor. Since the film may not be readily available, we print below William Luhr's continuity script for the opening sequence, based on the 100-minute release print of the film. Luhr explains:

> It [the script] records in greatest detail the film's dialogue; the placement, behavior, and movement of the characters; the camera movement; the lighting; and the continuity between the shots. It presumes all transitions between shots to be cuts, unless specifically noted (such as in the case of dissolves, fades, wipes, and the like). It gives little detail about the sets, props, and wardrobe beyond general descriptions ("Spade's office") and discusses music and background sound primarily when they motivate the plot.
>
> I have used the following standard abbreviations to describe the placement of the camera with relation to the main focus of the shot:
>
> | | |
> |---|---|
> | CS | close shot |
> | MCS | medium close shot |
> | MS | medium shot |
> | LS | long shot |
> | ELS | extreme long shot (25) |

■ ■ ■

THE CONTINUITY SCRIPT

The film opens, after the "Warner Bros." logo, in the middle of a camera pullback from a medium shot to a long shot of the Maltese Falcon statuette. It is darkly lit with a harsh shadow to screen right. The credits appear in a series of vaseline dissolves against this shot. The lighting, the wavy, uneven dissolves, and the ponderous music give a sinister effect. At the end of the credits the following words are scrolled up against a closer shot of the Falcon.

In 1539 the Knight Templars of Malta, paid tribute to Charles V of Spain, by sending him a Golden Falcon encrusted from beak to claw with rarest jewels—but pirates seized the galley carrying this priceless token and the fate of the Maltese Falcon remains a mystery to this day—

SAN FRANCISCO, EXTERIOR, DAY

1. ELS: *San Francisco Bay, framed by part of the Golden Gate Bridge, with title* "SAN FRANCISCO" *superimposed.*

   DISSOLVE.

2. ELS: *San Francisco, different view, seen from the Bay, with* "Golden Gate Bridge" *in large letters on top of a structure.*

   DISSOLVE.

3. ELS: Golden Gate Bridge.

   DISSOLVE.

4. ELS: San Francisco. *Camera pans right from bridge.*

   DISSOLVE.

SPADE'S OFFICE, INTERIOR, DAY

5. CS: *Spade's office window, with* "SPADE AND ARCHER" *in mirror image on it, the Golden Gate Bridge in the background. Camera tilts down to a MCS of Spade rolling a cigarette. A door is heard opening.*

   SPADE
   (*without looking up*)
   Yes, sweetheart?

6. LS: *Effie standing by office door. The back of Spade's head and shoulders is in the foreground of the frame.*

EFFIE
There's a girl who wants to see you. Her name's Wonderly.

SPADE
Customer?

7. CS: *Effie, low angle.*

EFFIE
I guess so. You'll want to see her, anyway. She's a knockout.

8. MCS: *Spade, still rolling the cigarette.* SPADE: Shoo her in, Effie darling, shoo her in.

9. LS : Effie and Spade, as in 6. Effie turns and opens office door, letting Brigid in, who walks toward Spade as Effie leaves. Spade rises to greet her.

EFFIE
Will you come in, Miss Wonderly?

BRIGID
Thank you.

10. MS: *Spade on right behind desk, Brigid on left, reverse angle of 9.*

SPADE
Won't you sit down, Miss Wonderly?

BRIGID
She moves to left side of desk and sits down. Spade sits also.
Thank you. I inquired at the hotel for the name of a reliable private detective. They mentioned yours.

SPADE
Suppose you tell me about it from the very beginning.

11. MCS: *Brigid on left, facing camera; Spade on right, from side.*

> BRIGID
> I'm from New York.

> SPADE
> Uh-huh.

> BRIGID
> I'm trying to find my sister. I have reason to believe
> that she's here in San Francisco with a man by the
> name of Thursby, Floyd Thursby. *(Spade lights
> cigarette. Brigid is nervously avoiding eye contact.)* I
> don't know where she met him. We've never been as
> close as sisters ought to be. If we had, perhaps
> Corinne would have told me that she was planning
> on running away with him. Mother and Father are
> in Honolulu. It would kill them, I've got to find her
> before they get back home.

12. MCS: *reverse angle of 11.*

> BRIGID
> They're coming home the first of the month.

> SPADE
> You've had word of your sister?

13. CS: *Brigid, still nervous.*

> BRIGID
> A letter from her about two weeks ago. It said noth-
> ing except that she was all right. I sent her a
> telegram begging her to come home. I sent it to the
> general delivery here. That was the only address she
> gave me. I waited a week and no answer came so I
> decided to come here myself. I wrote her that I was
> coming.

14. MCS: *as in 12.*

> BRIGID
> I shouldn't have done that, should I?

> SPADE
> Oh, it's not always easy to know what to do. You
> haven't found her?

15. CS: *Brigid, as in 13.*

> BRIGID
> No. I told her in my letter that I'd be at the St. Mark
> and for her to meet me there. I waited three whole
> days. She didn't come, didn't even send a message.

16. MCS: *Spade.*

> BRIGID
> *(Off)*
> It was horrible. Waiting.

17. CS: *Brigid, as in 13.*

> BRIGID
> I sent her another letter to general delivery.
> Yesterday afternoon I went to the post office.
> Corinne didn't call for her mail but Floyd Thursby
> did. He wouldn't tell me where Corinne was. He
> said she didn't want to see me. I can't believe that.
> He promised to bring her to the hotel if she'd come
> this evening. He said he knew she wouldn't. He
> promised to come himself if she didn't. He would—

18. MS: *Miles, from side angle, entering office. He sees Brigid and removes his hat.*

> MILES
> Oh excuse me.

19. MCS: *Brigid and Spade, as in 11.*

SPADE
Oh, it's all right, Miles. Come in.

20. MS: *Miles, as in 18. Camera follows him into office where he stands, screen left, behind Brigid. Spade stands, screen right. Brigid remains seated.*

SPADE
Miss Wonderly, my partner, Miles Archer.

(Addresses Archer)
Miss Wonderly's sister ran away from New York with a fellow named Floyd Thursby. They're here in San Francisco. Miss Wonderly has seen Thursby and has a date to meet him tonight. Maybe he'll bring the sister with him; the chances are he won't. Miss Wonderly wants us to find the sister, get her away from him, and back home. Right?

BRIGID
Yes.

Miles, who has been ogling Brigid from behind, lasciviously rolls his eyes and purses his lips for Spade to see. He then walks over and sits on the opposite side of the desk, facing Brigid, with Spade now in the center of the composition. The camera repositions slightly.

SPADE
Now it's, uh, a simple matter of having a man at the hotel this evening to shadow him when he leads us to your sister. If, after we've found her, she still doesn't want to leave him, well, we have ways of managing that.

MILES
Yeah.

> BRIGID
>
> Oh, but you must be careful. I'm deathly afraid of
> him, what he might do. She's so young. And his
> bringing her here from New York is such a serious . . .

21. MS: *Brigid, Spade, and Miles, reverse angle of 20.*

> BRIGID
>
> Mightn't he, mightn't he do something to her?

> SPADE
>
> Now just leave that to us. We'll know how to handle
> him.

22. CS: *Brigid as in 13.*

> BRIGID
>
> Oh, but I want you to know he's a dangerous man. I
> honestly don't think he'd stop at anything. I don't
> think he'd hesitate to . . . to kill Corinne if he
> thought it would save him.

23. MS: *Brigid, Spade, and Miles, as in 21.*

> MILES
>
> Could he cover up by marrying her?

> BRIGID
>
> He has a wife and three children in England.

> SPADE
>
> Yes, they usually do, though not always in England.

> *(He leans forward and starts taking notes.)*
> What does he look like?

24. CS: *Brigid as in 13.*

> BRIGID
>
> He has dark hair and thick, bushy eyebrows. He

talks in a loud, blustery manner. He gives the
impression of being a violent person.

25. MS: *Brigid and Spade, closer view of 21.*

> BRIGID
> He was wearing a light gray suit and a, a gray hat
> when I saw him this morning.

> SPADE
> What does he do for a living?

26. CS: *Brigid, as in 13.*

> BRIGID
> Why, I haven't the faintest idea.

27. MS: *Spade and Miles.*

> SPADE
> What time's he coming to see you?

> BRIGID
> *(off)*
> After eight o'clock.

> SPADE
> All right, Miss Wonderly. We'll have a man
> there.

> MILES
> *(leaning forward, eager to please)*
>
> I'll look after it myself.

28. CS: *Brigid, as in 13.*

> BRIGID
> Oh, thank you.

29. MS: *Brigid and Spade, as in 25.*

> BRIGID
> Uh, oh yes.
> *(Opens her handbag and searches for money. Spade watches
> attentively. Camera pans to show Miles, also impressed by the
> money in her bag.)*

30. CS: *Brigid, as in 13. She knows they are watching her bag.*

31. MS: *Brigid, Spade, and Miles, as in 21.*

> BRIGID
> Will that be enough?

Spade nods "Yes."

32. LS: *Brigid, Spade, and Miles. All three stand up and the camera moves with
Spade and Brigid as he escorts her to the door and she leaves.*

> BRIGID
> Thank you.

> SPADE
> Not at all. Oh, it'll help some if you meet Thursby in
> the lobby.

> BRIGID
> I will.

> MILES
> Hey, you don't have to look for me. I'll see you all
> right.

> BRIGID
> *(to Miles, as she shakes his hand)*
> Thank you.

(She then goes to the door and, as she leaves, shakes Spade's hand.)
Thank you so much.

SPADE
Good-bye.

33. CS: *Miles, examining the money. Spade enters frame and camera pulls back to MS.*

MILES
They're right enough. They have brothers in her bag.

*Camera continues to pull back as both move into the frame and
sit at their desks on opposite sides of the frame.*

SPADE
What do you think of her?

MILES
Oh she's sweet. Ah ha-ha, maybe you saw her first,
Sam, but I spoke first.

SPADE
You've got brains.

(Camera moves down to shadow image of the "SPADE AND
ARCHER" *window lettering in the floor)*
Yes you have.

DISSOLVE. (Luhr 27–32)

While you view the film or read the screenplay above, note what elements of the literary text the film keeps, drops, and adds. Be aware that "keep" refers not only to the narrative elements brought over to the film but also to reasonable substitutions for those elements. Also keep in mind the cinematic elements the filmmakers choose to employ. These elements are explained in Chapter 2: mise-en-scène, camerawork, editing, and sound. Your lists of what is kept, dropped, and added and of the elements of film should be as extensive as possible in order to understand better the relationship between Hammett's first chapter and the film's opening sequence.

Analysis of Film's Opening Sequence

Lists

Below are items from our lists. These lists are not comprehensive but offer examples of elements we think should be on any list.

> *Kept Elements of Narrative Include*
> > Exposition: the "facts" that explain Wonderly's problem to Spade and Archer
> > Characters: same names in same roles
> > > Sam Spade, detective
> > > Effie Perine, secretary
> > > Miss Wonderly, client
> > > Corinne Wonderly (named but not shown), client's sister
> > > Miles Archer, partner
> > > Floyd Thursby (named but not shown), Corinne's supposed companion
> > Setting: a San Francisco private detective's office during working hours
> > Point of view: third person limited
>
> *Dropped Elements of Narrative Include*
> > Some dialogue
> > Ashes on Spade's desk
> > Typewriter sounds
> > Window curtains
>
> *Added Elements of Narrative Include*
> > Thumbnail sketch of the myth of the Maltese Falcon
>
> *Elements of Film:* mise-en-scène (sets, costumes, lighting, makeup, props, placement of objects and people, and actors' gestures and movements), camerawork, editing, and sound

Kept Elements

Plot

Among the elements kept is the plot exposition—a term common to both literary and film study. The "facts" that Wonderly tells Spade in the chapter have essentially been kept in the film, except for a few minor drops and substitutions. For instance, Wonderly says that her parents are in Honolulu rather than in Europe. We are not certain why Huston or someone else made this change because as of yet we have not read any statement by him or anyone else concerning it; therefore, we can only suggest that the location was changed because it would be unlikely for Wonderly's parents to be vacationing in Europe during World War II. Ironically, the film opened in some cities in December 1941, the month of the Japanese attack on Pearl Harbor. Huston unintentionally moved the parents from one dangerous location to another. This is an example of outside events having nothing to do with the novel affecting its adaptation.

Characters

Although all the characters are kept, the performers' costumes, makeup, movement, and acting are not exactly like Hammett's description of how the characters dress, look, move, and speak. Humphrey Bogart is the extreme example of this type of alteration. As James Naremore observes:

> [c]learly Humphrey Bogart is the visual opposite of Hammett's Sam Spade. Spade, Hammett tells us, is a tall man with an "almost conical" body. When he takes off his shirt, "the sag of his big rounded shoulders" makes him resemble "a bear." Bogart's slight, swarthy appearance, his menacing smile, to say nothing of his famed low-life New York accent (he calls the falcon a "black boid") evoke an altogether different personality. (150)

Although Bogart does not look—nor perhaps sound—like Hammett's "blond satan," his dark hair, bushy eyebrows, penetrating eyes, craggy face, and deep, snarling voice project a politely controlled menace reminiscent of his literary counterpart. Like Hammett's Spade, Bogart wears a business suit; he speaks the same dialogue and moves around the office in a way similar to the Spade of the novel. Both Spades roll and light a cigarette, although Bogart rolls his at the beginning of the film's first scene whereas Hammett's character rolls his at the end of the book's first chapter.

Why don't the actors look like the characters described by Hammett? This substitution has to do with the Hollywood studio system. In the classical Hollywood period, roughly from the 1930s to the 1950s, each studio had a stable of actors under contract from which to draw for any given film. If the upcoming film was an adaptation, and the contract players available for the roles did not resemble the characters as described by the author, it was of little consequence to the studio. Renting actors from other studios or hiring free agents who closely resembled the described characters could be costly for the studio. A rented or hired actor might not have been as good a performer as the studio contract player. And it was simply easier for a studio to use its own players. If a studio assigned a contract player a role in a forthcoming film, the actor had to accept it or be placed on suspension without pay. Only a few stars could refuse a role and not be punished.

As several sources report, Huston first picked George Raft to play Sam Spade, but Raft, having clout, refused Huston because, as he

> wrote to Jack Warner [in charge of production at Warner Bros.] on June 6 [1941]: "As you know, I strongly feel that *The Maltese Falcon*, which you want me to do, is not an important picture and, in this connection, I must remind you again before I signed the new contract with you, you promised me that you would not require me to perform in anything but important pictures." (Behlmer 115)

Humphrey Bogart did not enjoy the same refusal status that Raft did at Warner Bros. in 1941. So he had to accept the role of Spade or continue on suspension for having refused a part in *Bad Men of Missouri* (Behlmer 115). Thus, Huston's use of an actor who did not look like Spade was dictated by the Warner Bros. studio system. As it turned out, Bogart and Huston became friends and worked on five more films together.

Still, critics fuss over actors' appearances. Jean-Loup Bourget comments that although "the Huston version is altogether remarkable thanks [in part] to Bogart" (178), "Sam Spade ought first to have been acted by George Raft, who, one imagines, would have been closer to Ricardo Cortez of *Dangerous Female* [the renamed first adaptation of *The Maltese Falcon*, directed by Roy del Ruth, (1930)]" (180). Cortez, Bourget believes, is closer in appearance and behavior to Hammett's Sam Spade than is Bogart, and Raft, at least, resembled Cortez (176). The choice of Bogart as Sam Spade illustrates the way in which the Hollywood studio system during the classical period of Hollywood filmmaking could affect the casting of an adaptation.

Setting

Another important kept element is the interior setting. The details of the story's setting are duplicated in the studio-constructed office, except for the ashes on Spade's desk, the typewriter and machine sounds, and the curtains on the office window. We discuss the significance of their absence later under dropped elements.

Point of View

Rudy Behlmer reports that Huston said:

> "[T]he book was told entirely from the standpoint of Sam Spade, and so too is the picture, with Spade in every scene. . . . The audience knows no more and no less than he does. All the other characters are introduced only as they meet Spade, and upon their appearance I attempted to photograph them through his eyes." (117)

An exception to Huston's observation that the film is told entirely from the standpoint of Spade occurs in the very next scene after the opening sequence, in which Archer is killed. This scene is not in the novel but was inserted into the film at the request of Jack Warner. Spade is not present in the scene, so it is told from the standpoint of Archer's killer, whose identity is not revealed at that point in the film (Behlmer 119). Nevertheless, Huston's generalization about the film's point of view is essentially accurate for the opening sequence. For the most part, the camera is positioned in back of Spade and views the action from his vantage point. However, occasionally the camera is placed at other points in the scene. One important camera position is behind Miss Wonderly in the shot/reverse shot series that conveys her conversation with Spade. We should keep in mind that unlike novelists of the period who had a range of points of view from which to choose, film directors, certainly in 1941, were mainly restricted to variations of the third person.

Although the third person point of view is kept, the camera obviously does not present the action in the opening sequence exactly as it is presented in the first chapter. For example, if a director were to present the first shot of Spade exactly as the narrator describes him in the first paragraph of the chapter, the camera might present a *straight-on close-up* of the actor playing Spade looking straight into the camera, possibly expressionless, and framed perhaps by a blank wall. The camera might tilt upward from his jaw to his hairline and back down again, ranging over his several "v-shaped" facial features. Instead, in Huston's sequence, the camera presents a *straight-on, level, medium close-up* of Bogart, who is *framed* by the bottom half of an office-building window, sitting in a chair at his desk, looking down toward his fingers as he rolls a cigarette, pre-occupied in his endeavor, frowning in concentration, and not looking like a blond satan. The sound of a door clicking open is heard. The hypothetical shot in our example makes a static, dull, descriptive cinematic introduction to Spade, but the actual shot in the sequence makes a dynamic, engaging, dramatic cinematic introduction.

Topics

The topics that will be developed into themes over the course of the novel are brought over to the opening sequence of the film. Archer's unbridled greed, his frank sexuality, and his one-upmanship are retained, although the sexuality is subdued somewhat because of film censorship, as we explain under dropped elements.

Dropped Elements

Let us now consider the elements in the chapter dropped from the film. Among them is some of the dialogue in the opening sequence. The script omitted from Wonderly's dialogue the stops, starts, and fragmented sentences. Behlmer explains the choice to modify the dialogue:

> The Maltese Falcon was previewed on September 5, 1941, and the next morning Jack Warner sent a memo to Hal Wallis in which he said:
>
> "Last night after the preview, I thought for about an hour, and believe we should positively make over the opening close-ups of Mary Astor [in Spade's office] and tell the audience what the hell it is all about instead of picking up with a lot of broken sentences with confusing words. . . .
>
> "Many of the [preview] cards [audience-opinion forms] stated they were very confused in the beginning, and I am sure we throw them off. Therefore why be so clever, as we have a hell of a good picture. . . . We should do these retakes the first thing Monday."
>
> On September 10, Bogart was excused from the shooting of his next picture *All Through the Night,* and along with Mary Astor and Jerome Cowan, reported to Stage 6 to retake the opening scene in the office of Spade and Archer. Brigid's speech regarding her sister and Floyd Thursby was rewritten and simplified by Huston. For example, in the original shooting the dialogue began:

SPADE
Now what can I do for you Miss Wonderly?

MISS WONDERLY
(hurriedly)
Could you—? I thought—I—that is—

SPADE
Suppose you tell me about it from the very beginning.

MISS WONDERLY
That was in New York.

SPADE
Yes?

MISS WONDERLY
I don't know where she met him in New York. She's five years younger than I—only seventeen—we didn't have the same friends. I don't suppose we've ever been close as sisters should be. Mamma and Papa are in Europe. It would kill them. I've *got* to get her back before they come home.

In the revised scene, the exposition is clearer:

SPADE
Won't you sit down, Miss Wonderly?

MISS WONDERLY
Thank you. I inquired at the hotel for the name of a reliable private detective. They mentioned yours.

SPADE
Suppose you tell me about it from the very beginning.

MISS WONDERLY
I'm from New York.

SPADE
Uh-huh.

MISS WONDERLY
I'm trying to find my sister. I have reason to believe that she's here in San Francisco with a man by the name of Thursby.

> Floyd Thursby. I don't know where she met him. We never
> have been as close as sisters ought to be. If we had, perhaps
> Corinne would have told me that she was planning on running
> away with him. Mother and Father are in Honolulu. It will kill
> them. I've got to find her before they get back home. They're
> coming home the first of the month.

The entire dialogue up to Archer's entrance was modified in this way. (121–22)

Thus, Huston's rewriting of the opening scene was done for a practical reason: The preview audience couldn't follow Hammett's broken dialogue. More important to notice is that a film industry practice—the use of audience analysis as a way to pretest the film before its release—affected the novel's screen adaptation.

The broken elements of Wonderly's dialogue in the first chapter suggest she is nervous in telling her story to Spade, and her nervousness plays a significant part later in the plot. Nonetheless, stops, starts, and fragmented sentences are easier to make sense of while we are reading the dialogue in Hammett's novel than while we are listening to the dialogue in the film. To compensate for dropping the jagged lines, Mary Astor explains, "I hyperventilated before going into most of the scenes. It gave me a heady feeling, of thinking at cross purposes" (Behlmer 119). Her slightly breathless delivery suggests nervousness, too.

One other dialogue change is important to discuss. In the novel, after Wonderly has left the office, Archer expresses a sexual interest in her. Spade replies, "You'll play hell with her, you will." The line is dropped in the film for a practical reason. The Production Code Administration categorized the word "hell" as profanity and forbid its use. In the film, Spade just replies, "You've got brains. Yes you have." Cinema production in the United States from early on has had to deal with various forms of internal and external censorship. These include the Hays Office, the 1930 Production Code, the Legion of Decency, and today's Motion Picture Association of America's rating system. As in the case here, changes in screen content are sometimes made for the purpose of satisfying censors.

Also dropped from the opening sequence is Hammett's description of the wind-driven ashes on Spade's desk and of the background typewriter and machine noises. In the film, a close-up shot of the desktop with ashes fluttering across it and the sound track playing the diegetic noises of the typewriter and machine within the story are needless and distracting to the viewer.

The office window is without a curtain. Not having a curtain allows the audience to see plainly the stenciled lettering of "Spade and Archer" on the glass pane. The lettering plays a minor role in the film, as we discuss under added elements.

Added Elements

So far we have discussed changes made for essentially practical reasons. However, other sorts of changes are made because they convey the filmmakers' interpretation, or vision, of Hammett's text. Among the elements not in the first

Not having a curtain on the office window allows the audience to see plainly the stenciled reverse lettering of "Spade and Archer" on the glass panes in *The Maltese Falcon.*

chapter of the novel that are added to the opening sequence of the film are the titles, the images over which the titles are superimposed, and the theme music playing while the images and titles are shown. These elements are unrelated to the world of the story and are called nondiegetic elements. The characters Spade, Perine, Wonderly, and Archer are unaware that these elements exist; only we viewers of the film can read the titles, look at the images, and listen to the music.

However, the titles include more than a simple listing of names and professional roles against a neutral background, so they merit attention. Most significant of these additions is the thumbnail sketch of the myth of the Maltese Falcon. Behlmer explains:

> Jack Warner . . . requested a short written prologue giving the background and history of the Falcon on a title following the opening credits. The background was partially based on fact. Hammett stated that "somewhere I had read of the peculiar rental agreement between Charles V [of Spain] and the Order of the Hospital of St. John of Jerusalem [the Knights of Malta]." This agreement of 1530 specified that rent for the Island of Malta would be an annual tribute on All Saints Day of a single falcon. The rest of the history seems to be Hammett's romantic embellishment. (120)

After reading the account of the myth, we know what the statuette is, why it was made, and that it is missing. This information provides us with more than we know about the Falcon after reading the first chapter of the novel. Yet after watching the rest of the opening sequence, we do not know how the Maltese

Falcon connects to the Wonderly case. Still, providing this information in the film is a departure for Huston. Following Hammett, Huston usually avoids explanations, forestalls connections, and plunges the viewer into the characters' world of mystery and suspense. In this case, however, Huston, at Warner's urging, uses the thumbnail sketch to identify the Maltese Falcon and to evoke viewer interest in it as an old, elusive treasure. Warner's request for the addition of the thumbnail sketch in *The Maltese Falcon* is another example of the influence of the production company on the screen adaptation.

Even though the credits are not significant to the narrative, their animated presentation is. In each of the nine close-up shots in which the credits appear, they swiftly swirl onto the screen, quickly solidify, and then suddenly dissolve in the same way. This swirling takes place against the still, solid background of the statuette and obscures it to a degree. The swirling makes a credit appear initially unclear; we have to wait until it forms into something we can read and interpret. Then it dissolves into something new and unclear; we have to wait again until it forms once more into something we can read and interpret. In a similar way, one could argue that Spade listens patiently for Wonderly to explain her complicated story and then quickly and accurately gives a succinct paraphrase of her situation. In the next sequence of the film, which is an adaptation of the second chapter of the novel, "Death in the Fog," Spade's understanding of Wonderly's situation suddenly dissolves for both himself and the viewer. Eventually Spade forms a new understanding of her situation, but that, in turn, also dissolves. This pattern repeats itself through the entire film and novel. The credit animation is a correlative for Spade's predicament; it prefigures how he must constantly make and remake sense of the other characters and their actions throughout the film.

After the credits and the myth of the Maltese Falcon have appeared, four exterior, extreme long shots of San Francisco dissolve into one another and show from various standpoints one of that city's famous icons, the recently built Golden Gate Bridge, spanning the inlet to San Francisco Bay and towering above the city's other buildings. The shots tell us where we are and serve as a bit of a travelogue. A "bit" is all we get, for the shots leave us no other architecture or landscape to ponder. As in the first chapter of the novel, the city plays virtually no role in the opening sequence except that it is shown as the city in which the action is set. The viewer has been told briefly where she or he is, and Huston gets on with his story.

The transition shot from the Golden Gate Bridge to the detectives' office is a close-up interior shot of a window with "REHCRA DNA EDAPS" stenciled on, a reverse spelling of the title of the first chapter of the novel, "SPADE AND ARCHER." The shot shifts the setting from the exterior of the city to the interior of the detectives' office. This shot appears to be a way for Huston to tell the viewer that his film adaptation is, in his mind, a mirror image of the novel. At the end of the opening sequence, the tilted-down, close-up shot of the window's shadow cast on the floor of the office is a "negative" copy of the original window. Again, this appears to be a way for Huston to tell the viewer that his film adaptation is a cinematic copy of the novel. The long, dark lettering also ominously foreshadows the very short future of the partnership. This future is revealed to the reader in the next chapter of the novel and to the viewer in the next sequence of the film.

Except for lighting, we touch on most of the important elements of mise-en-scène under the analysis of kept elements. The quality of the lighting of the statuette of the Maltese Falcon and of the office set is essentially *hard*, creating clearly defined shadows, crisp textures, and sharp edges. The design of the lighting is *low key*, producing strong contrasts between the light and dark areas in the shot. This style of lighting is usually associated with the dim, gloomy, sinister world of murder mysteries, crime stories, detective stories, and spy stories. The shot of the statuette is a close-up. This shot gives us some sense of what it looks like, although our view of the statuette is partially obscured by the credits and thumbnail sketch of its story. The shots of the characters in the office vary from close-up to long shot. The long shots introduce the characters as they enter Spade's office and meet him. The close-ups and medium close-ups focus on the characters' reactions to each other as they talk. The editing of the medium close-up and close-up shots move from one character's reaction to another in a shot/reverse-shot pattern that is typical for depicting conversation. As Bordwell and Thompson point out about the film editing in the opening sequence, "[t]he viewer is not supposed to notice all this. Throughout, the shots present space to emphasize the cause-and-effect flow—the characters' actions, entrances, dialogue, reactions" (317). Huston's style of shooting, both the type of shots and the rhythm of the editing, are analogous to Hammett's straightforward prose style.

The theme music, composed by Adolph Deutsch, that we hear over the credits is, as Behlmer suggests:

> [a] subtle and properly mysterious score that was devoid of bombast. The Warners music style of that time usually was thick textured, with heavy brass and strings surging to the foreground. Deutsch was relatively unobtrusive in his approach and gave the edge more to the mood and colorings his use of woodwinds evoked. He told me recently that he consciously avoided "the Wagnerian approach" and that he did not want obvious leitmotifs overpowering the picture. (120)

Instead of imposing a typical Warner Bros. music style on the film, Deutsch composed an unobtrusive score that complements the low-key style of the camerawork.

Once the transition, interior, close-up shot of the office window with "Spade and Archer" stenciled on it appears, the theme music stops, and the only sounds are produced by objects being moved and the dialogue of the characters. These are diegetic sounds.

As several film critics have noted, Huston's *The Maltese Falcon* comes at the beginning of a period in film history in which the style of *film noir* flourished. This film style is another, larger context in which to study the film. *Film noir* is French for "black film." The term refers to a specific style of film made in Hollywood during the 1940s and '50s. This style features a sinister, vicious, and violent urban world of vice and crime, populated by base and neurotic characters and emphasizing dreary settings, dark shadows, and high contrasts of light and dark. Since film styles supply conventions that can affect adaptations, it is worth noting a few *film noir* elements that appear in the opening sequence. The swirling-credit animation can suggest cigarette smoke and urban fog, two atmospheric motifs. The shadowy lighting and the mysterious theme music create a dark, ominous mood that fits a detective story. And as in other films of this genre, a client hires a private investigator to end an illicit affair.

The First Chapter and the Opening Sequence

We have discussed many differences between the novel's first chapter and the film's opening sequence, and some of the practical and interpretative reasons behind those differences. Now we are in a position to draw a conclusion about the relationship between the chapter and the opening sequence. There are three broad choices: the film is a close, loose, or an intermediate adaptation. After considering all three types, we decide the opening sequence is a close adaptation of the first chapter. Most of the elements of narrative in the first chapter are kept. Only a few elements are dropped, mostly for practical reasons, and the elements that are added are elements of film. Huston appears to agree when he says, "[I]t was simply a matter of editing Dashiell Hammett's book. It's his book on the screen and it took me all of three weeks to write the screenplay" (Prately 63).

Huston's remarks about his adaptation suggest he took it for granted that there was a story capable of being translated from one medium to another. He further believed he had identified that story, and was confident that he had filmed it. As Huston explained in an interview with Gene D. Phillips:

> After Allen Rivkin and I finished the screenplay of *The Maltese Falcon* [1941], I asked to direct it. Dashiell Hammett's book had been filmed twice before, but the previous screen adapters didn't have the faith in the story that we did. Our script simply reduced the book to a screenplay, without any fancy additions of our own. (37)

Rivkin, by the way, is not acknowledged as a co-writer of the screenplay in the film's credits and in most commentary on the film. However, he is a source for Behlmer concerning the process by which Huston wrote the screenplay:

> An account given by Huston and verified by writer Allen Rivkin, who at the time shared a secretary with Huston, goes as follows: Huston gave the novel to the

secretary and told her to recopy the text, but to break it down routinely into script format with the usual scene numbers and shot descriptions. . . .

Eventually Huston tightened the narrative and eliminated a few scenes, . . . but he retained an unusually large amount of the dialogue, style, and ambiance used by Hammett. . . . Fortunately, the novel lends itself to dramatization, being primarily a series of brilliant dialogues. (112–13)

Huston closely adapted the dialogue, style, and ambiance from the first chapter of Hammett's novel in the opening sequence of the film. Those three elements of narrative, to repeat Huston, are "what is up on the screen."

Microcosmic and Macrocosmic Analyses

In introducing a method for investigating the relationship between a literary work and the film adapted from it, we have confined ourselves to one chapter of a novel and to one sequence of a film. This specific application of the method we call the **microcosmic application.** In a microcosmic application, students of adaptation investigate in fine detail a small part of the literary text and the corresponding part of the film. They seek to articulate the relationship between the two.

However, we do not claim that the small part of the literary text and the corresponding part of the film stand for the whole literary text or for the whole film. For example, sometimes one student concludes the adaptation under discussion is close, a second student says it is loose, and a third student thinks it is intermediate. We find out each student has investigated a separate, small part of the literary text and of the film. Each investigation is accurate, but each student has hastened to generalize from his or her specific study. Through analyzing such opposing claims, the students discover that most adaptations are uneven. At times, a certain passage in the literary text is closely adapted in the corresponding sequence in the film. At times, a passage is loosely adapted in the sequence. At times, a passage is intermediately adapted.

To help students realize the unevenness in any given adaptation and to avoid confusion, a reckoning is required. To accomplish this reckoning and to complement the microcosmic application of the method, we have the **macrocosmic application.** In a macrocosmic application, the student investigates the whole literary text, paragraph by paragraph, stanza by stanza, or dialogue by dialogue. Then the student investigates the whole film, sequence by sequence, scene by scene, and even shot by shot. The student aims to articulate a more complete relationship between the whole literary text and the whole film. In such a study, the student weighs the uneven adapted passages and sequences. He or she slowly determines if the general trend of the adaptation is close, loose, or intermediate. Then the student categorizes the adaptation appropriately.

Subsequent chapters employ not only microcosmic but also macrocosmic applications of the method to help you come to an extensive understanding of the wide-ranging relationships between the whole literary text and the whole film adapted from it. Now that you have become familiar with the method, apply it to other films. At the end of Chapters 5–10 you will find recommended pairings of texts and films.

TOPICS FOR DISCUSSION

1. Take another section from Hammett's *The Maltese Falcon* and, using the method described, examine how it is transferred to the screen in the 1941 Huston version.

2. Look at several other characters besides Sam Spade in *The Maltese Falcon* (1941). How well do you think the actors fit the parts based on your own reading of their roles in Hammett's novel? Offer a plausible explanation for the casting whenever you think the actor doesn't quite fit the part.

3. In this chapter, we report the influence Jack Warner had on the opening sequence of the film. Do you consider his influence beneficial or detrimental to the narrative and cinematic elements of the opening sequence?

4. In Topic 1 we suggest you analyze another adapted section of *The Maltese Falcon* (1941). Is the adaptation of this section as close as the adaptation of the first chapter of the novel? If not, would you characterize it as loose or intermediate? Is it possible for two chapters from the same literary text to be adapted differently?

WORKS CITED

BEHLMER, RUDY. " 'The Stuff That Dreams Are Made of':*The Maltese Falcon.*" *The Maltese Falcon: John Huston, Director.* Ed. William Luhr. New Brunswick: Rutgers University Press, 1995. 112–24.

BORDWELL, DAVID, AND KRISTIN THOMPSON. *Film Art: An Introduction.* 7th ed. New York: McGraw-Hill, 2004.

BOURGET, JEAN-LOUP (writing as Jacques Segond). "On the Trail of Dashiell Hammett (The Three Versions of *The Maltese Falcon*)." *The Maltese Falcon: John Huston,* *Director.* Ed. William Luhr. New Brunswick: Rutgers University Press, 1995. 176–80.

HAMMETT, DASHIELL. *The Maltese Falcon.* New York: Vintage, 1992.

LUHR, WILLIAM. "Tracking *The Maltese Falcon:* Classical Hollywood Narration and Sam Spade." *The Maltese Falcon: John Huston, Director.* Ed. William Luhr. New Brunswick: Rutgers University Press, 1995. 161–75.

Maltese Falcon, The. Dir. John Huston. Perf. Humphrey Bogart and Mary Astor. Warner Bros., 1941.

NAREMORE, JAMES. "John Huston and *The Maltese Falcon.*" *The Maltese Falcon: John Huston, Director.* Ed. William Luhr. New Brunswick: Rutgers University Press, 1995. 149–60.

PHILLIPS, GENE D. "Talking with John Huston." *John Huston Interviews.* Ed. Robert Emmet Long. Jackson: University Press of Mississippi, 2001. 36–43.

PRATELY, GERALD. *The Cinema of John Huston.* New York: A. S. Barnes and Company, 1977.

5 THE NOVEL

At the first Academy Awards in Hollywood, the screenwriter Benjamin Glazer received an Oscar for adapting the silent film *Seventh Heaven* (1927). This early recognition of adaptation as an Oscar category is not surprising given the many adaptations made early in film history. In fact, a history of adaptation would start just a few years after the invention of cinema itself. Among the earliest examples is *The Death of Nancy Sykes* (1897), an episode derived from Charles Dickens's novel *Oliver Twist*.

The adaptation of printed texts continues to this day. Although estimates vary, several commentators agree that about one-third of all modern commercial films have come from literary sources. Brian McFarlane cites Morris Beja's calculation that since the first Academy Awards, adaptations have won three-fourths of the Oscars for best picture (*Novel* 8). In the 2003 Academy Award competition, all five nominations for Best Picture were adaptations: *Gangs of New York, The Lord of the*

Peter Jackson
accepting the 2004
Oscar for directing
*The Lord of the
Rings: The Return
of the King.*

Rings: The Two Towers, The Hours, The Pianist, and *Chicago,* which won. In the 2004 Academy Awards, four out of five nominations for Best Picture were adaptations: *Mystic River, Seabiscuit, Master and Commander: The Far Side of the World,* and *Lord of the Rings: Return of the King,* which won.

Literary texts of all kinds are a great source for films, but it has been the novel that has provided the bulk of the material. It's been estimated that half of all film adaptations come from novels. This is not surprising since the novel and narrative film share so many storytelling elements. Both use settings, characters, plot, actions, themes, and symbols to tell their stories.

There has long existed a symbiotic relationship between the novel and film. The novel not only offered early filmmakers story material but also provided them with narrative techniques. Sergei Eisenstein claims that film methods such as montage, dissolve, close-up, pan, and parallel action (where two stories unfold at the same time and the camera switches back and forth from one to another) owe a debt to narrative techniques used by the novelist Charles Dickens. Today the borrowing goes both ways. Alain Robbe-Grillet, for example, has produced several novels in which the story imitates a series of camera shots connected by jump cuts and other editing devices.

Classic novels once adapted because they were well known to the public, such as Dickens's *A Christmas Carol,* are now mainly remembered because of their film adaptations. Where once some novels were intentionally written to become best sellers, they are now intentionally written to become box office hits. In some cases, publishers look at the novel they accept as the first draft of a screenplay, sell the screen rights, and use the movie to market the book. A common practice is to place a famous face from the movie on the cover of a reissued novel to sell thousands of additional books. A case in point is Richard Russo's novel *Nobody's Fool* (1994). The original paperback edition carried on its cover the photograph of a man dressed in bib overalls sitting on the porch of a house typical of those in a small upstate New York town, which was the setting of the novel. But after screenwriter and director Robert Benton adapted the novel into a film, the publisher placed a photograph of Paul Newman as the lead character, Donald Sullivan, on the cover. Once the film left the movie theaters, the original photograph was reinstated.

The use of the film to sell the novel is an example of the "tie-in"—a marketing strategy that links book and film and other commodities in a circle of profitability. In today's era of multimedia corporations, executives think beyond the adaptation to a host of other ways of exploiting the literary story. The starting point may be the book and then the adaptation released domestically and worldwide, but soon the marketing moves to the videocassette and DVD, to TV and cable rights, to an audiocassette tape and CD of the film's soundtrack, to computer and video games, to the Internet, and to other marketable commodities, anything from T-shirts to toys. All of these forms lead away from the book, but they also lead some people back to it.

Filmmakers have been adapting novels for over a century, but how have they been able to transpose stories to the extent that audiences recognize the novel on the screen and reviewers find it imperative to compare the novel to the film? What techniques have filmmakers used to refashion the novel into cinematic terms?

Some Fundamentals of Novel Adaptation

Length to Length

Let's begin with some basic math. Novels tend to be long. Contemporary novels average 300 to 400 pages; nineteenth-century novels run even longer. Herman Melville's *Moby-Dick,* for example, was first published in England in three volumes and runs to more than 800 pages in some modern editions.

A major concern of the adapter of a novel running from 150 to 1,000 pages is that feature films last about two hours. One page of a screenplay takes about a minute to show on the screen, so the average script consists of 120 to 125 pages. How does a filmmaker transfer a novel into a screenplay when the screenplay is roughly two-thirds *shorter* in length?

Cutting

Clearly, the adapter has to cut elements from the story. This lesson was learned early in the film business when Erich Von Stroheim seemed determined to film virtually every sentence of Frank Norris's approximately 300-page novel *McTeague.*

The result was a nine-hour film adaptation called *Greed* (1924). Executives at Metro-Goldwyn-Mayer concluded that no film exhibitor would show a film that long and no audience would sit through it. MGM had the film cut down to just a quarter of its original length, with a running time of approximately 2 hours and 15 minutes. The making of *Greed* is a cautionary tale for all adapters of novels: Not every sentence can be filmed; there is no such thing as a one-to-one correspondence between a novel and a film; and, therefore, dropping some narrative elements is essential.

In an interview, Joel Engel asked screenwriter Nicholas Meyer how he wrote a screenplay for Miguel Cervantes' 1000-page novel *Don Quixote:*

> JE: It must have been a long screenplay.
>
>   NM: Actually, it was about 130 pages, normal size. What I did—this is the way I adapt novels . . . —I got a notebook and reread the book, putting down a sentence for every page. I turned a 1000-page novel into a 100-page outline, with a page number next to each sentence. That way, you learn the book real well. Then you can read the book in outline form and say, "That I like, this I don't like, this I need, that I don't need." (98)

Meyer's method was to reduce each page of this 1000-page novel to a sentence and then from the sentence outline to make further cuts. But even in a less extreme case, significant **cutting** and **condensing** are necessary. The cutting and condensing can begin with elements the novel carries at length and in abundance: exposition, settings, characters, scenes, dialogue, and subplots.

Visualizing, Double-Tasking, and Voicing Exposition

Most traditional novels begin with exposition, in which the setting is described, background is given, characters are introduced, and the initial conflict is suggested. Film is good at visualizing exposition. According to Robert Giddings, "Moving pictures take you there, to the very place, and show you who is who and what is what" (xiv). Marshall McLuhan explains that

> film has the power to store and convey a great deal of information. In an instant it presents a scene of landscape with figures that would require several pages of prose to describe. In the next instant it repeats, and can go on repeating, this detailed information. The writer, on the other hand, has no means of holding a mass of detail before his reader in so large a bloc or gestalt. . . . (Giddings xiv)

The traditional novel's opening description of place can be conveyed through a visualization of the locale, and long descriptions of character can be communicated almost instantly through the film actor's body and movements, face and facial expressions, voice and speech patterns.

Another way of compressing the novel's initial exposition is to make the opening film sequence serve a double purpose: The scene visualizes the exposition *while the screen credits are displayed.* For example, *Gods and Monsters* (1998), directed by Bill Condon and adapted from Christopher Bram's novel *Father of Frankenstein*, begins with credits superimposed or "titled over" the opening film footage. The film tells the story of the last days of James Whale, the director of *Frankenstein* and other horror movies, who, retired, lonely, and in ill health develops a relationship with Clay Boone, a young gardener. The opening credits are superimposed over scenes showing the muscular Clay waking up in a battered trailer. Clay is characterized by his belongings—cigarettes, a lighter with a Marine insignia, a beer bottle, work boots, and a muscle shirt. He gets into his pickup filled with garden tools and drives along a highway showing ocean, palm trees and 1950s vintage cars to a wealthy landscaped residence. Some three minutes into the film, the credits end just after revealing Whale inside the house looking out at the new yardman, an aging homosexual shown separated from the object of his attention by glass, curtain, and drape. These particular scenes with superimposed screen credits are an economical use of film time. They replicate the work of the novel's exposition by visualizing the time, place, characters, and initial situation, while also identifying the film title, director, major actors, screenwriter, and so on.

The voiceover, a film technique commonly used to establish point of view, is also used to convey exposition economically. Some interesting uses of the *voiceover to convey exposition* can be found in Pip's opening remarks in *Great Expectations* (1946); in Nick Carraway's voiceover during the first sixteen minutes of *The Great Gatsby* (1974); in Scout's voiceover in both young and old voices in *To Kill a Mockingbird* (1962); and in the voiceovers of Henry Hill and his wife, Karen, in *Goodfellas* (1990).

Using Versions of Intertitle Cards

Another substitution for the novel's exposition is the use of *intertitle cards*, familiar to viewers of silent films. The thumbnail sketch provided at the beginning of *The Maltese Falcon* to identify the falcon and its myth is an example of this device. Likewise, in both the 1932 and 1957 adaptations of Hemingway's *A Farewell to Arms*, intertitle cards are used to express some of the novel's exposition. The 1932 version, directed by Frank Borzage, identifies the war and two of its fronts.

> Disaster as well as victory is written for every nation on the record of the first World War, but high on the rolls of glory two names are inscribed—The Marne and The Piave.

The 1957 version, directed by Charles Vidor, offers more extensive exposition.

> We tell a story out of one of the wildest theaters of World War I—the snow-capped Alpine peaks and muddy plains of northern Italy.
> Here between 1915 and 1918 the Italians stood against the German and Austrian invaders. No people ever fought more valiantly, no nation ever rose more gallantly out of defeat to victory.

> But our story is not of war alone. It is a tale also of a love between an American boy and an English girl who bade their tragic farewell to arms while the cannon roared.

Intertitle cards are rarely used in modern movies, and when they are, they are highly abbreviated, usually to a line of text on the screen indicating the time and place of the action: Venice, New Year's Day, 2006. This modern use orients the viewer in telegraphic form, combining narrative function with film economy.

Skipping the Exposition

Sometimes novels begin with dozens of pages describing the setting, the characters, and the initial situation. In contrast to this lengthy exposition, contemporary films often start with an intense conflict. This is because filmmakers feel they have only a dozen minutes or so to capture the audience. As a consequence, adapters may read for the first important dramatic conflict in a novel and start with that, skipping introductory material and adding any necessary background or **backstory** at strategic points later in the film.

This technique is described by Stuart Ian Burns:

> [A] good beginning might not present itself until some time into the novel. In *Kramer versus Kramer,* the writer begins with over 40 pages of background information before there is a suitable beginning for the screenplay. . . .

In this adaptation, the novel's exposition is skipped so that the film adaptation can start with a compelling dramatic situation. Of course, that dramatic situation also serves to introduce the story's time and place and to set the tone.

Moby Dick (1956), directed by John Huston, dispenses with Herman Melville's prefatory material on the whale and eliminates most of the first chapter, which consists of Ishmael's lengthy musings on why he is going to sea. In their place, the screenwriter Ray Bradbury invents a scene with background music showing Ishmael heading downhill toward water while his voiceover describes a few of his motives for going to sea. The film quickly moves to Melville's Chapter 2, the first dramatic scene of the novel, where Ishmael encounters the inhabitants of the Spouter Inn.

A more recent example of skipping opening narrative material occurs in Jane Campion's 1996 adaptation of Henry James's *The Portrait of a Lady.* In the novel, Isabel Archer, a high-spirited American girl, is courted by a number of men and eventually agrees to marry one of them. The novel begins with a tea at an estate north of London where Lord Warburton is first made aware of the newly arrived Isabel, but it is not until the novel's twelfth chapter that Warburton proposes to her. The film, however, starts with Warburton's marriage proposal, an elision of nearly 100 pages. Most film adaptations of novels find their beginnings not on page one but somewhere in the body of the novel.

Cutting Characters

One element almost always reduced in an adapted novel is the cast of characters. For example, *Gone with the Wind* (1939) was intended by its makers as a close adaptation, primarily because the novel was a best seller and many in the audience were sure to know the story. However, one might ask, "How can it be a close adaptation?" when the novel ran to 1000 pages. Screenwriter Linda Seger explains one area where the story was cut.

> In the film *Gone with the Wind,* you know the characters of Scarlett O'Hara, Rhett Butler, Melanie, Ashley, Aunt Pittypat, Dr. Meade, Prissy, and Mammy. If you read the book, you would be introduced to several other important characters, such as Archie, Will, and the governor. In the book, Scarlett's mother, Ellen, was a very important figure whose values and kindnesses and images of what it meant to be a Southern lady served as both an example to Scarlett and as a reason for her considerable guilt about much of her behavior. Yet Ellen was rarely seen in the film. She needed to be sacrificed because of the length of the novel. (3)

Similarly, Robert Benton's screen adaptation of Russo's *Nobody's Fool* drops approximately twenty characters to help make the 549-page novel fit the 110-minute film. In *Midnight in the Garden of Good and Evil* (1997), directed by Clint Eastwood, half of the novel's 106 characters were either cut or combined. Usually, the adapter has no choice but to reduce a novel's cast of characters because of film length.

Cutting Scenes

Besides characters, the adapter often drops unnecessary scenes that do not advance the plot or are not essential in revealing or developing a character. Burns offers an example of scenes cut in Francis Ford Coppola's 1972 adaptation of Mario Puzo's novel.

> The first quarter of the novel of *The Godfather* deals with the young Vito [the character played by Marlon Brando] going to America and his early days in New York. These are very interesting, but in screenplay terms they do not drive the character or story forward—a scene with a member of his extended family in the film demonstrates that he is a man of experience to fear and respect.

The Godfather cuts much of the material about Vito's early life and uses a scene to compensate for the omission, but it's worth mentioning that the Vito material plays an important role in *The Godfather: Part 2* (1974) and contributes to the success of that film.

Cutting or Reducing Subplots

A subplot is a minor action running parallel to and contributing to the main plot. Some novelists create several subplots to give impetus, support, and interest to the main plot. Usually, if a novel has a great many characters, a good number of their stories will be carried by these minor actions. So one way to reduce the novel is to eliminate or compress subplots.

For example, in F. Scott Fitzgerald's novel *The Great Gatsby*, Nick Carraway carries on a romantic relationship with Jordan Baker that parallels the relationship between Jay Gatsby and Daisy Buchanan. However, in the 1976 adaptation of the novel that subplot is greatly reduced by cutting key scenes and dialogue involving Carraway and Baker. Similarly, in Russo's *Nobody's Fool*, the sixty-year-old Sully, the main character, has a long-standing affair with Ruth, a woman in her late forties, who is married to a jealous husband. Ruth has two grown children, one of whom is married to another jealous husband. Sully's love interest in Ruth is omitted, along with her relatives and their stories, as a way to shorten the length of the film.

Combining Scenes

Sometimes an adapter decides not to cut narrative elements but to combine them as a way to condense. For example, in James's *Portrait of a Lady*, Lord Warburton first proposes marriage to Isabel in Chapter 12 and then asks once again in Chapter 14 when he is rebuffed. Campion's film version combines the two proposal scenes. Both contain important dialogue, but they are somewhat redundant, so combining and condensing them makes sense. In John Berendt's novel *Midnight in the Garden of Good and Evil*, there are four trials of Jim Williams for murder—three in Savannah and one in Macon. In Eastwood's adaptation, the four trials are combined into one extended trial, which takes up a good part of the movie. Another example of combining scenes occurs in *Tom Jones* (1963), directed by Tony Richardson, in which the novel's many scenes set at an inn are conflated into one extended inn scene.

Burns identifies another use of this technique in *The Pelican Brief* (1993), directed by Alan J. Pakula, an adaptation of John Grisham's mystery novel.

> In *The Pelican Brief*, Darby Shaw rings the journalist, Gray Grantham, on a number of occasions to get his attention. In the film, we view only two of these calls, and these are re-written to include important information and imply the existence of the other communications (this strategy is used frequently in adaptations, usually with the immortal line—"Why do you keep calling me?").

Combining scenes, then, is a timesaving way to retain elements of the novel.

Truncation

Another strategy to shorten a scene is to **truncate** it or to show only a slice of it to suggest the whole. Two common scenes in novels that lend themselves to *truncation* are classroom and courtroom scenes. Just the final words of a lecture, a bell ringing, and students exiting the classroom are enough to suggest the character is a student or a teacher. For example, *Marathon Man* (1976), directed by John Schlesinger, an adaptation of William Goldman's novel, conveys a classroom scene by starting it at the last minute: "It begins with 'Well, class . . .' and the bell ringing, leading to another scene" (Burns). Likewise, a courtroom scene need not be dramatized in full but can be sketched with a few quick shots: the accused person standing, a judge's sentence, the pounding of a gavel, and the character led off to jail. The truncated scene is another economical device used for retaining narrative elements.

Dialogue

Good dialogue accomplishes a number of things at once. It advances the story by communicating information from one character to another; it reveals the characters' values or traits; and it reveals or suggests their inward and outward feelings and thoughts. However, the time limitations of the feature film dictate that, in most cases, the novel's dialogue must be pruned or cut. In carrying a scene over from the book, the screenwriter often simply rewrites the essential dialogue into the fewest number of words while advancing the plot and the audience's knowledge of the characters.

Screenwriter Scott Frank explains that another alternative is to make the camera take the place of dialogue whenever possible.

> Some of my favorite novels are told mostly through dialogue. Screenplays are also told a lot through the dialogue, but key things that can be done visually are done. In a book, two people just saying things, and saying them in an interesting way, and thinking about interesting things can be good reading. You can't do that in a movie. (Engel 280)

"You can't do that in a movie" because film is primarily a visual medium that tells its story using pictures. Screenwriter Nicholas Meyer explains:

> In many ways I think it helps to be illiterate as a screenwriter. The best of them think in pictures, not words. What makes Steven Spielberg great is that he thinks in pictures. That's not pejorative. For me, coming from a verbal and playwriting background, I have to go through a double process. First, I think in dramatic terms about what's going on, and I wind up thinking about words and dialogue and so forth. Then I have to think of ways to get rid of words and dialogue and make it into pictures. When sound first came to Hollywood, they brought out all these playwrights, because they needed help with the talk. They tell this one guy to write this one scene of a marriage breaking up. He did—ten pages; brilliant dialogue. They gave it to Billy Wilder, who allegedly solved the problem with one scene, no words: Man and his wife get into an elevator, the man is wearing his hat. The elevator stops at another floor, an attractive young tootsie gets in. Cut to the lobby: elevator doors open, man has removed his hat. End of marriage. No words. (Engel 98–99)

The Wilder example demonstrates how a screenwriter can visualize a situation in a way that makes dialogue unnecessary. In general, the screenwriter cannot keep all the dialogue from a novel because a feature film is a shorter form that stresses visual imagery, so it is necessary to cut or sharpen dialogue or to replace the information it conveys with camera shots.

Continuity and Coherence

To shrink the novel down to feature-length size, adapters cut, combine, condense, and truncate. But once the novel has been whittled down, the adapter has to worry about **continuity and coherence.** When background, characters, scenes, settings, and dialogue are cut or abbreviated, causality or motivation may be reduced or eliminated. After cutting elements, transitional material may be added to make the film coherent to the viewer. For example, *Get Shorty* (1995), directed by Barry Sonnenfeld and adapted from Elmore Leonard's novel, concerns Chili Palmer, a loan shark for the Miami mob, who pursues a defaulting client to Hollywood. In the novel, one whole scene describes Chili's estranged wife purchasing a leather coat for her husband. That scene is dropped from the film, so when Chili discovers his leather jacket has been stolen from a restaurant cloakroom, the extent of his anger is unexplained. A line is added in which Chili mentions to the maitre d' that his wife bought the coat for him in New York, implying that it has sentimental as well as cash value. In this case, a character's emotion is explained by a scene in the novel that is dropped from the film, so a line of film dialogue is added to compensate for the omission and make Chili's emotion coherent.

Rearrangement

Some traditional novels have a beginning, a middle, and an end with events generally presented in chronological order, but a film adapter need not stick to a novel's temporal arrangement. The adapter may reorder events for any number of reasons—to build suspense, to create clearer causality, or to fit the demands of a film genre. To understand **rearrangement,** it is helpful to recall the distinction between story and plot explained in Chapter 2. The story refers to the settings, characters, and events presented in chronological order. The plot is the way the settings, characters, and events are represented in terms of causal and temporal order. The adapter can abstract settings, characters, and events from a novel but not follow the novel's presentation of these elements. The adapter can construct his or her own arrangement.

Sometimes the adapter rearranges the elements of the novel in order to begin with a highly charged dramatic scene. There may be no scene like this in the novel until the very end, so the ending of the novel may be moved to the beginning of the film and serve as the present. After this, past events are shown that lead up to the opening. This is called a **framed narrative:** The story begins in a narrative present, stops, and then backs up to a past narrative that eventually catches up to the narrative present and moves beyond it. Allan Rowe identifies an example of narrative rearrangement in *The Ice Storm* (1997), directed by Ang Lee, an adaptation of Rick Moody's novel of the same name.

> *The Ice Storm,* for instance, starts with its [the novel's] ending (the morning after
> the storm), and then tells us what happened up to that moment, but eschews any
> of the conventional signifiers of the flashback, such as the dissolve. This technique
> reinforces a sense of inevitability in the actions and reactions presented—we know
> how it is all going to end. (116)

The film begins in the present just short of the novel's ending and then backs up
to the period leading up to the storm and its aftermath. The two time frames
come together and then move on chronologically.

Another example of rearrangement is found in Volker Schlöndorff's *Swann
in Love* (1984), an adaptation of the first volume of Marcel Proust's *Remembrance
of Things Past.* Charles Swann, an educated bachelor, is obsessed with Odette de
Crecy, a courtesan, and eventually succeeds in marrying her although Swann's
sexual jealousy continues. According to John Orr,

> [t]hough Proust's narrative of Swann's life . . . works chronologically, the film
> version reverses the author's narrative sequence by starting with the climax to
> Swann's suspicions of Odette's liaisons with both men and women, and then
> tracing the early blossoming of their affair through flashback. (7)

Opening with a powerful scene that stresses the inevitability of an outcome is
just one reason a filmmaker may have for rearranging the presentation of
events in a novel.

Beyond Cutting: Finding Correlatives

Novels contain many narrative elements that are relatively easy to transpose
from the page to the screen. Settings, characters, dialogue, and events lend
themselves to display, but some elements of the novel are virtually impossible
to transfer and require cinematic equivalents where possible.

Orr identifies three problematic areas where cinematic equivalents need to
be found:

> In fiction, narrative language is used to describe consciousness, but the camera has
> no analogous convention for rendering thought. Consequently, . . . the narrative
> language of feeling, attitude, and judgment in the novel often becomes more
> ambiguous and problematic when rendered through the image. (2)

In other words, novels can tell us *directly* what a person is thinking or feeling,
but films cannot unless a voiceover or some other intrusive cinematic device is
used. It is true that sometimes the camera can focus on a facial expression, a
body movement, or a hand gesture to express inner thoughts, but these images
are much more ambiguous in conveying thought and feeling than the narrator
of a novel simply telling the reader directly.

For example, in *The Red Badge of Courage* (1951), directed by John Huston,
Henry Fleming, an untried soldier, is shown marching toward his first battle. In
the novel, the limited-omniscient narrator tells us directly that Fleming is scared.

However, there is no good way for the camera to show Fleming's anxiety visually because he is trying to hide his fear from the other soldiers marching beside him. Huston's answer to this problem is to use a disembodied voiceover—like the voice of God—to directly inform viewers of Henry's inner feelings.

Orr identifies a second problem—the lack of flexibility in handling multiple points of view: "[T]he camera usually works from a series of fixed viewpoints. Though this can be changed with rapid cutting or tracking, nonetheless the fluid interchangeability of the point of view which is a feature of the classic novel up to Henry James is less easy" (2).

A third problem with adaptation also involves point of view. In film, it is difficult to convey a distinctive narrative voice. According to McFarlane,

> The narrative in a novel is conveyed through two kinds of voices: those attributed to various characters in direct speech and that of the author's narration. . . . In the film adaptation, actors can be given the words of characters, either direct from the novel, or in some modified form; it is considerably more challenging for the filmmaker to render that other voice, that of authorial narration, which, in the novel, will be our guide as to what we make of the words spoken by the characters. (*Words* 15)

In the novel, there is always a distance between the teller and the tale. The teller of the tale mainly uses word choices to show the attitude of the narrator toward the characters or the action. However, in narrative film, the camera tells the tale almost as an objective viewer—it shows us events unfolding before our eyes. How is the camera able to convey the precise judgments of the novel's authorial voice?

First-Person Narration

The most problematic point of view to replicate is first-person narration. As already discussed in Chapter 2, devices such as the voiceover, narrative frame, dissolve, and point-of-view shots are commonly used to identify the camera with the narrator's perspective. Perhaps the most commonly used technique in first-person narrated films is the voiceover, either in the voice of a participant in the story or someone outside the story. The voiceover is often used extensively at the beginning of the film, returned to intermittently, and then used again at the end.

Another technique for bringing out a literary narrator's inner thoughts is to have the character talk to him or herself out loud or to another character who is present but not listening. For example, in Hemingway's novel *A Farewell to Arms*, Frederick Henry, the first-person narrator, expresses directly to the reader his inner feelings about his dying lover Catherine, but in the 1932 film adaptation of this novel, those inner feelings are externalized by having Frederick talk to himself out loud in a busy restaurant and then outside the hospital room where his beloved Catherine lay dying.

A third technique for revealing a narrator's inner thoughts (expressed in either the first or third person) is to rewrite them into dialogue. In *The Great Gatsby*, Nick Carraway meditates on the moment when the Dutch sailors first spied Long Island:

> [G]radually I became aware of the old island here that flowered once for Dutch sailors' eyes—a fresh, green breast of the new world. . . . [F]or a transitory enchanted moment man must have held his breath in the presence of this continent, . . . face to face for the last time in history with something commensurate to his capacity for wonder. (182)

The film translates this meditation into unlikely dialogue between Nick and Gatsby.

> *Nick:* Can you imagine what this old island must have looked like to those Dutch sailors when they first saw it? Fresh green. Like a dream of a new world.
>   *Gatsby:* They must have held their breath. Afraid it would disappear before they could touch it.

Whatever technique is used, the novel's first-person point of view is difficult to transfer. One famous experiment in replicating first-person narration was to have the camera follow a character who is in every scene and show the viewer only what this character could see.

> There has been only one major film . . . that tried to duplicate the first person narration so useful to the novel, Robert Montgomery's *Lady in the Lake* (1947). The result was a cramped, claustrophobic experience: we saw only what the hero saw. In order to show us the hero, Montgomery had to resort to a battery of mirror tricks. (Monaco 46)

Another film that seeks to approximate first-person narration is *Double Indemnity* (1944), directed by Billy Wilder. The film begins with the camera showing Walter Neff speeding in his car through the streets of Los Angeles at dawn, entering his insurance company's building, going to his office, starting a Dictaphone, and narrating the events not only of earlier that night, but also of several months before. The office scene dissolves into the past, and the camera associates itself with Neff's point of view. We see Neff in all reported events, and, because of his extensive voiceover, we understand them from his point of view. Virtually the entire film is seen through his eyes.

The replication of a text's first-person point of view is difficult in cinema. One problem is that the voiceover is intrusive and distracting. It tends to divert the audience's attention from what is seen to what is said and thus reduce the immediacy of the film experience. And because viewers identify so closely with the camera, the audience tends to forget the first-person narrator and thus to lose the sense that events are filtered through a single consciousness. Rendering the inner thoughts and feelings of characters, moving quickly among multiple points of view, and transposing distinctive authorial voices are all problems that pose challenges for the adapter of the novel.

Outside Factors

"Production determinants," according to McFarlane, are those factors "which have nothing to do with the novel but may be powerfully influential upon the film" (*Novel* 10). What are some outside factors that may be responsible for major shifts in a novel's adaptation?

First of all, keep in mind, as John Izod reminds us, that "the adaptation of literature into film is almost always a commercial enterprise" (95). Adaptation is commercial because it takes a great deal of money to produce a film. A recent estimate is an average of more than one hundred million dollars to produce, market, and advertise a big studio feature film. Since films cost a lot to make and to market, they require a good box office return.

C. Kenneth Pellow describes how the novelist Robert Penn Warren realized the box office imperative might affect an adaptation. Warren was watching the making of *All the King's Men* (1949), an adaptation of his novel of the same name, directed by Robert Rossen.

> "When the editing of the film was being done, Bob [Rossen], out of courtesy, invited me in. He ran off several different endings, then asked me which I liked best. I said the second, or third, or whatever it was, but added that none of the endings had a meaning like my novel—this said in the friendliest way. And Bob replied, 'Son, when you are dealing with American movies you can forget, when you get to the end, anything like what you call Irony—then it's cops and robbers, cowboys and Indians.' " (6–7)

Here the director emphasizes to the novelist that the American movie is directed at a much larger audience than the novel's and that filmmakers must keep in mind what a mass audience understands and what it wants to see. An ironic or ambiguous ending is generally not appealing to a mass audience. The box office success of the adaptation will be reduced if the director does not pay attention to the general public's expectations, level of awareness, and taste.

In many cases, the author of a novel addressed a different historical and cultural audience than the one addressed by the novel's adapter. Jane Austen's nineteenth-century readership was familiar with language, customs, and forms that many individuals today would not understand. The adapter of a novel must prune or cut altogether historical or cultural features that would be confusing or incomprehensible to a modern mass audience and find a way to update or contemporize retained period references.

Moreover, the adapter intent on the widest distribution has to make decisions about whether the story of the novel meets contemporary standards of decency as defined by industry rules and guidelines and by a sense of public morality. It may be offensive to some readers of a novel to read graphic descriptions of a sex scene, but the offensiveness of that scene will be magnified in a close adaptation because of film's power to visualize and because of the sexual mores of a mass audience. A film containing nudity, sexual scenes, or offensive language will be reviewed by industry censors and penalized (depending on the period of its release) by ratings that will affect viewership. Thus, the adapter may choose to change the story to fit the sexual mores of a contemporary mass audience.

On the other hand, the contemporary filmmaker has the freedom to address sexual material more openly and explicitly than an author from a previous century. This appears to be the case in *Grand Isle* (1991), directed by Mary Lambert, an adaptation of Kate Chopin's *The Awakening*, a novel published in 1899. In the novel, the main character, Edna Pontellier, a married woman and mother, develops an extramarital relationship with Alcée Arobin, a gambler and notorious womanizer. Their growing intimacy intensifies into a kiss:

> They continued silently to look into each other's eyes. When he leaned forward and kissed her, she clasped his head, holding his lips to hers.
>
> It was the first kiss of her life to which her nature had really responded. It was a flaming torch that kindled desire. (106)

In the novel, the kiss doesn't lead to the sexual act. However, in the film, after Edna and Alcée kiss, he pulls her to the floor by the fire, opens her blouse and caresses her breasts. They make love.

At the end of the novel, Edna commits suicide by swimming out into the Gulf of Mexico and drowning. We are told in the novel that she leaves her bathing suit behind. But in the film, the camera shows Edna disrobing and then an extended sequence with her swimming naked out to sea. The sexual acts and nudity implied but not described in the book are visualized by a 1990s filmmaker who can go beyond the moral restrictions of a century before. However, because of those scenes, the movie received a VM rating for very mature audiences, a classification that generally reduces the audience. The decisions filmmakers make in adapting sexual material from a novel can have an impact on the number of people who see the film.

The adapter may also choose to take into account other sensitive issues such as those that pertain to race, religion, ethnicity, and political events or to public controversies such as those over homosexuality or abortion. For example, the anti-Semitic references in Hemingway's *The Sun Also Rises* are left out of the 1957 film adaptation, directed by Henry King. *The Last of the Mohicans* (1992), directed by Michael Mann, an adaptation of one of James Fenimore Cooper's Leather-Stocking novels, leaves out Natty Bumppo's designations of Native Americans as savages, heathens, or barbarians. *Spider-Man* (2002), directed by Sam Raimi, an adaptation of the comic book, originally contained scenes in which the lead character climbs the World Trade Center, but these shots were dropped when the film was released eight months after the destruction of the World Trade Center on September 11, 2001.

The costly production of films and the consequent need for a mass audience to pay for them can change an adaptation's ending. The conflict established at the beginning of the film, and intensified in the middle, needs to be resolved. According to Burns, a film "ending is either 'upbeat', 'downbeat' or ambiguous." It is often the case that adaptations end with more upbeat endings than the ones offered by the novels from which they are derived. For example, John Steinbeck's novel *The Grapes of Wrath*, published in 1939, concerns the Joads, a poor farming family from the Dust Bowl, who are forced off their land during the Depression and migrate from Oklahoma to California where they endure the sufferings of the unemployed and homeless. The novel ends with a devastating strike in which the migrant workers are defeated and the Joad family faces starvation. In the final image, Rose of Sharon, who has lost her stillborn baby, bares her breast and lets her starving Pa breastfeed. But *The Grapes of Wrath* (1940), directed by John Ford, replaces that downbeat ending with Ma Joad's inspirational speech that tells people they can overcome any crisis: "We'll go on forever, Pa. We're the people." One could claim that before Ma gives her optimistic speech, viewers glimpse the possibility of a downbeat ending. In this reading, the film gives two endings, but, in typical Hollywood fashion, the upbeat one comes last.

Two famous nonadaptations that appear to be exceptions to the Hollywood rule that films end on an upbeat note are *Butch Cassidy and the Sundance Kid* (1969) and *Thelma and Louise* (1991). In both films, the two title characters, who have earned the audience's sympathy by the end, are allowed to die. But in both cases, the death is not visualized but implied. Butch and Sundance come out of a church to face an army, but the barrage of bullets that apparently meets them is heard only on a freeze frame showing them still alive, and Thelma and Louise are shown driving off a cliff, as if their car will continue on through the air toward a greater degree of freedom.

During the reign of the Hollywood studio system, downbeat endings were sometimes required in order to punish the wrongdoer. For example, *High Sierra* (1941), directed by Raoul Walsh and adapted from W. R. Burnett's novel, ends with the ex-con Roy Earle being shot to death, but this "downbeat" ending is acceptable in the film since Earle is a gangster who has killed and robbed and must be brought to justice.

Sometimes the ending is changed to fit film audiences' expectations of a character. For example, at the very end of Thomas Harris's novel *Hannibal*, Agent Clarice Starling rescues Hannibal Lector from a sure and torturous death—he was to be eaten alive by sixteen giant pigs. While rescuing Hannibal, Clarice is shot twice by a dart gun carrying morphine. Hannibal carries Clarice away, treats her with drugs, and through psychoanalytic and other techniques that include having Clarice's enemy, Krendler, eat his own brains, Hannibal, in a sense, takes her over. The book ends with Hannibal and Clarice living as lovers in Buenos Aires.

When Jodie Foster was offered the opportunity to continue in the role of Clarice that she had made famous in *The Silence of the Lambs* (1991), she declined the offer on the grounds that Clarice's character had been betrayed. As it turned out, *Hannibal* (2001), directed by Ridley Scott, changed the ending of the novel so that after the sautéed brains scene, Clarice continues to try to capture Hannibal by handcuffing herself to him; he escapes the handcuffs by cutting off his hand rather than Clarice's. It is an implied act of love on his part, and one that she takes in, but she is still kept in her role on the "right" side of the law, and what we might call the coherence of the Hannibal and Clarice "franchise" remains intact for future filming and marketing.

McFarlane describes another example of a novel's ending being changed in the film for external reasons:

> In a 1938 film version of *Wuthering Heights,* producer Sam Goldwyn, director William Wyler, or scriptwriters Ben Hecht and Charles MacArthur, or all four, have chosen to omit the second half of Emily Brontë's novel, thus eliminating the processes of Heathcliff's revenge and the reconciliation of important conflicting emotional elements. . . . Perhaps the decision was dictated by so external a matter as what would work best to promote its leading lady Merle Oberon (Cathy); perhaps it was felt unwise to kill off the film's major star half-way through. The point is that, while the film is a handsome romantic melodrama, in certain critical ways it can scarcely be regarded as a serious version of the Brontë novel. The emphases, the governing narrative motifs, of the original have been replaced by others in the interests—it can be argued—of the inner consistency and coherence of a commercial film. (*Words* 7)

The point here is that sometimes an adaptation's form is influenced or even dictated by commercial considerations that supersede artistic preferences.

Adapters cut, combine, condense, truncate, and rearrange narrative elements; they find cinematic equivalents, contemporize references, and adjust the plot and ending of the novel to fit the film medium and to appeal to a mass audience.

We look now at a specific adaptation—Harper Lee's semiautobiographical novel *To Kill a Mockingbird*—chosen because it is a book most students have read. In what follows, we are not trying to present a full discussion of the cinematic choices made in transferring the story to film. Instead, we discuss omitted or compressed story elements that are responsible for shifts in narrative and thematic emphasis.

TO KILL A MOCKINGBIRD (1960), by Harper Lee

The novel *To Kill a Mockingbird* became an immediate best seller when it was published in 1960. It won the Pulitzer Prize in 1961. Since then, it has become a staple in high school English classes and has gained critical stature as a coming-of-age novel that addresses many different kinds of intolerance.

To Kill a Mockingbird is set in the small town of Maycomb, Alabama, during the Depression. The story is told through a first-person narrator—the mature Jean Louise "Scout" Finch who looks back to events she experienced as a six-year-old girl. Scout's father, Atticus Finch, is an honest lawyer and a widower, who is raising his two children with the help of Calpurnia, the family's black maid. Scout, her ten-year-old brother, Jem, and their friend, Dill, are fascinated by Boo Radley, the mysterious recluse next door who has been hiding in his house for years. They imagine Boo as some kind of bogeyman who eats raw squirrels and lurks in the neighborhood at night. But they gradually discover that Boo acts as a friend to them, leaving gifts in a hollow tree and mending Jem's torn pants.

Part 1 of the novel concerns Scout, Jem, and Dill's childhood escapades and their growing knowledge of the adult world, but Part 2 is mainly concerned with the trial of Tom Robinson, a young African-American who has been falsely accused of raping Mayella Ewell, a white woman. Atticus agrees to defend Tom and, in the months before the trial, racial tensions grow. The children are taunted at school by those against Atticus defending a black man, and a mob goes to the jail attempting to lynch Tom, but Atticus refuses to drop the case. At the trial, Atticus establishes clear proof of Tom's innocence, but the all-white jury is so prejudiced it delivers a guilty verdict. Atticus promises to appeal, but Tom doesn't believe he can win on appeal and is killed trying to escape from prison. Returning home from a Halloween party, Scout and Jem are murderously attacked by Robert E. Lee Ewell, father of the woman who falsely accused Tom. In rescuing the children, Boo pushes Ewell, who falls on top of his own knife. When Atticus learns of Ewell's death, he thinks that his son killed him and insists to Sheriff Heck Tate that Jem be turned in. However, when he learns that the reclusive Boo killed Ewell, Atticus agrees with the Sheriff that it is best to let the matter go.

TO KILL A MOCKINGBIRD (1962), Directed by Robert Mulligan

Made just two years after the book was published, To Kill a Mockingbird was a popular film success. It was nominated for eight Academy Awards and won in three categories—notably best actor for Gregory Peck and best adapted screenplay for Horton Foote. Some claim the movie would have won best picture had it not been competing against Lawrence of Arabia, the winner that year.

Here is a fairly complete list of plot and character elements kept, added, and dropped in the adaptation.

KEPT ELEMENTS
CHARACTERS
Finch Household
Atticus Finch

Scout (Jean Louise Finch)
Jem (Jeremy Finch)
Calpurnia (the maid)
Neighborhood
    Dill (Charles Baker Harris from Meridian, Mississippi)
    Aunt Rachel Haverford (Dill's aunt), renamed Aunt Stephanie in film
    Boo Radley (Arthur)
    Mr. Radley (father)
    Maudie Atkinson (neighbor)
    Mrs. Henry Lafayette Dubose
    Jessie (unnamed maid)
    Tim Johnson (dog)
    Zeebo (garbage collector, referred to)
School
    Walter Cunningham, Jr. (of the Cunninghams from Old Sarum
        neighborhood)
    Cecil Jones (referred to)
Trial People
    Tom Robinson (the accused)
    Helen Robinson
    David Robinson (Sam in book)
    Mr. Walter Cunningham (father)
    Heck Tate (sheriff)
    Judge Taylor
    Reverend Sykes
    Mayella Ewell (accuser)
    Bob Ewell (father of Mayella)
    Mr. Gilmer (solicitor for Ewell)
    Clerk
    Foreman
    Crowds outside and inside the courtroom
    Dr. Reynolds
SETTINGS
    Both novel and movie begin in 1932, but the book covers three
        years while the film compresses time to a year and a half.
    Maycomb, seat of Maycomb County, Alabama
    Finch residence
    Radley residence—including backyard
    Maudie Atkinson's residence
    Dubose residence
    Tom Robinson's place
    Town square
    Outside of jail
    Courthouse and courtroom interior

SITUATIONS
Neighborhood life
 Father-too-old segment
 Dill's appearance in collard patch
 Rolling of tire
 Shooting the rabid dog
 Finding things in tree hole
 Going off to school
 Young Walter Cunningham fight and subsequent luncheon at the
  Finches'
 Boo Radley raid
Trial
 Atticus's defense of Tom Robinson outside jail
 Trial of Tom Robinson
 Informing Helen Robinson that Tom is dead
 The Halloween attack by Ewell on Scout and Jem
 Boo's rescue and Jem's injury
 Heck versus Atticus on porch deciding not to involve Boo in
  Ewell's death

ADDED ELEMENTS
 Montage of child's toy box and contents during opening screen credits
 Scout's humming
 Music score
 Drawing title
 Tearing up picture of mockingbird
 Voiceover of mature Scout looking back at events
 Reference to Crash of '29
 Scout and Jem, falling asleep, talk about their dead mother while
  Atticus sits listening on the porch
 Scout asking to see the watch and Atticus offering pearls
 Jem, Scout, and Dill go to see basement where Boo was once kept
  and see beginning of trial hearings in the courthouse
 Atticus taking kids to the Robinsons'
 Threat scene of Bob Ewell twice—offstage in book
 Bob Ewell scares kids
 Tom Robinson is transported by car from Abbottsville
 Jem, in bed, overhears Atticus's decision to defend Tom in jail
 Bird notes and whippoorwill
 Mr. Townsend
 Spence (Tom Robinson's father)
 Elements of Film: mise-en-scène (sets, costumes, lighting, makeup,
  props, placement of objects and people, and actors' gestures and
  movements), camerawork, editing, and sound

DROPPED ELEMENTS
CHARACTERS
Finch Family
Uncle Jack Finch, M.D. (Atticus's brother)
Aunt Alexandra (Scout's aunt who visits)
Uncle Jimmy (Alexandra's husband)
Frances Hancock (Scout's cousin)
Henry
Cousin Ike Finch (sole surviving Confederate veteran)
Neighborhood
Mrs. Radley
Nathan Radley (older son who lived in Pensacola, returns home, and takes over)
Mr. Conner (Maycomb's ancient beadle)
Miss Stephanie Crawford (gossip—her name is used for Aunt Rachel)
Henry Lafayette Dubose
Dr. Frank Buford (father of Maudie Atkinson)
Foot-washing Baptists who pass through neighborhood
Mr. Avery (boarder who pees off porch)
Eula May (telephone operator)
Mr. Harry Johnson (owner of Tim Johnson, rabid dog)
School
Miss Caroline Fisher (Scout's first-grade teacher who stays at Maudie's)
Burris Ewell (goes to school first day)
Miss Gates (Scout's second-grade teacher)
Little Chuck Little (Scout's classmate in second grade)
Elmer Davis (classmate)
Black Church
Eunice Ann Simpson (girl left tied to chair in basement of church)
Lula (black woman who opposes Cal taking white children to church)
Carlow Richardson
Missionary Society
Mrs. Merriwether
Mrs. Farrow
Trial
Link Deas (employer of Tom Robinson)
Mr. Underwood (newspaper owner)
Ruth Jones (social worker who tells Atticus that Ewell blames him for losing WPA job)
Miss Blount (sixth-grade teacher)
Mr. Dolphus Raymond (drunk who lives with a black woman and has children)

Mr. X. Billups
Tenshaw Jones
Emily Davis
Byron Waller
Jack Slade
Tutti and Frutti Garber
Agnes Boone (butterbean in pageant)
Mrs. Crenshaw (local seamstress)
Estelle (sent rolls after court proceedings)

SETTINGS

Finch homestead at Finch's Landing on Christmas
Calpurnia's black church
Inside of neighbors' houses
School rooms

SITUATIONS

Visit to Finch's Landing on Christmas
First day at school for Scout with teacher and Burris
Mr. and Mrs. Radley die (at different times) and Nathan takes over
Dill runs away from Mississippi to the Finch residence
Playacting of children of Boo material
Mrs. Dubose material—lesson in real courage
Building the snowman
The fire at Maudie's house
All the Aunt Alexandra material during trial

To Kill a Mockingbird is a relatively short novel of less than 300 pages in the Warner edition. Still, many of its narrative elements were dropped or altered to fit the parameters of the feature-length film, and those modifications are responsible for changes in narrative emphases.

Setting

Both book and movie are set in the fictional town of Maycomb, Alabama, and both show three main locations: (1) the Finch neighborhood (including the Finch house, the Radley residence and backyard, and Maudie Atkinson's front yard); (2) Tom Robinson's house; and (3) the town square and courthouse. Both stories begin in 1932, but the book covers three years while Foote compresses the period to a year with summers on both sides.

Characters

The plot summary and list of kept elements make it clear that the film keeps the novel's essential characters. These include the lawyer Atticus Finch and his children, Scout and Jem, and their friend Dill; Calpurnia the maid; Boo Radley, the mysterious neighbor, and Maudie Atkinson, the helpful one; Tom Robinson, the black man accused of rape by Mayella Ewell; Judge Taylor, who asks Atticus to take the case, and Sheriff Heck Tate, who investigates it; Walter Cun-

Atticus and Scout embracing in *To Kill a Mockingbird* (1962).

ningham, who owes money to Atticus but supports the lynch mob; and the racist Bob Ewell who is the father and abuser of Mayella and the attacker of Jem and Scout.

However, the novel contains approximately sixty-eight characters. Of these, forty characters are dropped, and some of the kept characters are reduced in importance. Although the dropped characters are minor (except perhaps for Aunt Alexandra), still the sheer number of characters omitted reduces the viewer's sense of the social complexity of Maycomb. Perhaps to compensate for this, the film uses crowds during the lynch scene and before, during, and after the trial, but these mostly anonymous crowds are not equivalent to the novel's more detailed and nuanced portrayal of the many people living in this small Southern community.

Scenes

The book consists of two parts, with Part 1 devoted primarily to the children and their world, and Part 2 devoted to Tom Robinson's trial. The main childhood scenes of Part 1 are retained. They include the opening discussion of Atticus's age, Dill's appearance in the collard patch, rolling the tire onto Boo's porch, Jem finding Boo's gifts in a tree hole, Scout going off to school, the Walter Cunningham fight and luncheon, and the night raid on the Radleys. Also kept are the main scenes dealing with the trial of Tom Robinson in Part 2: Atticus agreeing to take on the case, his defense of Tom Robinson from the mob outside the jail, the trial of Tom Robinson itself, and then Atticus informing Helen Robinson that Tom is dead. The novel's ending is also kept: the Halloween attack by Ewell on Scout and Jem, Boo's rescue, Jem's injury, and Heck and Atticus's discussion about whether to report Boo's involvement in Ewell's death.

Atticus defending the jailed Tom Robinson from a lynch mob in *To Kill a Mockingbird.*

Significantly, the film cuts a number of childhood scenes, including the Boo Radley drama, the Morphodite Snowman, and Mrs. Merriweather's play. These cuts, combined with other changes, shift the film's emphasis from the children to the trial and the trial lawyer. The film's focus on a white lawyer battling on behalf of a falsely accused black man reflects the civil rights era in which the movie was made.

Point of View

The novel is narrated by a mature Jean Louise Finch who is looking back to events that occurred over a three-year period starting when she was six years old. The filmmakers use several devices to replicate first-person narration. The opening music by Elmer Bernstein suggests a child's piano tune, and the sequence begins with a montage of childhood objects: a toy box is opened and its assorted contents are shown—marbles, crayons, a timepiece, and a penknife. Six-year-old Scout hums on the voiceover and presumably *her* hands rub a crayon over paper that reveals the film's title. Screen credits are displayed while other objects from the box are shown. The child draws a bird and then tears the paper in two, perhaps suggesting the killing of the mockingbird referred to in the title. Scout's humming is eventually replaced by her grown-up voice saying, "Maycomb was a tired old town even in 1932 when I first knew it." The childlike piano tune, the montage of childhood items, and the voiceover of the young girl and older woman are used to foreground Scout as the first-person narrator who is recalling events as they looked through her six-year-old eyes. The voiceover by the offscreen, never-seen adult is brought back intermittently to remind us of the first-person narration and for purposes of story transition.

Although many critics have criticized Lee's use of point of view because six-year-old Scout's observations sometimes sound as if they belong to a more mature intelligence, the novelist still uses Scout consistently as the character whose eyes filter the events described. One problem with the film's use of Scout as the point-of-view character is that sometimes she is not present in scenes. For example, Jem, not Scout, is the one to accompany Atticus twice to Tom Robinson's house (the first time Scout goes, but falls asleep and does not see anything; the second time she doesn't come). Again, Jem is the one shown discovering Boo's treehold and taking care of his gifts. Another problem is that the film does not sustain the illusion that Scout is the central consciousness because the camera sometimes uses shot/reverse shots to focus attention on Jem. For example, we watch Jem, not Scout, react to Atticus's shooting of the rabid dog and to Atticus's defense of Tom during the final courtroom scene.

Moreover, the film suffers the failings of all cinematic attempts to replicate first-person texts. Audiences identify with the camera and see events as being presented objectively. Even when reminded, they are disinclined to remember that what they see unfolding is filtered through a narrator's eyes. But in addition to that common problem with narrated films, this particular film's attempt to make Scout the one who tells the story is inconsistent because she drops from some scenes, and the camera sometimes identifies with Jem's point of view.

Symbol

The film retains the symbol of the mockingbird emphasized in the novel's title. In the novel, when Atticus is finally persuaded to give Jem and Scout air rifles, he warns them "it's a sin to kill a mockingbird" (90). Maudie reiterates this lesson.

> "Your father's right," she said. "Mockingbirds don't do one thing but make music for us to enjoy. They don't eat up people's gardens, don't nest in corncribs, they don't do one thing but sing their hearts out for us. That's why it is a sin to kill a mockingbird." (90)

In the film, it is Atticus, not Maudie, who explains to the children the meaning of the mockingbird.

> [My daddy] told me . . . that I could shoot all the blue jays I wanted if I could hit 'em but to remember t'was a sin to kill a mockingbird . . . because mockingbirds don't do anything but make music for us to enjoy, don't eat people's gardens, don't nest in the corn cribs, don't do one thing but just sing their hearts out for us.

The mockingbird is identified as a creature that does not cause harm and through its song is beneficial to others. With this meaning in mind, the title *To Kill a Mockingbird* could refer to Tom Robinson, who doesn't cause the harm he is accused of and, in fact, is helpful to his accuser, but who is shot seventeen times when trying to escape. It could also refer to Boo Radley, who, while intending no harm, kills to help Jem and Scout and is ultimately spared by the mockingbird principle. In the film, Sheriff Tate says, "To my way of thinking, taking the one man [Boo] who has done you [Atticus] and this town a big service, and dragging him with his shy ways into the limelight, to me, that's a sin. It's a sin." And when Tate leaves, Scout says to Atticus: "Mr. Tate was right. . . . Well, it [turning Boo in] would be sort of like shooting a mockingbird, wouldn't it."

Historical References

One thing film has a hard time showing is a novel's extensive use of historical detail. One important context for Lee's novel is the history of race relations in the South. The novel contains many references to the Civil War that link the racial division in Maycomb to the past. But the novel makes even more specific connections between past and present by linking the Atticus Finch family and their neighbors the Duboses to the Confederacy. For example, when Atticus explains to Scout and Jem why he took on the Robinson case, one that is likely to fail, he says, "Simply because we were licked a hundred years before we started is no reason for us not to try to win" (76). This answer reminds Scout of cousin Ike Finch, who "was Maycomb County's sole surviving Confederate veteran" (76). She recounts how her relative liked to "rehash the war," mentioning General Hood, Stonewall Jackson, and the Missouri Compromise. The film's cutting of references to the Confederacy and its connections to the Dubose and Finch families means that the racial divide in Maycomb is not rooted, as it is in the novel, in the historical divisions of the South.

Theme

It can be argued that the novel offers two main themes—the necessity for courage and for tolerance—and that the film keeps both. However, the *primary* emphasis in both is on the necessity of dealing tolerantly with the "other." The novel repeatedly shows the community's tendency to draw racial, class, and religious boundaries and to dehumanize and discriminate against anyone who is different: blacks, the mentally disabled, people from a different class, Jews, the weak, the elderly, the ill, bigots, snobs, religious zealots, and others. Atticus advises Scout: "If you can learn a simple trick, Scout, you'll get along a lot better with all kinds of folks. You never really understand a person until you consider things from his point of view— . . . until you climb into his skin and walk around in it" (30). Atticus's lesson and the novel's primary theme are the need for compassion and human understanding for "all kinds of people."

To Kill a Mockingbird is generally regarded as a close to intermediate adaptation of the novel, but clearly the film is a reinterpretation of the story. As with any novel, there is the necessity to cut characters, scenes, dialogue, settings, and historical detail. But Foote's decisions of what to cut tended to deemphasize the childhood material of Part 1 and give greater emphasis to the courtroom drama of Part 2. Cutting many of the Civil War and family ref-

Courtroom scene from *To Kill a Mockingbird.*

erences dehistoricizes the racial conflict in Maycomb, and reducing the number of minor characters—crowd scenes notwithstanding—dilutes the novel's powerful sense of community. Omitting characters that represent different versions of the "other" reinterprets the novel's broad lesson about the need to combat *different kinds* of intolerance and to "get along better with all kinds of folks" (30).

This is not to say that the film is unsuccessful. The movie is well regarded and is viewed by many critics as a film classic, mainly because of its excellent acting performances. Gregory Peck conveys Atticus's quiet but passionate love for justice and his children, and the two nonprofessional child actors, Mary Badham as Scout and Philip Alford as Jem, act in such a natural and unaffected way that they give highly believable performances. Brock Peters plays Tom Robinson in a way that never makes us question his innocence, and James Anderson plays Ewell in a way that never makes us question his malevolence.

The novel's Maycomb, which was modeled on Monroeville, Alabama, Lee's hometown, had become too modernized by 1962 to convey the Depression-era story, so the producer Alan J. Pakula and the director Robert Mulligan had a replica town built on Universal's back lot. From pictures taken at Monroeville's courthouse and footage shot of the town, set designers were able to recreate the setting in Hollywood. The town and courtroom settings and Russell Harlan's black-and-white cinematography give the film the authentic feel of small-town life in the Deep South during the Depression.

However, the film's cutting of characters and events dealing with childhood coupled with its emphasis on the trial and on the trial lawyer pushes the adaptation toward a courtroom drama and tapers the novel's layered lesson on the need for compassion for all kinds of people to the need for racial tolerance.

The Novella

Most novels adapted to feature-length films are abbreviated in some way—characters and events are dropped, exposition is shortened, dialogue is cut or condensed. But there are novels short enough that they need not be reduced. In fact, some believe that the short novel or *novella* is the ideal length for an adapted screenplay.

The **novella** can be defined as a short novel or as a long short story; but whatever reference point is used, there is consensus that its length falls somewhere in between. Most novellas consist of 80 to 120 pages; feature-length screenplays average between 120 to 125 pages. This means that given a novella amenable to adaptation a screenwriter could decide to stay fairly close to the text without cutting a great deal as with the novel or adding a great deal as with the short story.

When watching a screen version of a novel, the student of adaptation may decide to start with questions about what was cut and how those cuts affect the relationship of text to film. With a short story, the student may begin with what material was added and how the additions shift the story's narrative emphases. But a novella does not provide a clue as to which set of questions would be most useful to begin with because its length does not necessarily require extensive cutting or adding. Instead, the student asks the general questions that can apply to any adaptation: What story elements does the novella contain that do or do not lend themselves to cinematic display? What are some of the thousand decisions made by filmmakers in realizing the story using cinematic conventions? What is the screenwriter's interpretation? What are the practical difficulties in bringing the story to film? What outside determinants have an effect on the film?

In the next case study, we look at Norman Maclean's first-person novella *A River Runs Through It* and the film of the same name directed by Robert Redford. What's interesting about this adaptation is that at 104 pages the book is quite manageable as a feature-length film. But Redford and scriptwriter Richard Friedenberg decide to cut many of the first-person meditations about fly-fishing and religion, add episodes and minor characters, enlarge some character roles, and rearrange events. In cutting, adding, and rearranging, they are able to magnify the subject from the concern of one man for his lost brother to a larger concern over the loss of an older, more innocent America. Where some novels are reduced in scope in their cinematic retellings, Friedenberg and Redford reshape this novella's story into a cinematic version that is in many ways far more expansive and ambitious than the original story.

John Maclean (Tom Skerritt) teaching casting for fly-fishing to his two sons, Paul and Norman, in *A River Runs Through It* (1992).

A RIVER RUNS THROUGH IT (1976),
by Norman Maclean

Norman Maclean's autobiographical novella *A River Runs Through It* tells the story of his relationship to his younger brother, Paul, as they grew up in Montana. The author covers the years when the brothers grew from adolescence to adulthood, with emphasis given to Paul's sudden and sad death. The story is part *memoir* and part *elegy*.

 River is set in the small cities and towns and on the large trout rivers of Montana from just after the beginning of the twentieth century to the summer of 1937. According to Norman, the narrator, during this time the modern world of automobiles still coexists with a nature so pristine it is linked in his mind to the primordial past:

> I had to be careful driving toward the river so I wouldn't high-center the car on a boulder and break the crankcase. . . . The boulders on the flat were shaped by the last ice age only eighteen to twenty thousand years ago, but the red and green precambrian rocks beside the blue water were almost from the basement of the world and time. (83–84)

 Occupying this setting are three main characters: Norman, Paul, and their father, John, a Scottish Presbyterian minister. The father plays a key role in his sons' development. He instructs the boys—from on high in the pulpit and from hip-deep in the Big Blackfoot River—about the difficult tenets of both religion and fly-fishing. "In our family," he tells his sons, "there was no clear line between religion and fly fishing" (1). But if the teacher and the lessons are the same, the sons seem to absorb them differently and to move in different directions. Although physically tough, Norman is essentially intellectual, obedient, and serious-minded, interested in bookish pursuits that will eventually lead him to become a professor of English and the author of *River*. Paul is more physically reckless and wild, a hard-living newspaper reporter whose drinking, gambling, fighting and womanizing lead him into deadly trouble.

The problem for both Norman, the model son, and his father, the stern but wise minister, is how to help Paul out of his troubles. The problem is echoed in the subplot that concerns Jessie, Norman's wife, and her alcoholic, snobby brother, Neal, who also needs help that no one can supply. Since the Maclean family consists of people unable to express their deeper feelings, it is unclear to Norman and his father what Paul really needs or wants. But even if they knew, the father raises the question, would he or Norman be able or willing to provide it:

> Either we don't know what part to give or maybe we don't like to give any part of ourselves. Then, more often than not, the part that is needed is not wanted. And even more often, we do not have the part that is needed. (81)

The story's interrelated themes, then, are the inability to know and to aid those we love. The father says, "It is those we love and should know who elude us" (104). And Norman sadly echoes his father's sentiment: "Now nearly all those I loved and did not understand when I was young are dead" (104). However, there is something positive offered. Simply put, nature can, at least temporarily, make us forget our troubles and bring us into communion with others. Fishing the great Montana trout rivers is the Macleans' entrance into nature, and thus, the only help Norman and his father can offer Paul.

A RIVER RUNS THROUGH IT (1992), Directed by Robert Redford

One important change from the novella to the film is a time shift. Maclean's *River* is set mainly in 1937, when Norman is thirty-four; the film is set mainly in 1926, when Norman is twenty-three. Richard Friedenberg, the screenwriter, explains the decision to move the story back eleven years:

> The Norman in the novella is a settled man, married, a father in the midst of comfortable success, far removed from the curiosity and anguish of youth. The actual story is propelled by Paul's anguish and darkness in a youth he can't leave. I faced

The Maclean brothers carry a stolen boat to a river to ride the rapids in *A River Runs Through It.*

a beautiful book that I could only see as a movie about a middle-aged professor explaining the sadness of his brother's life, interspersed with fifteen-page exegeses on the art and religion of fly fishing. . . .

I finally realized that to make "my" Norman dimensional I needed to put him back in the twenties when he returned from college, uncertain of his future and ashamed of his uncertainty. It was the time when he learned he'd been accepted into the graduate program at the University of Chicago, the time when he met and wooed Jessie. (5–6)

The decision to make Norman twenty- rather than thirty-something affects the film's dramatic situations and themes. The male bonding among Norman, Paul, and their father that takes place in the book is somewhat deemphasized in the film in order to accommodate Paul and Norman's growing up and coming of age, especially professionally and romantically. Thus, characters such as the Macleans' boyhood friends are added to the film to dramatize their early years, and Jessie, Norman's romantic interest, is given more dimension in the film than she ever had in the novella, where, as his wife, she is hardly mentioned. As Friedenberg explains it, the time change allows the film to focus on

the rise of Norman from uncertainty to purpose, from boyhood to manhood, set against Paul's downward arc, from competent journalist to lost artist, from worldly lover to stubborn child, unable to mature, beautiful on the river but damned in life. To me that was a story a film could tell. A movie. (6)

A second major change in the film has to do with the reordering of Maclean's narrative. His *River* is a series of remembered episodes that, although thematically connected, are not presented in strict chronological order. The screenwriter and director, however, chose to rearrange these episodes in chronological order. They chose to drop redundant episodes, such as the first fishing trip with Neal, and some theoretical, nonfigurative, nondramatic passages that essentially cannot be filmed, such as Norman's meditation on the river, part of the "fifteen-page exegeses on the art of religion and fly-fishing" that Friedenberg refers to. They also chose to add actual episodes of Norman and Paul's growing up and coming of age as told to them by Maclean and his surviving boyhood friends. They add these episodes in chronological order in order to present a sequential and more coherent story.

But an even more important change is Redford's choice to expand the focus of the story from Maclean's nuclear family to the landscapes, townscapes, and townspeople of Montana and the American West. The widening of focus first appears in the film's opening montage sequence. The series consists of Philippe Rousselot's fourteen brief shots showing still, black-and-white, mostly archival photographs of Montana life of about the film's time period. The straight-on angle shots run from four to eight seconds, track forward to bring us closer to examine the detail in the typically extreme long-shot photographs, then dissolve into the next still life.

The first two shots are of photographs showing Norman and Paul as youngsters alone and then with their parents. Although the people in the photographs are not the actual Macleans but the actors who portray them, the two film photographs are modeled on two real photographs of the Maclean family (Friedenberg 9, 17). Following these shots is a series of photographs showing Montana life in the first quarter of the twentieth century. They consist of a river running through a countryside, a dirt street running through a town, another dirt street, a horse and wagon on a dirt street, a town situated at the foot of a mountain range, a gang of loggers sitting and standing on a pile of logs, a gang of loggers standing in a camp, a church situated near a bridge over a river, people sitting and standing in a field, people standing in front of a city hall draped with large U.S. flags, a woman and two boys standing on a tree-lined street, and finally another church. The effect of the still photographs in the montage sequence is to suggest that this family story takes place in a civic- and religious-minded community whose livelihood is closely tied to nature.

Accompanying the montage sequence are the film's credits, a voiceover, and the music theme. The credits are lettered small, centered in the lower half of the shot, and are unobtrusive. They provide an excuse for placing the montage sequence at the beginning of the film. Robert Redford reads all of the film's voiceovers. He speaks the narrative lines of the older Norman Maclean who, after all, is the author of the novella, just as Redford is the auteur of the film. The voiceover occurs with the second, third, and fourth photographs. With the photograph of the family, the older Norman states, "In our family, there was no clear line between religion and fly fishing." With the photograph of the river, he states, "We lived at the junction of great trout rivers in Missoula, Montana." Both lines are oral interpretations of the first two sentences of the novella. With

Paul (Brad Pitt), John (Tom Skerritt), and Norman (Craig Sheffer) Maclean fly-fish together in *A River Runs Through It.*

the photograph of the dirt street running through a town, Norman says, "Indians still appeared out of the wilderness to walk the honkytonks of Front Street." This line is new to the film.

The three lines link three major themes to be explored in the film. First is religion, with its emphasis, courtesy of their father, on salvation, grace, and art. Second is fly-fishing, with its emphasis, courtesy of Paul, on genius, luck, and a code suggested by Paul's instruction to Neal that there are three things for which the Macleans are never late: work, church, and fly-fishing. Third is the wilderness, which, in spite of the white migration to the far west, is still thriving in the first decade of the twentieth century. Part of that wilderness is the people who live in it. These include not only the Native Americans mentioned in the voiceover but also the loggers in the woods camps and the townspeople in the foothill settlements pictured in the photographs. Norman, Paul, and their parents know these people. The montage sequence is meant to give us a glimpse of them at the beginning of the film, so that later when they are reintroduced in detail, we will recognize that they, too, are part of the community remembered and elegized in the film.

The film's theme music, by Mark Isham, begins before the montage sequence and ends with it. The theme is a vibrant melody of strings, woodwinds, and horns, played in a slow tempo that keeps pace with the tracking shots in the montage sequence and that anticipates the leisurely pace with which the film progresses. It evokes a solemn, haunting mood that may be felt as echoing the elegiac mood of the film, as well as the novella. Both the film and the novella end with Norman's moving statement of loss: "I am haunted by waters."

In addition to the montage sequence, a second method of expanding the focus of the novella from the Maclean family to the Montana townspeople is to add to the film specific social scenes not in the novella, such as the July 4th dance where Norman awkwardly meets Jessie, and the picnic where Norman strolls with his mother, Clara, and talks with various, mildly comical towns-people. These added scenes broaden the memoir/elegy to include a communal way of life that, like Paul, Jessie, John, and Clara, has vanished for Norman.

In short, the film dramatizes the novella's central conflict and its interrelated themes: the inability to know and to aid those we love; and the ability of nature, at least temporarily, to make us forget our troubles and bring us into communion with others. The novella emphasizes the relationship between religion and fly-fishing, brotherly love, and male bonding. The film also emphasizes religion and fly-fishing, but is less interested in brotherly love and male bonding and more interested in the brothers' coming of age, the courtship romance, and the vanished, early twentieth-century Montana way of life set within pristine nature.

Another way to state the relationship between the novella and the film is to say that the film is more dramatic, chronologically coherent, and thematically expansive than the novella. Maclean's memoir/elegy focuses on the loss of one man, Paul. The film retains the memoir subject and elegiac tone but expands the meaning of the loss to include the community and the land. Some, perhaps most, of the elements of narrative in the work of literature are kept in the film, other elements are dropped for primarily practical reasons, and still more elements are added for interpretative reasons. Thus, the film is an intermediate-to-close adaptation of Maclean's novella. The film does not conform exactly to Maclean's novella nor does it use the text as a point of departure. The film keeps to the book but enlarges it.

As mentioned above, the film, like the book, mourns the death of a young man, but, more importantly, the film mourns the loss of his family, of his community, and of a pastoral way of life that no longer exists even in Montana. "It [Montana] was a world with dew still on it, more touched by wonder and possibility than any I have known since," the older Norman says in one of the film's voiceovers. The past tense is appropriate because that dew-covered world, as the filmmakers discovered, no longer exists.

According to Jay Carr of *The Boston Globe,*

> Pollution kept the filmmakers out of the real Big Blackfoot River. . . . When he got around to filming, Mr. Redford had to use five Montana rivers to substitute for the book's Blackfoot, which he found to be "a diseased river" due to pollution. This behind-the-scenes detail fits right in with the film's theme of grace glimpsed and lost, and a country losing chunks of its great natural heritage every day. "What I hoped the feeling [of the film] would be is a sense of loss, a part of our history that won't be returned because we've grown out of it and lost our innocence," he [Redford] says. (33)

And Maclean writes, "What a beautiful world it was once" (56). Thus, the film expands the novella to include the loss of American nature and the way a community had of living in harmony with it.

Both Maclean's novella and the film are part of what John Cawelti calls the "[n]ew western stories [that] mark a revival of the genre in print, film, and on TV" (1). Cawelti explains that the "sense of the end of the heroic West haunts such major works of the new western fiction as Norman Maclean's [stories]. . . . Maclean evokes a lost world of skill with tools and heroic physical labor and shows how powerful an experience it was to be initiated into such a world" (6).

The loss of American nature and the way a community had of living in harmony with it are favorite themes for Redford. Redford remembers how he first learned of *River:*

> In 1981, on a visit to Montana, I had a discussion about Western writers, with my friend Tom McGuane [the novelist]. We debated the authenticity issue: living it and knowing it versus just loving it. Several names were thrown around—Wallace Stegner, Ivan Doig, B. Guthrie, Vardis Fisher—before McGuane suggested he could settle the question by having me read *A River Runs Through It,* by Norman Maclean. "This is the real thing," he said.
>
> I distrust such proclamations, but when I read the first sentence . . . I thought I might be in for something. When I looked at the last line, I knew it. And when I finished reading the novella, I wanted to bring it to the screen. (1)

In a 1992 interview with Wes D. Gehring, Redford mentioned that he "coupled his interest in the personal grace expressed by Maclean with the 'opportunity to say [via beautiful images from rural Montana] that this is the way our environment was when we took it for granted, and for the most part, it's gone.' (The environmental message is a given in all of [Redford's] populist pictures)" (9).

Redford's addition of community life to the film and his emphasis on the loss of the pristine nature of the American West broaden Maclean's memoir and elegy. Unlike some filmmakers who adapt novellas, Redford was not content with a close adaptation. Although he told Maclean's story virtually in its entirety, he also decided to add to it as an adapter would with a short story. But the literary form of Maclean's novella did not dictate Redford's decision. Adding was a matter of Redford's artistic choice, not the form's demands.

Summary

The novel is a prose fiction that in its modern form usually consists of between 300 and 400 pages, though it can run much longer. Some elements of the novel, such as setting and character, lend themselves to cinematic display, but others, such as point of view, are difficult to transpose. Unlike the short story, the adapter of the novel is forced to cut, condense, combine, or truncate narrative elements to accommodate the average running time of a feature film. These changes result in different narrative emphases in the film. Beyond the issues of cutting and transfer, the adapter has to deal with outside determinants that have nothing to do with the novel but that nevertheless affect its adaptation. Commercial filmmaking is costly and requires a mass audience. The screenwriter, director, producer, and others may change a novel's beginning or end, or adjust the story to the taste, morals, and understanding of the general public in order to address the daunting economics of the film business.

▪▪▪▪ TOPICS FOR DISCUSSION

1. Identify an element of a novel that critics have labeled uncinematic (such as first-person narration or an ironic verbal style) and discuss how filmmakers address the issue in a specific adaptation.

2. Take an episode from a novel that was dropped from its adaptation and explain why you think the scene was *not* shot and the reasons why you think it should be included. Describe the scene and explain where and how you would add it to the film. How would this addition contribute to the film story or change its meaning?

3. Choose a long novel that has been adapted to film and identify the settings, scenes, characters, dialogue, exposition and other narrative elements that were cut. What is the overall effect of these omissions?

4. Nicholas Meyer explains that he wrote a screenplay for Miguel Cervantes' 1000-page novel *Don Quixote* by rereading the novel, putting down a sentence for every page, and turning a 1000-page novel into a 100-page outline. He read the outline and determined what he liked, needed, and did not need. From the filmography, choose a novel, read a chapter, write down a sentence for each page, and determine what narrative elements you like and do not like. Then compare your adaptation outline with the adaptation of the chapter in the film.

5. In Chapter 4, the credit portion of the opening sequence of *The Maltese Falcon* is analyzed to show how its content and structural elements *foreshadow,* or prefigure, a later development in the film. In this chapter, the credit portion of the opening sequence of *A River Runs Through It* is also analyzed to show not only how its content and structural elements foreshadow later developments in the film but also how they contribute to a new narrative emphasis. Analyze the credit portion of the opening sequence of a film adaptation (such as *Double Indemnity*) to show how its content and structural elements foreshadow a later development in the film and/or contribute to a new narrative emphasis. How does the credit portion of the film relate to the original story?

6. Choose a scene from a novella that is kept in the film adaptation. Describe the scene in some detail and explain its relationship to the over-

all text. Why do you think the scene was included? What are some important differences between the text scene and the film scene? What do these differences add up to? State a relationship between the literary and cinematic scenes.

7. With the novella, the filmmaker is not faced with the necessity and the challenge of either dropping or adding substantial elements of narrative to the novella to fit the running time of the feature film. Instead, the adapter can drop, or add, or do nothing at all. Take a novella with which you are familiar and determine whether you would drop narrative elements, add them, or do nothing with them at all, if you were going to make a film adaptation of it.

8. Robert Redford said of the novella *A River Runs Through It* that, "when I read the first sentence . . . I thought I might be in for something. When I looked at the last line, I knew it. And when I finished reading the novella, I wanted to bring it to the screen." Although Redford's observation may apply to any literary work, choose a novella, read the first and last lines of the text, and decide if you would like to bring this work to the screen.

WORKS CITED

BURNS, STUART IAN. 1996. *Film Adaptation*. 24 September 2002 <http://feelinglistless.blogspot.com/2002_09_15_feelinglistless_archive.html#81817594>.

CARR, JAY. "Redford's River Runs Deep." Rev. of *A River Runs Through It,* dir. Robert Redford. *The Boston Globe.* 16 Oct. 1992, city ed., arts & film: 33.

CAWELTI, JOHN G. "What Rough Beasts—New Westerns." *ANQ* 9 (1996): 4–16. Expanded Academic ASAP Dutchess Community Coll. Lib., Poughkeepsie, New York. 10 Dec. 2001 <http://web5.infotrac.galegroup.com/itw/i>.

CHOPIN, KATE. *The Awakening*. Ed. Nancy A. Walker. 2nd ed. New York: Bedford/St. Martin's, 2000.

EISENSTEIN, SERGEI. "Dickens, Griffith, and the Film Today." *The Film Form.* Ed. and trans. Jay Leyda. New York: Harcourt, 1947.

ENGEL, JOEL. *Screenwriters on Screenwriting.* New York: MJF Books, 1995.

Farewell to Arms, A. Dir. Frank Borzage. Perf. Gary Cooper, Helen Hayes, and Adolph Menjou. Paramount, 1932.

Farewell to Arms, A. Dir. Charles Vidor. Perf. Rock Hudson, Jennifer Jones, and Vittorio De Sica. 20th Century Fox, 1957.

FITZGERALD, F. SCOTT. *The Great Gatsby.* New York: Scribner's, 1925.

FRIEDENBERG, RICHARD. Preface. *A River Runs Through It: Bringing a Classic to the Screen.* By Friedenberg. Livingston, Montana: Clark City Press, 1992. 5–18.

GEHRING, WES D. "The Populist Films of Robert Redford." *USA Today* 127 (1999): 62. Expanded Academic

ASAP. Dutchess Community Coll. Lib., Poughkeepsie, New York. 10 Dec. 2001 <http://web2.infotrac.galegroup.com/itw/i>.

GIDDINGS, ROBERT, ET AL. *Screening the Novel: The Theory and Practice of Literary Dramatization.* New York: St. Martin's Press, 1990.

Great Gatsby, The. Dir. Jack Clayton. Perf. Robert Redford, Mia Farrow, and Sam Waterston. Paramount, 1974.

IZOD, JOHN. "Words Selling Pictures." Orr 95–103.

LEE, HARPER. *To Kill a Mockingbird.* New York: Warner, 1960.

MACLEAN, NORMAN. *A River Runs Through It and Other Stories.* Chicago: The University of Chicago Press, 1976. 1–104.

MCFARLANE, BRIAN. *Novel to Film: An Introduction to the Theory of Adaptation.* Oxford: Oxford University Press, 1995.

———. *Words and Images: Australian Novels into Film.* Victoria, Australia: Heinemann, 1983.

MONACO, JAMES. *How to Read A Film: Movies, Media, Multimedia.* 3rd ed. New York: Oxford University Press, 2000.

ORR, JOHN, AND COLIN NICHOLSON, EDS. *Cinema and Fiction: New Modes of Adapting 1950–1990.* Edinburgh: Edinburgh University Press, 1992.

PELLOW, C. KENNETH. *Films as Critiques of Novels: Transformational Criticism.* Lewiston, New York: Mellen Press, 1994.

REDFORD, ROBERT. Introduction. *A River Runs Through It: Bringing a Classic to the Screen.* By Richard Friedenberg. Livingston, Montana: Clark City Press, 1992. 1–2.

River Runs Through It, A. Dir. Robert Redford. Perf. Craig Sheffer, Brad Pitt, Tom Skerritt, and Emily Lloyd. Columbia, 1992.

ROWE, ALLAN. "Film Form and Narrative." *An Introduction to Film Studies.* Ed. Jill Niemes. 2nd ed. London: Routledge, 1999.

SEGER, LINDA. *The Art of Adaptation: Turning Fact and Fiction into Film.* New York: Henry Holt, 1992.

To Kill a Mockingbird. Dir. Robert Mulligan. Perf. Gregory Peck. Universal, 1962.

■■■ SELECTED FILMOGRAPHY OF NOVEL ADAPTATIONS

LOUISA MAY ALCOTT. *Little Women* (1886–89).
GEORGE CUKOR. *Little Women* (1933).
GILLIAN ARMSTRONG. *Little Women* (1994).

JANE AUSTEN. *Emma* (1814–16).
AMY HECKERLING. *Clueless* (1995).
DOUGLAS MCGRATH. *Emma* (1996).

JANE AUSTEN. *Mansfield Park* (1814).
PATRICIA ROZEMA. *Mansfield Park* (UK 1999).

JANE AUSTEN. *Pride and Prejudice* (1813).
ROBERT Z. LEONARD. *Pride and Prejudice* (1940).
ANDREW BLACK. *Pride and Prejudice* (2003).

JANE AUSTEN. *Sense and Sensibility*
(1811).
ANG LEE. *Sense and Sensibility* (1995).

LOUIS BEGLEY. *About Schmidt* (1997).
ALEXANDER PAYNE. *About Schmidt*
(2002).

PETER BENCHLEY. *Jaws* (1974).
STEVEN SPIELBERG. *Jaws* (1975).

RAY BRADBURY. *Fahrenheit 451* (1953).
FRANÇOIS TRUFFAUT. *Fahrenheit 451*
(UK 1966).

CHARLOTTE BRONTË. *Jane Eyre* (1848).
ROBERT STEVENSON. *Jane Eyre* (1944).
FRANCO ZEFFIRELLI. *Jane Eyre* (1996).

EMILY BRONTË. *Wuthering Heights*
(1847).
WILLIAM WYLER. *Wuthering Heights*
(1939).
PETER KOSMINSKY. *Wuthering Heights*
(1992).

ANTHONY BURGESS. *A Clockwork
Orange* (1962).
STANLEY KUBRICK. *A Clockwork Orange*
(UK 1971).

JANE CAMPION. *The Piano: A Novel*
(1994).
JANE CAMPION. *The Piano* (Aus. 1993).

KATE CHOPIN. *The Awakening* (1899).
MARY LAMBERT. *Grand Isle* (1991).

ARTHUR C. CLARKE. *2001: A Space
Odyssey* (1968).
STANLEY KUBRICK. *2001: A Space
Odyssey* (1968).

MAX ALLAN COLLINS, ET AL. *The Road
to Perdition* (1998).
SAM MENDES. *The Road to Perdition*
(2002).

JOSEPH CONRAD. *The Duel* (1908).
RIDLEY SCOTT. *The Duellists* (1977).

JAMES FENIMORE COOPER. *The Last of
the Mohicans* (1826).
MICHAEL MANN. *The Last of the Mohicans* (1992).

DANIEL DEFOE. *Moll Flanders* (1722).
PEN DENSHAM. *Moll Flanders* (1996).

PHILIP K. DICK. *Do Androids Dream of
Electric Sheep?* (1968).
RIDLEY SCOTT. *Blade Runner* (1982).

CHARLES DICKENS. *David Copperfield*
(1849–50).
GEORGE CUKOR. *David Copperfield*
(1935).

CHARLES DICKENS. *Great Expectations*
(1860–61).
DAVID LEAN. *Great Expectations*
(UK 1946).

CHARLES DICKENS. *Nicholas Nickleby*
(1838–39).
DOUGLAS MCGRATH. *Nicholas Nickleby*
(2002).

JAMES DICKEY. *Deliverance* (1970).
JOHN BOORMAN. *Deliverance* (1972).

GIUSEPPE TOMASI DI LAMPEDUSA. *The
Leopard* (1958).
LUCHINO VISCONTI. *The Leopard*
(It. 1963).

ISAK DINESEN. *Out of Africa* (1937).
SYDNEY POLLACK. *Out of Africa* (1985).

DAPHNE DU MAURIER. *Rebecca* (1938).
ALFRED HITCHCOCK. *Rebecca* (1940).

LAURA ESQUIVEL. *Like Water for Choco-
late* (1989).
ALFONSO ARAU. *Like Water for Choco-
late* (Mex. 1992).

WILLIAM FAULKNER. *The Sound and the
Fury* (1929).
MARTIN RITT. *The Sound and the Fury*
(1959).

HENRY FIELDING. *Tom Jones* (1749).
TONY RICHARDSON. *Tom Jones* (UK 1963).

F. SCOTT FITZGERALD. *The Great Gatsby* (1925).
FRANCIS FORD COPPOLA. *The Great Gatsby* (1974).

GUSTAVE FLAUBERT. *Madame Bovary* (1857).
CLAUDE CHABROL. *Madame Bovary* (Fr. 1991).

E. M. FORSTER. *Howards End* (1910).
JAMES IVORY. *Howards End* (UK 1992).

E. M. FORSTER. *A Passage to India* (1924).
DAVID LEAN. *A Passage to India* (UK 1984).

E. M. FORSTER. *A Room with a View* (1908).
JAMES IVORY. *A Room with a View* (UK 1985).

JOHN FOWLES. *The French Lieutenant's Woman* (1969).
KAREL REISZ. *The French Lieutenant's Woman* (UK 1981).

GRAHAM GREENE. *The Quiet American* (1955).
PHILLIP NOYCE. *The Quiet American* (2002).

JUDITH GUEST. *Ordinary People* (1976).
ROBERT REDFORD. *Ordinary People* (1980).

THOMAS HARDY. *Tess of the d'Urbervilles* (1891).
ROMAN POLANSKI. *Tess* (Fr./UK 1979).

NATHANIEL HAWTHORNE. *The Scarlet Letter* (1850).
VICTOR SJÖSTRÖM. *The Scarlet Letter* (1926).
ROLAND JOFFÉ. *The Scarlet Letter* (1995).

PETER HEDGES. *What's Eating Gilbert Grape* (1991).
LASSE HALLSTRÖM. *What's Eating Gilbert Grape* (1993).

JOSEPH HELLER. *Catch-22* (1961).
MIKE NICHOLS. *Catch-22* (1970).

ERNEST HEMINGWAY. *A Farewell to Arms* (1929).
FRANK BORZAGE. *A Farewell to Arms* (1932).

ERNEST HEMINGWAY. *The Sun Also Rises* (1926).
HENRY KING. *The Sun Also Rises* (1957).

S. E. HINTON. *The Outsiders* (1967).
FRANCIS FORD COPPOLA. *The Outsiders* (1983).

KAZUO ISHIGURO. *The Remains of the Day* (1983).
JAMES IVORY. *The Remains of the Day* (UK/US 1993).

HENRY JAMES. *The Bostonians* (1886).
JAMES IVORY. *The Bostonians* (UK/US 1984).

HENRY JAMES. *The Europeans* (1878).
JAMES IVORY. *The Europeans* (UK 1979).

HENRY JAMES. *The Golden Bowl* (1904).
JAMES IVORY. *The Golden Bowl* (2000).

HENRY JAMES. *The Portrait of a Lady* (1881).
JANE CAMPION. *The Portrait of a Lady* (UK/US 1996).

HENRY JAMES. *Washington Square* (1889).
AGNIESZKA HOLLAND. *Washington Square* (1997).

HENRY JAMES. *The Wings of the Dove* (1902).

IAIN SOFTLEY. *The Wings of the Dove* (US/UK 1997).

FRANZ KAFKA. *The Trial* (1925).
DAVID HUGH JONES. *The Trial* (UK 1993).

THOMAS KENEALLY. *Schindler's List* [also published as *Schindler's Ark*] (1982).
STEVEN SPIELBERG. *Schindler's List* (1993).

KEN KESEY. *One Flew Over the Cuckoo's Nest* (1962).
MILOS FORMAN. *One Flew Over the Cuckoo's Nest* (1975).

STEPHEN KING. *The Shining* (1977).
STANLEY KUBRICK. *The Shining* (1980).

W. P. KINSELLA. *Shoeless Joe* (1982).
PHIL ALDEN ROBINSON. *A Field of Dreams* (1989).

JERZY KOSINSKI. *Being There* (1970).
HAL ASHBY. *Being There* (1979).

MILAN KUNDERA. *The Unbearable Lightness of Being* (1982).
PHILIP KAUFMAN. *The Unbearable Lightness of Being* (1988).

CHODERLOS DE LACLOS. *Les Liaisons dangereuses* (1782).
STEPHEN FREARS. *Dangerous Liaisons* (US/UK 1988).
ROGER KUMBLE. *Cruel Intentions* (1999).

D. H. LAWRENCE. *Sons and Lovers* (1913).
JACK CARDIFF. *Sons and Lovers* (UK 1960).

D. H. LAWRENCE. *Women in Love* (1920).
KEN RUSSELL. *Women in Love* (UK 1969).

DENNIS LEHANE. *Mystic River* (2001).
CLINT EASTWOOD. *Mystic River* (2003).

PIERRE LOUŸS. *That Obscure Object of Desire* (1898).
LUIS BUÑUEL. *That Obscure Object of Desire* (Fr./Sp. 1977).

BERNARD MALAMUD. *The Natural* (1952).
BARRY LEVINSON. *The Natural* (1984).

HERMAN MELVILLE. *Moby-Dick* (1851).
JOHN HUSTON. *Moby Dick* (1956).

MARGARET MITCHELL. *Gone with the Wind* (1936).
VICTOR FLEMING. *Gone with the Wind* (1939).

ALBERTO MORAVIA. *The Conformist* (1951).
BERNARDO BERTOLUCCI. *The Conformist* (It./Fr./W.G. 1970).

TONI MORRISON. *Beloved* (1988).
JONATHAN DEMME. *Beloved* (1998).

VLADIMIR NABOKOV. *Lolita* (1955).
STANLEY KUBRICK. *Lolita* (US/UK 1962).
ADRIAN LYNE. *Lolita* (US/Fr. 1997).

PATRICK O'BRIAN. *The Far Side of the World* (1970) and other novels in the Aubrey/Maturin series.
PETER WEIR. *Master and Commander: The Far Side of the World* (2003).

MICHAEL ONDAATJE. *The English Patient* (1992).
ANTHONY MINGHELLA. *The English Patient* (1996).

GEORGE ORWELL. *Nineteen Eighty-Four* (1949).
MICHAEL RADFORD. *Nineteen Eighty-Four* (UK 1984).

BORIS PASTERNAK. *Doctor Zhivago* (1956).

DAVID LEAN. *Doctor Zhivago* (1965).

RICHARD PECK. *Don't Look and It Won't Hurt* (1972).

ALLSION ANDERS. *Gas Food Lodging* (1992).

MARIO PUZO. *The Godfather* (1969).

FRANCIS FORD COPPOLA. *The Godfather* (1972).

HENRI-PIERRE ROCHÉ. *Jules et Jim* (1953).

FRANÇOIS TRUFFAUT. *Jules et Jim* (Fr. 1962).

PHILIP ROTH. *The Human Stain* (2000).

ROBERT BENTON. *The Human Stain* (2003).

J. K. ROWLING. *Harry Potter* Books 1–3 (1997–99).

CHRIS COLUMBUS. *Harry Potter and the Sorcerer's Stone* (2001).
Harry Potter and the Chamber of Secrets (2002).

ALFONSO CUARÓN. *Harry Potter and the Prisoner of Azkaban* (2004).

RICHARD RUSSO. *Nobody's Fool* (1993).

ROBERT BENTON. *Nobody's Fool* (1994).

MARY SHELLEY. *Frankenstein* (1818).

JAMES WHALE. *Frankenstein* (1931).

NICHOLAS SPARKS. *The Notebook* (1996).

NICK CASSAVETES. *The Notebook* (2004).

JOHN STEINBECK. *The Grapes of Wrath* (1939).

JOHN FORD. *The Grapes of Wrath* (1940).

BRAM STOKER. *Dracula* (1897).

WERNER HERZOG. *Nosferatu the Vampyre* (W.G./Fr. 1979).

WILLIAM STYRON. *Sophie's Choice* (1979).

ALAN J. PAKULA. *Sophie's Choice* (1982).

AMY TAN. *The Joy Luck Club* (1990).

WAYNE WANG. *The Joy Luck Club* (1993).

WILLIAM MAKEPEACE THACKERAY. *The Luck of Barry Lyndon* (1844).

STANLEY KUBRICK. *Barry Lyndon* (UK 1975).

WILLIAM MAKEPEACE THACKERAY. *Vanity Fair* (1848).

MIRA NAIR. *Vanity Fair* (UK/US 2004).

J. R. R. TOLKIEN. *The Lord of the Rings* trilogy (1954–55).

PETER JACKSON. *The Lord of the Rings: The Fellowship of the Ring* (NZ/US 2001).
The Lord of the Rings: The Two Towers (NZ/US 2002).
The Lord of the Rings: The Return of the King (NZ/US 2003).

MARK TWAIN. *The Adventures of Huckleberry Finn* (1884).

STEPHEN SOMMERS. *The Adventures of Huck Finn* (1993).

ANNE TYLER. *The Accidental Tourist* (1985).

LAWRENCE KASDAN. *The Accidental Tourist* (1988).

ALICE WALKER. *The Color Purple* (1982).

STEVEN SPIELBERG. *The Color Purple* (1985).

ROBERT PENN WARREN. *All the King's Men* (1946).

ROBERT ROSSEN. *All the King's Men* (1949).

H. G. WELLS. *The War of the Worlds*
(1896).
BYRON HASKIN. *The War of the Worlds*
(1953).

IRVINE WELSH. *Trainspotting* (1994).
DANNY BOYLE. *Trainspotting* (UK 1996).

EDITH WHARTON. *The Age of Innocence*
(1920).
MARTIN SCORSESE. *The Age of
Innocence* (1993).

OSCAR WILDE. *The Picture of Dorian
Gray* (1891).

ALBERT LEWIN. *The Picture of Dorian
Gray* (1945).

VIRGINIA WOOLF. *Mrs. Dalloway* (1925).
MARLEEN GORRIS. *Mrs. Dalloway*
(UK/US 1997).

MICHAEL CUNNINGHAM. *The Hours*
(1998).
STEPHEN DALDRY. *The Hours* (2002).

VIRGINIA WOOLF. *Orlando* (1928).
SALLY POTTER. *Orlando* (UK 1992).

RICHARD WRIGHT. *Native Son* (1940).
PIERRE CHENAL. *Native Son* (1951).

NOVELLA ADAPTATIONS ■■■

JAMES M. CAIN. *Double Indemnity*
(1936).
BILLY WILDER. *Double Indemnity* (1944).

JAMES M. CAIN. *The Postman Always
Rings Twice* (1934).
PIERRE CHENAL. *Le Dernier Tournant*
(Fr. 1939).
LUCHINO VISCONTI. *Ossessione*
(It. 1943).
TAY GARNETT. *The Postman Always
Rings Twice* (1946).
BOB RAFELSON. *The Postman Always
Rings Twice* (1981).

ALBERT CAMUS. *The Stranger* (1942).
LUCHINO VISCONTI. *The Stranger*
(It. 1967).

TRUMAN CAPOTE. *Breakfast at Tiffany's*
(1958).
BLAKE EDWARDS. *Breakfast at Tiffany's*
(1961).

JOSEPH CONRAD. *Heart of Darkness*
(1901).
MICHAEL HERR. *Dispatches* (1977).

FRANCIS FORD COPPOLA. *Apocalypse
Now* (1979).
NICOLAS ROEG. *Heart of Darkness* (1994).

STEPHEN CRANE. *The Red Badge of
Courage* (1895).
JOHN HUSTON. *The Red Badge of
Courage* (1951).

ROALD DAHL. *James and the Giant
Peach* (1961).
HENRY SELICK. *James and the Giant
Peach* (1996).

CHARLES DICKENS. *A Christmas Carol*
(1843).
EDWIN L. MARIN. *A Christmas Carol*
(1938).
BRIAN DESMOND HURST. *Scrooge*
(UK 1951).
CLIVE DONNER. *A Christmas Carol*
(UK 1984).

FYODOR DOSTOYEVSKY. *The Double*
(1846).
BERNARDO BERTOLUCCI. *Partner*
(It. 1968).

GRAHAM GREENE. *The Third Man* (1950).

CAROL REED. *The Third Man* (UK 1949).

ERNEST HEMINGWAY. *The Old Man and the Sea* (1952).

JOHN STURGES. *The Old Man and the Sea* (1958).

HENRY JAMES. *Daisy Miller* (1878).

PETER BOGDANOVICH. *Daisy Miller* (1974).

HENRY JAMES. *The Turn of the Screw* (1898).

JACK CLAYTON. *The Innocents* (UK 1961).

JACK LONDON. *The Call of the Wild* (1903).

WILLIAM A. WELLMAN. *The Call of the Wild* (1935).

KEN ANNAKIN. *Call of the Wild* (1972).

THOMAS MANN. *Death in Venice* (1912).

LUCHINO VISCONTI. *Death in Venice* (It. 1971).

HORACE MCCOY. *They Shoot Horses, Don't They?* (1935).

SYDNEY POLLACK. *They Shoot Horses, Don't They?* (1969).

HERMAN MELVILLE. *Bartleby the Scrivener* (1856).

JONATHAN PARKER. *Bartleby* (2001).

HERMAN MELVILLE. *Billy Budd* (1891).

PETER USTINOV. *Billy Budd* (USA/UK 1962).

JACK SCHAEFER. *Shane* (1949).

GEORGE STEVENS. *Shane* (1953).

OUSMANE SEMBENE. *Xala* (1974).

OUSMANE SEMBENE. *Xala* (1975).

JOHN STEINBECK. *Of Mice and Men* (1937).

LEWIS MILESTONE. *Of Mice and Men* (1939).

REZA BADIYI. *Of Mice and Men* (1981).

GARY SINISE. *Of Mice and Men* (1992).

JOHN STEINBECK. *The Red Pony* (1938).

LEWIS MILESTONE. *The Red Pony* (1949).

ROBERT LOUIS STEVENSON. *The Strange Case of Dr. Jekyll and Mr. Hyde* (1886).

JOHN S. ROBERTSON. *Dr. Jekyll and Mr. Hyde* (1920).

ROUBEN MAMOULIAN. *Dr. Jekyll and Mr. Hyde* (1931).

VICTOR FLEMING. *Dr. Jekyll and Mr. Hyde* (1941).

MARIO SOFFICI. *El hombre y la bestia (The Man and the Beast)* (Sp. 1951).

JEAN RENOIR. *La Testament du Docteur Cordelier (The Testament of Dr. Cordelier* (Fr. 1959).

ROY WARD BAKER. *Dr. Jekyll and Sister Hyde* (UK 1971).

STEPHEN FREARS. *Mary Reilly* (1996).

H. G. WELLS. *The Invisible Man: A Grotesque Romance* (1897).

JAMES WHALE. *The Invisible Man* (1933).

H. G. WELLS. *The Time Machine* (1895).

GEORGE PAL. *The Time Machine* (1960).

SIMON WELLS. *The Time Machine* (2002).

6 THE SHORT STORY

The short story, as its name suggests, is a brief fiction written in prose. Although the short story is brief, meaning usually between 500 and 15,000 words, it involves the same narrative elements found in the novel and the novella. However, the typical plot has fewer scenes and is more compact than either the novel or the novella. The setting is usually sketched rather than described at length. And the characters are limited in number and less developed, their qualities more likely disclosed by the central action than by elaborate analysis from the narrator.

The brevity of the short story poses a unique challenge for the filmmaker. With the novel, the filmmaker must drop elements of narrative to shorten the story to fit the running time of the feature film, which is usually 80 to 120 minutes. Even a relatively short novel of 140 pages is just too long a narrative to be wholly contained within a feature film. However, with the short story, the filmmaker must add or expand narrative elements to lengthen the story to fit the running time of the feature film.

Director and screenwriter Christopher Nolan sees in this challenge an advantage that the short story holds over the novel:

> I think the short story can be a very good jumping off point for a feature. I think novels very often are too complex, too dense to begin with, so you are always trying to weed things out. Risking losing the things that attract you to that material in the first place. The nice thing about a short story is that a simple scene, a simple concept, . . . lends itself quite naturally to . . . expansion to feature size. ("Christopher Nolan")

Three Strategies for Expanding the Short Story into a Feature Film

The filmmaker usually accomplishes Nolan's "expansion to feature size" by using one or more of three different strategies.

1. **Concentration strategy.** The filmmakers keep most of the elements of narrative from the short story; concentrate those elements at the beginning, middle, or end of the film; and add invented elements to the rest of the film.

2. **Interweaving strategy.** The filmmakers keep most of the elements of narrative from the short story; disperse those elements throughout the film, although not necessarily in their original order; and interweave either invented elements or invented expansions to already existing elements.

3. **Point-of-departure strategy.** The filmmakers drop most of the elements of narrative from the short story; keep perhaps the plot premise, a character's name, or just the title; and, using these elements as a point of departure, add an invented narrative.

We illustrate the three strategies by briefly discussing an example of each. If you are asked to read one of the short stories mentioned and to view the companion film, follow the method for studying an adaptation illustrated in Chapter 4.

Concentration Strategy

The Killers, directed by Robert Siodmak and adapted from Ernest Hemingway's short story of the same name, illustrates the concentration strategy. When employing this strategy, filmmakers keep most of the narrative elements from the short story; concentrate them at the beginning, middle, or end of the film;

and add story elements to the rest of the film. In their use of the strategy in *The Killers*, the filmmakers concentrate the kept elements at the beginning of the film and attach entirely new material for the rest of the film.

"THE KILLERS" (1927), by Ernest Hemingway

Ernest Hemingway's "The Killers" tells the story of the attempted murder of Ole Andreson by two gunmen, Al and Max, one evening at a diner in a small town. While they wait for Andreson to show up, the gunmen intimidate the diner employees, George and Sam, and a young customer, Nick Adams. Andreson does not show up at the diner as expected. Their plans stymied, Al and Max leave. Adams goes to Andreson's boardinghouse room to warn him about the men, but Andreson refuses to do anything. Adams is so upset by the incident he decides to leave town.

The personalities of the main characters are disclosed in the confrontation between the would-be killers and their would-be victims. Al and Max, the would-be killers, are vaudevillian in their dress and comic patter and yet sadistic in their intimidation. George, Nick, and Sam, the would-be victims, behave submissively. Ole appears mysterious because of his vague statements about his past and his decision neither to fight, nor run, nor hide.

The small town, Summit, plays a role in the short story because of its size. In such a rural settlement of the 1920s, the urban gunmen stand out, and someone like Ole, with a dishonest past, can hide out there. Its name may suggest the peak of emotional crisis for those in the diner and for Ole.

The story is narrated in the present tense, using the dramatic point of view. The narrator does not confine what is seen or heard to any one character, does not explain to the reader what any of the characters think or feel, and reports only how they look and what they say and do. Most of the narrative is dialogue. The descriptions of the characters, their actions, and the setting are brief, straightforward, and not detailed, as if they were stage directions in a play. The short story reads like a performance text, such as a one-act play or a short film script.

The short story's theme is a variation on a familiar one of Hemingway's— grace under pressure. By their intimidation, Al and Max supply a "pressure" that is unwarranted but must be endured so long as the two control the situation with their guns. George, Nick, and Sam exhibit sensible "grace" under pressure, even after Al and Max leave the diner and are no longer a threat.

The story's incompleteness is another one of its features. The killers do not get to kill anybody. Their intended victim chooses neither to fight, nor run, nor hide. One of their hostages makes plans to leave town, but there is no way to tell if he does. The incomplete actions create the unresolved narrative tension on which the story ends. On the one hand, the ending is ironic because this is a crime story, and in this genre a crime is committed and the criminals are hunted down. The ending could be a deliberate strategy by Hemingway to make "The Killers" a *parody*, or criticism, of the formulaic crime story. On the other hand, the unresolved ending creates the feeling in some readers that the story is unfinished. This feeling played a part in its adaptation, as we mention below.

THE KILLERS (1946), Directed by Robert Siodmak

The first scene in the opening sequence of the film is an invention. The scene is divided into three shots. The first is a straight-on, medium close-up shot of the backs of two men sitting inside a car and driving at night along a road illuminated by the headlights of the car, with the sound track playing the noises of the engine running and the tires rolling on the pavement. The second shot is a straight-on close-up of a sign announcing Brentwood (Summit renamed), illuminated by the headlights of the car, with the sound track still playing the noises of the engine and the tires. The third shot is a slightly high-angled, extreme long shot of two men walking down a Brentwood street at night that becomes a straight-on close-up shot as the characters move down the street and up to the camera. Streetlights create pools of bright light. The men's bodies cast long, dark shadows on the pavement. They walk to a closed, darkened filling station, peer inside briefly, and then set their sights on the open, well-lighted interior of the diner located across the street. Sharp shadows cross their lighted faces as they gaze at the diner. These motifs of light and dark are typical conventions of *film noir* and signal to viewers the dark, somber genre of crime film they are beginning to watch. As the men walk, the credits flash on the screen, partially obscuring their progress down the street but for the most part not interfering with the viewers' general perception of the scene. The sound track plays Miklos Rozsa's theme music. The arrival of the two men is not in the short story, but is implied by the setting and the characters and thus is an invented expansion on already existing narrative elements.

The short story narrative occupies only the second and third scenes of the opening sequence or about 8 minutes of a 103-minute film. The second scene begins with a straight-on, interior long shot of Al and Max entering the diner. The third scene begins with a high-angle, exterior long shot of Nick Adams running to tell Pete Lund (Ole Andreson renamed) about the killers. The third scene ends with a close-up, interior shot of Pete in his boardinghouse room listening to the sounds of the killers climbing the stairs. (This last detail is invented since the killers never find Ole in the story.)

In the second and third scenes, most of the elements of narrative from the short story are kept. The plot, the six major characters, the diner and boardinghouse settings, the third-person point of view, and the theme of grace under

Al, Max, and George in the diner, illuminated by low-key lighting typical of *film noir,* from the second scene of *The Killers* (1946).

pressure are retained. The several minor drops and **substitutions** are changes that speed up the narrative. Dropped are several repetitious actions in the lunchroom; two characters, a nameless lunchroom customer and the boarding-house manager; a number of lines of dialogue, including a degrading reference to Sam; Nick's decision to leave town; and the narrative feature of incomplete-ness. Substituted are some lines of dialogue, Nick's route to the boardinghouse, the town's name, and Ole Andreson's name. The structural elements of film flesh out (in the *film noir* style of the first scene) the sketchy descriptive details of the characters, actions, and setting in the short story.

After the third scene, beginning with the close-up shot of Pete listening to the sounds of feet climbing the stairs in the boardinghouse, the rest of the film is a 90-minute addition that develops another plot, introduces new characters and settings, brings in new themes, yet continues in the same *film noir* style. In the film, once Al and Max find and kill Pete (Ole) in his boardinghouse room, an insurance investigator traces Pete's life back to find out why he was mur-dered. Essentially, Pete, a former boxer, has gotten himself mixed up with a gangster, has participated in a robbery, and has become romantically involved with the gangster's girlfriend. Themes of greed, lust, betrayal among thieves, and inevitable revenge emerge. The impetus for this huge addition is, in the short story, Ole Andreson's statement to Nick in Ole's room: "I got in wrong," and, in the film, Pete Lund's statement to Nick: "I did something wrong." What Ole/Pete has done wrong, to whom, when, and where is narrated in the rest of the film. This massive addition shifts the overall film adaptation from close-to-intermediate to loose. The result of this huge addition is a virtually new story.

As Carlos Clarens observes:

> After the opening, *The Killers* became a caper story about a meticulously planned holdup—closer in fact to W. R. Burnett [a crime novelist] than to Hemingway, although not surprising, since [the screenwriter and director] John Huston had written the scenario [for *The Killers*]. . . . Since *High Sierra* (1940), [an adaptation of a Burnett crime novel of which Huston wrote the screenplay and Raoul Walsh directed] Huston's work had borne the acknowledged influence of Burnett and would continue through the forties to deal with the failed efforts of mismatched adventurers [including *The Maltese Falcon* (1941), which we discussed in Chapter 4]. (199)

The length of Hemingway's short story led the filmmakers to add new narrative elements in order to make a feature film; they had no other choice. These added elements affect the meaning of the film. Frank Laurence, in his book *Hemingway and the Movies,* suggests:

> Anthony Veiller's [the credited screenwriter—Huston is uncredited] responsibility was to make a popular entertainment out of a sophisticated story. It was natural to give [Ole Andreson] the major role in the screenplay and let Nick Adams be a very minor part. Just as obvious is the reason why [Ole] had to be killed in the movie. What kind of gangster movie would it be where the killers simply go away when their intended victim does not show up on time where he should be?
>
> You certainly could not call such a movie *The Killers.* Possibly it did not so much seem to Anthony Veiller, Robert Siodmak, and Mark Hellinger [the producer] that they were changing the nature of Hemingway's story as that they were finishing it for him. Many readers feel that the story is not finished. They feel this partly because they wish for a very different kind of story than Hemingway intended. They are used to one kind of gangster story and do not readily imagine another kind. (191)

For some readers and viewers, especially the screenwriters, the director, and the producer, the consequence of the addition of narrative elements is the necessary finishing of an incomplete short story; for others, the consequence of the additions is the superfluous padding of an already completed short story. Either way, the filmmakers' interpretation of Hemingway's short story illustrates the concentration strategy of adapting a short story to a feature film. The filmmakers keep most of the narrative elements; concentrate them at the beginning, middle, or end of the film; and add new elements to the rest of the film.

Interweaving Strategy

The Swimmer, directed by Frank Perry and adapted from John Cheever's story of the same name, illustrates the interweaving strategy. When employing this strategy, the filmmakers keep most of the elements of narrative from the short story; disperse those elements throughout the film, although not necessarily in their original order; and interweave either invented elements or expansions on already existing elements.

"THE SWIMMER" (1964), by John Cheever

Cheever's "The Swimmer" is the story of Ned Merrill's summer Sunday afternoon swimming expedition from a friend's house to his own house located across the county. He uses for water the chain of luxurious in-ground swimming pools that belong to his affluent friends and acquaintances. As he plunges into the clear, chemically well-balanced water, Ned leaves his wife, Lucinda, poolside, complaining that she had drunk too much the previous night. He expects to find his daughters playing tennis when he arrives home later in the day. For the first half of his swim-trek, old friends warmly greet Ned as a surprise but a welcome guest. However, for the last half, old acquaintances and a spurned lover coolly snub him as a disrupting interloper. Late Sunday evening, when he gets home, neither his wife nor his daughters are in the house or on the tennis court, and the house is locked and abandoned.

At each pool stop along the way, the trend of the conversations suggests Ned has been away awhile and has not kept up with the latest news. Some of the people he speaks with have been trying to contact him but have been unsuccessful. In response to their questions concerning his whereabouts, he replies vaguely and promises to see them soon. When he mentions his wife, daughter, job, or house, they exchange ironic glances and say nothing. Something seems radically amiss with Ned. In conjunction with the increasingly cooler reception the pool owners give Ned, there is a growing perception that summer has gone and fall is here: red and yellow leaves drop, a chill is in the air, the constellations change, the pools reflect a "wintry light," and Ned— dressed only in a bathing suit—becomes gradually cold and exhausted. Whatever has happened to Ned at home or on the job, he has come undone before our eyes.

The story is narrated in the past tense, using the third-person restricted point of view. The narrator confines what is seen and heard to a single character, Ned, and explains only what Ned thinks and feels. Most of the story consists of narration and of descriptions of characters and setting, and the only dialogue consists of the brief exchanges mentioned earlier between Ned and those he meets. Cheever's writing style is plain, and his tone is neutral. His diction is concrete and specific, somewhere between formal and informal.

The question of what has happened to Ned is addressed by several critics. Stanley J. Kozikowski points out that the story

> accommodates various readings, particular and universal. Within its range of appeal, for instance, it has been read as suggestive autobiography, contemporary American Odyssey, dazzling literary structure, as a midsummer's nightmare, sacramental parody, realism yielding to fantasy, and Neddy Merrill dead in Hades. (367)

THE SWIMMER (1968), Directed by Frank Perry

Although Hemingway's "The Killers" and Cheever's "The Swimmer" are both short stories, their characteristics set them apart and may have led the filmmakers to choose different filming strategies. "The Killers" is quite short: its plot is compact, consisting of two scenes, two settings, and ten characters. "The Swimmer" is longer: its plot is episodic, consisting of many scenes, numerous characters, and various settings. One could say "The Swimmer" reads like a novel in miniature. To disperse the narrative spine of "The Killers" over the whole film would be to dilute the gradual building of suspense and dramatic tension. However, since "The Swimmer" is more episodic, it offers entry points for development and addition without disturbing the structure of the story. Accordingly, *The Swimmer* disperses the narrative spine of Cheever's short story over the 94 minutes of the film.

Many narrative elements of "The Swimmer" are kept. These include the overall plot of Ned's summer Sunday afternoon swimming expedition; many of the characters Ned meets along the way, as well as those only mentioned in passing such as Ned's wife, Lucinda, and their daughters; the settings of the various well-manicured backyards and well-maintained pools, in addition to the public pool Ned also swims and the dangerous highway he manages to cross at his own risk; the gradually changing seasons of late summer, fall, and early winter; the third-person point of view; and the gradual transformation of Ned.

The kept elements of the story have been reorganized. The film has Ned follow the same geographic course, but relocates his friends and neighbors so that Ned meets them in a different order and with a different cumulative effect. One of the significant reorderings is to have the public pool become the last pool Ned swims before returning to his house. At the public pool, Ned has humiliating encounters with a ticket-taker who refuses to let him onto the pool premises until he borrows the entrance fee from a shopkeeper, and with a pool custodian who refuses to let him into the pool until he thoroughly washes his dirty feet. These embarrassments are followed by an eye-stinging swim through the over-chlorinated, overcrowded, churning water. As he pulls himself laboriously out of the pool, he meets some of the shopkeepers in his town who deliver a final, sneering, crushing blow to his positive perception of himself. They criticize his wife's taste for imported gourmet foods, his daughters' disrespectful behavior, and his unpaid bills. Enraged, Ned knocks down one of the shopkeepers and crawls on all fours up a giant rock as a spider scurries away to safety from its destroyed web.

The kept elements of the story have also been expanded. The filmmakers' expansion includes extended dialogues. These do not merely repeat for emphasis but increase the number of clues from the short story that hint at but do not expose what happened to Ned at home and on the job. Thus, like Cheever's story, the film only suggests but does not explain Ned's personal problems. Among the expanded dialogues are two hostile conversations. In one, Mrs. Hammer, an added character, expels Ned from her property because he failed to visit her son, Ned's friend, while he was dying. In the other, Ned discovers that the crass Biswangers, also added characters, bought his hot dog wagon at a white elephant sale, and he gets into a physical fight with Mr. Biswanger over who owns it. Ned does not recollect either the death or the sale and is extremely puzzled by them and by the hostile reactions he receives.

Many elements are dropped. These include repetitious dialogue, superfluous characters, and redundant settings. Gone, for example, are the exclamations that everyone from the priest to the head of the Audubon group had drunk too much on Saturday night.

The script adds several new characters for Ned to meet. Most are minor poolside guests, including one interestingly enough played by Cheever himself. However, a few important characters are added, among them the shopkeepers; Julie Ann Hooper, the Merrills' now grown-up babysitter; and a flute-playing boy left home alone. At one of his pool stops, Ned meets some twenty-something men and women, including Julie Ann. Intrigued by Ned's description of his swimming expedition, Julie Ann leaves her friends and plunges into the next pool with him. As they walk between pools, they enter a wood. During Julie Ann and Ned's soft-focus gentle ramble through the sunlit woods, their slow-motion graceful romp at a steeplechase, and their nostalgic conversations about her fascination with him as a teenager, the film allows the viewer to see Ned as the debonair, athletic, young-at-heart gentleman he once was—and still wants to be—through the eyes of a

Ned Merrill (Burt Lancaster) and Julie Ann Hooper (Janet Landgard) approach a hurdle during their slow-motion graceful romp at a steeplechase in *The Swimmer* (1968).

formerly infatuated, starry-eyed teenager who has now grown up. Just after Julie Ann leaves, Ned encounters the lonely boy, who brings out his paternal side. The boy's absent mother and father are separated and he has been left in the care of a nurse. The boy's loneliness and self-confessed lack of athletic ability, including knowing how to swim, inspire Ned to encourage the boy to accompany him on a make-believe swim for the length of the cavern-like pool. They climb down into the pool, walk the pool floor, and move their arms in imitation of various strokes. Their "swim" amuses the boy, and it delights him that he "accomplished" it. As Ned follows the boy up the pool ladder, he advises him that "[i]f you make-believe hard enough, then it's true for you."

This advice is as telling about Ned as it is about the boy. James E. O'Hara observes:

> A generally overlooked weakness of the story is Cheever's refusal to open up Neddy's consciousness for the reader to any great extent. This reticence is essential, perhaps, to its shock ending, but also unfair to the reader. If we are finally to discover that Neddy's personal problems are much more serious than the events of the story had indicated, we deserve some advance warning in the form of insights provided by Neddy; but such hints are scarce and slight. (68)

Ned's advice to the boy is one of the film's several attempts to supply "advance warning" to the viewers and to assist them in realizing the seriousness of Ned's personal problems. Perhaps Ned knows that his daughters will not be home when he arrives and that the house will be locked up and abandoned. Yet he chooses to ignore these facts, to enjoy his swim, and to pretend that all is as it ought to be for his family and himself. Thus, his tears at the end of the film, as he kneels on the front steps of his abandoned house and pounds on the locked door, are possibly tears of bitter recognition that he cannot make believe hard enough and that what is true for him is his loneliness.

The practical considerations of making the feature film led the filmmakers to add new narrative elements; like Siodmak, they had no other choice. The significant additions make the film an intermediate-to-close adaptation of the short story. The consequence of these additions is to emphasize the drama of Ned's decline more clearly than Cheever does in the short story, yet the additions do not alter the portrayal of his decline. The film stays close to the story but illuminates it for the viewer. The film's interpretation of Cheever's short story illustrates the interweaving strategy of adapting a short story to a feature film. The filmmakers keep most of the narrative elements from the short story, disperse those elements throughout the film, and interweave either invented elements or expansions on already existing elements.

Point-of-Departure Strategy

Jonathan Nolan's short story "Memento Mori" and the film *Memento,* directed by his brother Christopher Nolan, illustrate the point-of-departure strategy. In this strategy, the filmmakers drop most of the narrative elements from the short

▸tory; keep perhaps the plot premise, a character's name, or just the title; and, using these rudiments as a point of departure, invent a new story. Because of its limited availability, "Memento Mori" is reprinted below.

■ ■ ■

"MEMENTO MORI" (2001)

by Jonathan Nolan

"What like a bullet can undeceive!"
—Herman Melville

Your wife always used to say you'd be late for your own funeral. Remember that? Her little joke because you were such a slob—always late, always forgetting stuff, even before the incident.

Right about now you're probably wondering if you were late for hers.

You were there, you can be sure of that. That's what the picture's for—the one tacked to the wall by the door. It's not customary to take pictures at a funeral, but somebody, your doctors, I guess, knew you wouldn't remember. They had it blown up nice and big and stuck it right there, next to the door, so you couldn't help but see it every time you got up to find out where she was.

The guy in the picture, the one with the flowers? That's you. And what are you doing? You're reading the headstone, trying to figure out who's funeral you're at, same as you're reading it now, trying to figure why someone stuck that picture next to your door. But why bother reading something that you won't remember?

She's gone, gone for good, and you must be hurting right now, hearing the news. Believe me, I know how you feel. You're probably a wreck. But give it five minutes, maybe ten. Maybe you can even go a whole half hour before you forget.

But you will forget—I guarantee it. A few more minutes and you'll be heading for the door, looking for her all over again, breaking down when you find the picture. How many times do you have to hear the news before some other part of your body, other than that busted brain of yours, starts to remember?

Never-ending grief, never-ending anger. Useless without direction. Maybe you can't understand what's happened. Can't say I really understand, either. Backwards amnesia. That's what the sign says. CRS disease. Your guess is as good as mine.

Maybe you can't understand what happened to you. But you do remember what happened to HER, don't you? The doctors don't want to talk about it. They won't answer my questions. They don't think it's right for a man in your condition to hear about those things. But you remember enough, don't you? You remember his face.

This is why I'm writing to you. Futile, maybe. I don't know how many times you'll have to read this before you listen to me. I don't even know how long you've been locked up in this room already. Neither do you. But your advantage in forgetting is that you'll forget to write yourself off as a lost cause.

Sooner or later you'll want to do something about it. And when you do, you'll just have to trust me, because I'm the only one who can help you.

EARL OPENS ONE EYE after another to a stretch of white ceiling tiles interrupted by a hand-printed sign taped right above his head, large enough for him to read from the bed. An alarm clock is ringing somewhere. He reads the sign, blinks, reads it again, then takes a look at the room.

It's a white room, overwhelmingly white, from the walls and the curtains to the institutional furniture and the bedspread. The alarm clock is ringing from the white desk under the window with the white curtains. At this point Earl probably notices that he is lying on top of his white comforter. He is already wearing a dressing gown and slippers.

He lies back and reads the sign taped to the ceiling again. It says, in crude block capitals, THIS IS YOUR ROOM. THIS IS A ROOM IN A HOSPITAL. THIS IS WHERE YOU LIVE NOW.

Earl rises and takes a look around. The room is large for a hospital—empty linoleum stretches out from the bed in three directions. Two doors and a window. The view isn't very helpful, either—a close of trees in the center of a carefully manicured piece of turf that terminates in a sliver of two-lane blacktop. The trees, except for the evergreens, are bare—early spring or late fall, one or the other.

Every inch of the desk is covered with Post-it notes, legal pads, neatly printed lists, psychological textbooks, framed pictures. On top of the mess is a half-completed crossword puzzle. The alarm clock is riding a pile of folded newspapers. Earl slaps the snooze button and takes a cigarette from the pack taped to the sleeve of his dressing gown. He pats the empty pockets of his pajamas for a light. He rifles the papers on the desk, looks quickly through the drawers. Eventually he finds a box of kitchen matches taped to the wall next to the window. Another sign is taped just above the box. It says in loud yellow letters, CIGARETTE? CHECK FOR LIT ONES FIRST, STUPID.

Earl laughs at the sign, lights his cigarette, and takes a long draw. Taped to the window in front of him is another piece of looseleaf paper headed YOUR SCHEDULE.

It charts off the hours, every hour, in blocks: 10:00 p.m. to 8:00 a.m. is labeled GO BACK TO SLEEP. Earl consults the alarm clock: 8:15. Given the light outside, it must be morning. He checks his watch: 10:30. He presses the watch to his ear and listens. He gives the watch a wind or two and sets it to match the alarm clock.

According to the schedule, the entire block from 8:00 to 8:30 has been labeled BRUSH YOUR TEETH. Earl laughs again and walks over to the bathroom.

The bathroom window is open. As he flaps his arms to keep warm, he notices the ashtray on the windowsill. A cigarette is perched on the ashtray, burning steadily through a long finger of ash. He frowns, extinguishes the old butt, and replaces it with the new one.

The toothbrush has already been treated to a smudge of white paste. The tap is of the push-button variety—a dose of water with each nudge. Earl pushes the brush into his cheek and fiddles it back and forth while he opens the medicine cabinet. The shelves are stocked with single-serving packages of vitamins, aspirin, antidiuretics. The mouthwash is also single-serving, about a shot-glass-worth of blue liquid in a sealed plastic bottle. Only the toothpaste is regular-sized. Earl spits the paste out of his mouth and replaces it with the mouthwash. As he lays the toothbrush next to the toothpaste, he notices a tiny wedge of paper pinched between the glass shelf and the steel backing of the medicine cabinet. He spits the frothy blue fluid into the sink and nudges for some more water to rinse it down. He closes the medicine cabinet and smiles at his reflection in the mirror.

"Who needs half an hour to brush their teeth?"

The paper has been folded down to a minuscule size with all the precision of a sixth-grader's love note. Earl unfolds it and smooths it against the mirror. It reads—

IF YOU CAN STILL READ THIS, THEN YOU'RE A FUCKING COWARD.

Earl stares blankly at the paper, then reads it again. He turns it over. On the back it reads—

P.S.: AFTER YOU'VE READ THIS, HIDE IT AGAIN.

Earl reads both sides again, then folds the note back down to its original size and tucks it underneath the toothpaste.

Maybe then he notices the scar. It begins just beneath the ear, jagged and thick, and disappears abruptly into his hairline. Earl turns his head and stares out of the corner of his eye to follow the scar's progress. He traces it with a fingertip, then looks back down at the cigarette burning in the ashtray. A thought seizes him and he spins out of the bathroom.

He is caught at the door to his room, one hand on the knob. Two pictures are taped to the wall by the door. Earl's attention is caught first by the MRI, a shiny black frame for four windows into someone's skull. In marker, the picture is labeled YOUR BRAIN. Earl stares at it. Concentric circles in different colors. He can make out the big orbs of his eyes and, behind these, the twin lobes of his brain. Smooth wrinkles, circles, semicircles. But right there in the middle of his head, circled in marker, tunneled in from the back of his neck like a maggot into an apricot, is something different. Deformed, broken, but unmistakable. A dark smudge, the shape of a flower, right there in the middle of his brain.

He bends to look at the other picture. It is a photograph of a man holding flowers, standing over a fresh grave. The man is bent over, reading the headstone. For a moment this looks like a hall of mirrors or the beginnings of a sketch of infinity: the one man bent over, looking at the smaller man, bent over, reading the headstone. Earl looks at the picture for a long time. Maybe he begins to cry. Maybe he just stares silently at the picture. Eventually, he makes his way back to the bed, flops down, seals his eyes shut, tries to sleep.

The cigarette burns steadily away in the bathroom. A circuit in the alarm clock counts down from ten, and it starts ringing again.

Earl opens one eye after another to a stretch of white ceiling tiles, interrupted by a hand-printed sign taped right above his head, large enough for him to read from the bed.

You can't have a normal life anymore. You must know that. How can you have a girlfriend if you can't remember her name? Can't have kids, not unless you want them to grow up with a dad who doesn't recognize them. Sure as hell can't hold down a job. Not too many professions out there that value forgetfulness. Prostitution, maybe. Politics, of course.

No. Your life is over. You're a dead man. The only thing the doctors are hoping to do is teach you to be less of a burden to the orderlies. And they'll probably never let you go home, wherever that would be.

So the question is not "to be or not to be," because you aren't. The question is whether you want to do something about it. Whether revenge matters to you.

It does to most people. For a few weeks, they plot, they scheme, they take measures to get even. But the passage of time is all it takes to erode that initial impulse. Time is theft, isn't that what they say? And time eventually convinces most of us that forgiveness is a virtue. Conveniently, cowardice and forgiveness look identical at a certain distance. Time steals your nerve.

If time and fear aren't enough to dissuade people from their revenge, then there's always authority, softly shaking its head and saying, We understand, but you're the better man for letting it go. For rising above it. For not sinking to their level. And besides, says authority, if you try anything stupid, we'll lock you up in a little room.

But they already put you in a little room, didn't they? Only they don't really lock it or even guard it too carefully because you're a cripple. A corpse. A vegetable who probably wouldn't remember to eat or take a shit if someone wasn't there to remind you.

And as for the passage of time, well, that doesn't really apply to you anymore, does it? Just the same ten minutes, over and over again. So how can you forgive if you can't remember to forget?

You probably were the type to let it go, weren't you? Before. But you're not the man you used to be. Not even half. You're a fraction; you're the ten-minute man.

Of course, weakness is strong. It's the primary impulse. You'd probably prefer to sit in your little room and cry. Live in your finite collection of memories, carefully polishing each one. Half a life set behind glass and pinned to cardboard like a collection of exotic insects. You'd like to live behind that glass, wouldn't you? Preserved in aspic.

You'd like to but you can't, can you? You can't because of the last addition to your collection. The last thing you remember. His face. His face and your wife, looking to you for help.

And maybe this is where you can retire to when it's over. Your little collection. They can lock you back up in another little room and you can live the rest of your life in the past. But only if you've got a little piece of paper in your hand that says you got him.

You know I'm right. You know there's a lot of work to do. It may seem impossible, but I'm sure if we all do our part, we'll figure something out. But you don't have much time. You've only got about ten minutes, in fact. Then it starts all over again. So do something with the time you've got.

EARL OPENS HIS EYES and blinks into the darkness. The alarm clock is ringing. It says 3:20, and the moonlight streaming through the window means it must be the early morning. Earl fumbles for the lamp, almost knocking it over in the process. Incandescent light fills the room, painting the metal furniture yellow, the walls yellow, the bedspread, too. He lies back and looks up at the stretch of yellow ceiling tiles above him, interrupted by a handwritten sign taped to the ceiling. He reads the sign two, maybe three times, then blinks at the room around him.

It is a bare room. Institutional, maybe. There is a desk over by the window. The desk is bare except for the blaring alarm clock. Earl probably notices, at this point, that he is fully clothed. He even has his shoes on under the sheets. He extracts himself from the bed and crosses to the desk. Nothing in the room would suggest that anyone lived there, or ever had, except for the odd scrap of tape stuck here and there to the wall. No pictures, no books, nothing. Through the window, he can see a full moon shining on carefully manicured grass.

Earl slaps the snooze button on the alarm clock and stares a moment at the two keys taped to the back of his hand. He picks at the tape while he searches through the empty drawers. In the left pocket of his jacket, he finds a roll of hundred-dollar bills and a letter sealed in an envelope. He checks the rest of the main room and the bathroom. Bits of tape, cigarette butts. Nothing else.

Earl absentmindedly plays with the lump of scar tissue on his neck and moves back toward the bed. He lies back down and stares up at the ceiling and the sign taped to it. The sign reads, GET UP, GET OUT RIGHT NOW. THESE PEOPLE ARE TRYING TO KILL YOU.

Earl closes his eyes.

They tried to teach you to make lists in grade school, remember? Back when your day planner was the back of your hand. And if your assignments came off in the shower, well, then they didn't get done. No direction, they said. No discipline. So they tried to get you to write it all down somewhere more permanent.

Of course, your grade-school teachers would be laughing their pants wet if they could see you now. Because you've become the exact product of their organizational lessons. Because you can't even take a piss without consulting one of your lists.

They were right. Lists are the only way out of this mess.

Here's the truth: People, even regular people, are never just any one person with one set of attributes. It's not that simple. We're all at the mercy of the limbic system, clouds of electricity drifting through the brain. Every man is broken into twenty-four-hour fractions, and then again within those twenty-four hours. It's a daily pantomime, one man yielding control to the next: a backstage crowded with old hacks clamoring for their turn in the spotlight. Every week, every day. The angry man hands the baton over to the sulking man, and in turn to the sex addict, the introvert, the conversationalist. Every man is a mob, a chain gang of idiots.

This is the tragedy of life. Because for a few minutes of every day, every man becomes a genius. Moments of clarity, insight, whatever you want to call them. The clouds part, the planets get in a neat little line, and everything becomes obvious. I should quit smoking, maybe, or here's how I could make a fast million, or such and such is the key to eternal happiness. That's the miserable truth. For a few moments, the secrets of the universe are opened to us. Life is a cheap parlor trick.

But then the genius, the savant, has to hand over the controls to the next guy down the pike, most likely the guy who just wants to eat potato chips, and insight and brilliance and salvation are all entrusted to a moron or a hedonist or a narcoleptic.

The only way out of this mess, of course, is to take steps to ensure that you control the idiots that you become. To take your chain gang, hand in hand, and lead them. The best way to do this is with a list.

It's like a letter you write to yourself. A master plan, drafted by the guy who can see the light, made with steps simple enough for the rest of the idiots to understand. Follow steps one through one hundred. Repeat as necessary.

Your problem is a little more acute, maybe, but fundamentally the same thing.

It's like that computer thing, the Chinese room. You remember that? One guy sits in a little room, laying down cards with letters written on them in a language he doesn't understand, laying them down one letter at a time in a sequence according to someone else's instructions. The cards are supposed to spell out a joke in Chinese. The guy doesn't speak Chinese, of course. He just follows his instructions.

There are some obvious differences in your situation, of course: You broke out of the room they had you in, so the whole enterprise has to be portable. And the guy giving the instructions—that's you, too, just an earlier version of you. And the joke you're telling, well, it's got a punch line. I just don't think anyone's going to find it very funny.

So that's the idea. All you have to do is follow your instructions. Like climbing a ladder or descending a staircase. One step at a time. Right down the list. Simple.

And the secret, of course, to any list is to keep it in a place where you're bound to see it.

HE CAN HEAR THE BUZZING through his eyelids. Insistent. He reaches out for the alarm clock, but he can't move his arm.

Earl opens his eyes to see a large man bent double over him. The man looks up at him, annoyed, then resumes his work. Earl looks around him. Too dark for a doctor's office.

Then the pain floods his brain, blocking out the other questions. He squirms again, trying to yank his forearm away, the one that feels like it's burning. The arm doesn't move, but the man shoots him another scowl. Earl adjusts himself in the chair to see over the top of the man's head.

The noise and the pain are both coming from a gun in the man's hand—a gun with a needle where the barrel should be. The needle is digging into the fleshy underside of Earl's forearm, leaving a trail of puffy letters behind it.

Earl tries to rearrange himself to get a better view, to read the letters on his arm, but he can't. He lies back and stares at the ceiling.

Eventually the tattoo artist turns off the noise, wipes Earl's forearm with a piece of gauze, and wanders over to the back to dig up a pamphlet describing how to deal with a possible infection. Maybe later he'll tell his wife about this guy and his little note. Maybe his wife will convince him to call the police.

Earl looks down at the arm. The letters are rising up from the skin, weeping a little. They run from just behind the strap of Earl's watch all the way to the inside of his elbow. Earl blinks at the message and reads it again. It says, in careful little capitals, I RAPED AND KILLED YOUR WIFE.

It's your birthday today, so I got you a little present. I would have just bought you a beer, but who knows where that would have ended?

So instead, I got you a bell. I think I may have had to pawn your watch to buy it, but what the hell did you need a watch for, anyway?

You're probably asking yourself, Why a bell? In fact, I'm guessing you're going to be asking yourself that question every time you find it in your pocket. Too many of these letters now. Too many for you to dig back into every time you want to know the answer to some little question.

It's a joke, actually. A practical joke. But think of it this way: I'm not really laughing at you so much as with you.

I'd like to think that every time you take it out of your pocket and wonder, Why do I have this bell? a little part of you, a little piece of your broken brain, will remember and laugh, like I'm laughing now.

Besides, you do know the answer. It was something you learned before. So if you think about it, you'll know.

Back in the old days, people were obsessed with the fear of being buried alive. You remember now? Medical science not being quite what it is today, it wasn't uncommon for people to suddenly wake up in a casket. So rich folks had their coffins outfitted with breathing tubes. Little tubes running up to the mud above so that if someone woke up when they weren't supposed to, they wouldn't run out of oxygen. Now, they must have tested this out and realized that you could shout yourself hoarse through the tube, but it was too narrow to carry much noise. Not enough to attract attention, at least. So a string was run up the tube to a little bell attached to the headstone. If a dead person came back to life, all he had to do was ring his little bell till someone came and dug him up again.

I'm laughing now, picturing you on a bus or maybe in a fast-food restaurant, reaching into your pocket and finding your little bell and wondering to yourself where it came from, why you have it. Maybe you'll even ring it.

Happy birthday, buddy.

I don't know who figured out the solution to our mutual problem, so I don't know whether to congratulate you or me. A bit of a lifestyle change, admittedly, but an elegant solution, nonetheless.

Look to yourself for the answer.

That sounds like something out of a Hallmark card. I don't know when you thought it up, but my hat's off to you. Not that you know what the hell I'm talking about. But, honestly, a real brainstorm. After all, everybody else needs mirrors to remind themselves who they are. You're no different.

THE LITTLE MECHANICAL VOICE PAUSES, then repeats itself. It says, "The time is 8:00 a.m. This is a courtesy call." Earl opens his eyes and replaces the receiver. The phone is perched on a cheap veneer headboard that stretches behind the bed, curves to meet the corner, and ends at the minibar. The TV is still on, blobs of flesh color nattering away at each other. Earl lies back down and is surprised to see himself, older now, tanned, the hair pulling away from his head like solar flares. The mirror on the ceiling is cracked, the silver fading in creases. Earl continues to stare at himself, astonished by what he sees. He is fully dressed, but the clothes are old, threadbare in places.

Earl feels the familiar spot on his left wrist for his watch, but it's gone. He looks down from the mirror to his arm. It is bare and the skin has changed to an even tan, as if he never owned a watch in the first place. The skin is even in color except for the solid black arrow on the inside of Earl's wrist, pointing up his shirtsleeve. He stares at the arrow for a moment. Perhaps he doesn't try to rub it off anymore. He rolls up his sleeve.

The arrow points to a sentence tattooed along Earl's inner arm. Earl reads the sentence once, maybe twice. Another arrow picks up at the beginning of the sentence, points farther up Earl's arm, disappearing under the rolled-up shirtsleeve. He unbuttons his shirt.

Looking down on his chest, he can make out the shapes but cannot bring them into focus, so he looks up at the mirror above him.

The arrow leads up Earl's arm, crosses at the shoulder, and descends onto his upper torso, terminating at a picture of a man's face that occupies most of his chest. The face is that of a large man, balding, with a mustache and a goatee. It is a particular face, but like a police sketch it has a certain unreal quality.

The rest of his upper torso is covered in words, phrases, bits of information, and instructions, all of them written backward on Earl, forward in the mirror.

Eventually Earl sits up, buttons his shirt, and crosses to the desk. He takes out a pen and a piece of notepaper from the desk drawer, sits, and begins to write.

I don't know where you'll be when you read this. I'm not even sure if you'll bother to read this. I guess you don't need to.

It's a shame, really, that you and I will never meet. But, like the song says, "By the time you read this note, I'll be gone."

We're so close now. That's the way it feels. So many pieces put together, spelled out. I guess it's just a matter of time until you find him.

Who knows what we've done to get here? Must be a hell of a story, if only you could remember any of it. I guess it's better that you can't.

I had a thought just now. Maybe you'll find it useful.

Everybody is waiting for the end to come, but what if it already passed us by? What if the final joke of Judgment Day was that it had already come and gone and we were none the wiser? Apocalypse arrives quietly; the chosen are herded off to heaven, and the rest of us, the ones who failed the test, just keep on going, oblivious. Dead already, wandering around long after the gods have stopped keeping score, still optimistic about the future.

I guess if that's true, then it doesn't matter what you do. No expectations. If you can't find him, then it doesn't matter, because nothing matters. And if you do find him, then you can kill him without worrying about the consequences. Because there are no consequences.

That's what I'm thinking about right now, in this scrappy little room. Framed pictures of ships on the wall. I don't know, obviously, but if I had to guess, I'd say we're somewhere up the coast. If you're wondering why your left arm is five shades browner than your right, I don't know what to tell you. I guess we must have been driving for a while. And, no, I don't know what happened to your watch.

And all these keys: I have no idea. Not a one that I recognize. Car keys and house keys and the little fiddly keys for padlocks. What have we been up to?

I wonder if he'll feel stupid when you find him. Tracked down by the ten-minute man. Assassinated by a vegetable.

I'll be gone in a moment. I'll put down the pen, close my eyes, and then you can read this through if you want.

I just wanted you to know that I'm proud of you. No one who matters is left to say it. No one left is going to want to.

EARL'S EYES ARE WIDE OPEN, staring through the window of the car. Smiling eyes. Smiling through the window at the crowd gathering across the street. The crowd gathering around the body in the doorway. The body emptying slowly across the sidewalk and into the storm drain.

A stocky guy, facedown, eyes open. Balding head, goatee. In death, as in police sketches, faces tend to look the same. This is definitely somebody in particular. But really, it could be anybody.

Earl is still smiling at the body as the car pulls away from the curb. The car? Who's to say? Maybe it's a police cruiser. Maybe it's just a taxi.

As the car is swallowed into traffic, Earl's eyes continue to shine out into the night, watching the body until it disappears into a circle of concerned pedestrians. He chuckles to himself as the car continues to make distance between him and the growing crowd.

Earl's smile fades a little. Something has occurred to him. He begins to pat down his pockets; leisurely at first, like a man looking for his keys, then a little more desperately. Maybe his progress is impeded by a set of handcuffs. He begins to empty the contents of his pockets out onto the seat next to him. Some money. A bunch of keys. Scraps of paper.

A round metal lump rolls out of his pocket and slides across the vinyl seat. Earl is frantic now. He hammers at the plastic divider between him and the driver, begging the man for a pen. Perhaps the cabbie doesn't speak much English. Perhaps the cop isn't in the habit of talking to suspects. Either way, the divider between the man in front and the man behind remains closed. A pen is not forthcoming.

The car hits a pothole, and Earl blinks at his reflection in the rearview mirror. He is calm now. The driver makes another corner, and the metal lump slides back over to rest against Earl's leg with a little jingle. He picks it up and looks at it, curious now. It is a little bell. A little metal bell. Inscribed on it are his name and a set of dates. He recognizes the first one: the year in which he was born. But the second date means nothing to him. Nothing at all.

As he turns the bell over in his hands, he notices the empty space on his wrist where his watch used to sit. There is a little arrow there, pointing up his arm. Earl looks at the arrow, then begins to roll up his sleeve.

"You'd be late for your own funeral," she'd say. Remember? The more I think about it, the more trite that seems. What kind of idiot, after all, is in any kind of rush to get to the end of his own story?

And how would I know if I were late, anyway? I don't have a watch anymore. I don't know what we did with it.

What the hell do you need a watch for, anyway? It was an antique. Deadweight tugging at your wrist. Symbol of the old you. The you that believed in time.

No. Scratch that. It's not so much that you've lost your faith in time as that time has lost its faith in you. And who needs it, anyway? Who wants to be one of those saps living in the safety of the future, in the safety of the moment after the moment in which they felt something powerful? Living in the next moment, in which they feel nothing. Crawling down the hands of the clock, away from the people who did unspeakable things to them. Believing the lie that time will heal all wounds—which is just a nice way of saying that time deadens us.

But you're different. You're more perfect. Time is three things for most people, but for you, for us, just one. A singularity. One moment. This moment. Like you're the center of the clock, the axis on which the hands turn. Time moves about you but never moves you. It has lost its ability to affect you. What is it they say? That time is theft? But not for you. Close your eyes and you can start all over again. Conjure up that necessary emotion, fresh as roses.

Time is an absurdity. An abstraction. The only thing that matters is this moment. This moment a million times over. You have to trust me. If this moment is repeated enough, if you keep trying—and you have to keep trying—eventually you will come across the next item on your list.

Jonathan Nolan's "Memento Mori" is the story of Earl's unusual state of affairs. Since a certain point in his life, when something happened to his brain, he has been unable to remember anything beyond a few minutes. However, he can remember what happened before his brain injury, such as the death of his wife. In short, he cannot make new memories since his injury. Thus, he resorts to reading notes and looking at taped-up pictures around the hospital room in which he lives to remind himself of who, what, when, where, and why he is. Earl spends most of the story in his room following a daily routine. However, toward the end of the story, Earl suddenly and inexplicably leaves the hospital, wakes up in another room, gets tattooed, is present at the scene of a murder, and is taken away in a car.

The story is told from two points of view. One point of view, printed in italics, is a chain of monologues in which a voice explains to Earl the physical and psychological conditions of his new way of life. The other point of view, printed in roman type, is an alternating chain of third-person descriptions of Earl's waking hours both in and out of the hospital. However, during the course of the short story, the voice in the italicized monologue occasionally shifts pronouns from the second person to the first-person plural. Thus, the voice briefly connects him/herself with Earl to suggest they are the same person. Possibly this voice is within Earl's mind all along. For example, as Earl leaves the murder scene in the back of a car, the voice in the italicized monologue suddenly shifts pronouns twice from "you" to either "we" or "us." In the back of the car, Earl discovers he has lost his watch. The italicized voice assures him that the watch does not matter to either of them because Earl's memory disability has collapsed the three conventional partitions of time—past, present, and future—and replaced them with "singularity. One moment. This moment" (193). According to the italicized voice, this significant, emotionally full moment incessantly begins again and again and appears to insulate the two of them from an emotionally empty future.

MEMENTO (2001), Directed by Christopher Nolan

Unlike *The Killers* and *The Swimmer*, *Memento* drops most of the narrative elements of the short story, keeps the plot premise, uses it as a point of departure, and adds a new story. In an interview with *New York Screenwriter Magazine*

Online, Christopher Nolan explains how he learned of his brother's developing short story:

> At the time he had not finished it and he actually told it to me verbally as we were driving from Chicago to Los Angeles. He had this image of this guy with this condition—as a central concept—looking for revenge and using his body to record information. For me that was the jumping off point and I said immediately, "Can I go and write a screenplay from this while you finish your story." In fact, I think I finished the film before he finished the short story. . . . I just took the concept and wrote my own screenplay from it. . . . I was very free and the story is very different from the film.

The film keeps the premise of Earl as a man whose wife has died, who has been unable to remember anything beyond a few minutes, who resorts to writing notes and taking pictures, who listens to someone who advises him, who yearns for revenge, yet whose actions seem without consequence. The film drops all the rest of the elements of narrative. It renames Earl as Leonard Shelby and gives him an identity as a former insurance investigator. It adds the revenge plot of Leonard's search for the man named John G. who murdered his wife; sordid characters, chief among them Teddy, a rogue policeman, and Natalie, the bartender girlfriend of a drug dealer, who assist Leonard in his search; sleazy settings, such as the abandoned building where Leonard kills not one but two men named John G., and the low-rent motel room where he stays; new symbols, such as some of his wife's remaining things, including a hair comb filled with strands of her hair and a well-thumbed paperback book, which she read several times; Leonard's self-tattooing with a needle and ball-point pen ink; and a unique way to tell the story: backwards.

The first sequence of the film begins by literally running backwards from frame to frame. For example, it starts with a series of close-ups of a Polaroid photograph that fades to blankness in a fanning hand. The photo is then placed

Leonard Shelby (Guy Pearce) showing one of the pictures he has taken to help himself identify his policeman "friend" in *Memento* (2001).

by that hand at the front of a Polaroid camera and is pulled back up into the camera. The series of close-ups and now extreme close-ups continue as a photograph is taken by a young blond-haired man; blood runs seemingly uphill in slow motion (although it actually runs along a floor; the camera is turned 90 degrees to make the horizontal look vertical and thus disorient the viewer even more); still lifes appear of a bullet casing, a pair of glasses, the back of a man's head lying on a bloody floor; a gun flies up into the young man's hand; the bullet casing rolls along the floor, then flies up into the air and into the gun; the man squats down and fires a bullet out of the other man, and the other man screams. After the first sequence, the rest of the color sequences run forward frame by frame in conventional order, but are arranged in reverse chronological order. In an interview with Chris Roberts, Christopher Nolan explains the purpose for the reverse-chronological order:

> If we apply [the protagonist's condition] to ourselves, we see how our systems are for placing ourselves in the world, in time and space. How do we know people can be trusted? I wanted to put the audience in his head, make them think that way, question things the way he does, so they come out of it with their head spinning, mulling it over, arguing about it with a friend. We thought a lot about how to keep an emotional thread running through it. We realized it was something which could become very cerebral and cold, or simply puzzling. So it was a challenge to the audience, to give them a narrative that works backwards but has a lot of forward logic to it.

The reverse-chronological scenes narrate the story of Leonard's search. The scenes take place in various interior and exterior settings. They are filmed in color and show Leonard dressed in a gray-green suit, wearing a shoulder holster, and driving a Jaguar. Alternating with these scenes is a second set of scenes that run in chronological order. These scenes are essentially a monologue of Leonard's explanations of his situation to someone on the telephone, the rogue policeman Teddy, as Leonard prepares to self-tattoo his thigh. The scenes take place either in Leonard's motel room or in flashbacks to various places he still remembers such as working on an insurance case of a man with a similar memory problem or staying at home with his wife. They are filmed in black and white; feature extreme close-ups, close-ups, and medium close-ups; and show Leonard in his underwear.

The black-and-white sequences counterpoint the color sequences. The former dramatize Leonard's claustrophobic self-absorption, his self-congratulatory rationalizations that explain the nature of his memory impairment, and his idiosyncratic, systematic method for controlling that impairment. The color sequences dramatize how Leonard functions in the world at large as he goes about his search assisted by the manipulative Natalie and Teddy. The alternating color and the black-and-white sequences can be seen as a parallel to the alternating voices in Jonathan Nolan's short story, but they are not adapted from those voices. Whether or not Leonard gets his man—or, more to the point, remembers getting his man—it is Leonard's "condition," as he prefers to call it, and the Nolan brothers' evoking of that condition for their respective audiences that are at the center of not only the film but also the short story; the brothers imagine his condition differently for the viewer and the reader.

Memento illustrates the point-of-departure strategy for adapting a short story. In this strategy, the adapter drops most of the narrative elements from the short story; keeps perhaps the plot premise, a character's name, or just the title; and, using these rudiments as a point of departure, adds a whole new story. The point-of-departure strategy is always a loose adaptation of a literary work.

Combining Strategies

At the end of the chapter, you will find pairings of short stories and their adaptations. We suggest you study some of these to discover what kind of strategy the filmmakers use to address the brevity of the short story. Keep in mind that some adaptations will combine several strategies

For example, *Rashômon* (1950), directed by Akira Kurosawa, combines the concentration and the interweaving strategies. In the concentration strategy, filmmakers choose to concentrate narrative elements at the beginning, middle, or end of the film. In the interweaving strategy, the filmmakers choose to disperse added narrative elements throughout the film. *Rashômon* uses both methods, but what distinguishes this combination is that the filmmakers choose to link the kept narrative elements of one story by using narrative elements from a second short story written by the same author. The film draws on both Ryunosuke Akutagawa's "Rashômon" and "In a Grove."

The film uses Akutagawa's "Rashômon" as a *framework story* for Akutagawa's "In a Grove." It concentrates some of the "Rashômon" material at the beginning and the rest at the end of the film. The filmmakers disperse the narrative spine of "In a Grove" over the middle of the film, sometimes interrupting it with references to "Rashômon."

Kurosawa links two short stories in a film, but sometimes filmmakers expand a short story by drawing on several of an author's works. For example, Chris Eyre, in *Smoke Signals* (1998), keeps most of the narrative elements from Sherman Alexie's short story "This Is What It Means to Say Phoenix, Arizona," disperses those elements throughout the film, and interweaves brief, minor elements of narrative from several other short stories from Alexie's collection *The Lone Ranger and Tonto Fistfight in Heaven.* Likewise, Alison Maclean, in *Jesus' Son* (1999), keeps many of the elements of narrative from several of Denis Johnson's short stories from his collection of the same name and links them in an order similar to the way they appear in the collection, giving her film an *episodic structure,* in which the same character goes through a succession of incidents that follow one another without a particular logical organization, much like a short story collection only on film. *Short Cuts* (1993), directed by Robert Altman, adapts several of Raymond Carver's short stories from different collections. The stories are linked in that they have similar plots, characters, settings, and themes. Another variation on the expansion of the short story material by drawing on several works is used by the author/director Rebecca Miller, who adapts three of her own short stories about women fleeing from men into a three-segment film entitled *Personal Velocity* (2002).

A final example of a film that combines the strategies mentioned above is *Blow-Up* (1966), directed by Michelangelo Antonioni and adapted from Julio Cortazar's short story "Las Babas del Diablo" (1964). "Las Babas del Diablo" tells the story of a photograph from its taking through its successive enlargements to its sudden revelation of an event that now horrifies the photographer. The event is a possible homosexual pickup of a boy that was interrupted when the photographer took the picture. *Blow-Up* concentrates a similar story in the last half of the film.

Blow-Up also interweaves new elements of narrative into Cortazar's story. "Las Babas del Diablo" describes the photographer's struggle (1) to make sense of the homosexual pickup, (2) to make sense of the bizarre situation in which the enlarged photograph unexpectedly and impossibly comes to life in clear images of moving figures, (3) to make sense of the revelation that the pickup now appears to succeed despite the photographer's efforts to prevent it, and (4) to make sense of the literary form his report of these fantastic incidents should take. In the film, the photographed event is not a pickup but a murder that is briefly interrupted when the photographer takes pictures of a couple embracing in a park near a line of trees in which the murderer is camouflaged. *Blow-Up* interweaves the photographer's struggle to make sense of his situation with a documentary-like look at a day in the life of a successful commercial photographer who has artistic ambitions, business distractions, personal aggravations, and professional frustrations. These additional elements of narrative provide an ordinary context for the photographer's struggle to make sense of the extraordinary circumstances in which he suddenly finds himself.

The film makes so many substitutions of plot, character, setting, and theme that it gives the impression that the filmmakers have dropped most of Cortazar's narrative elements and, like Nolan in *Memento,* added a whole new story. For example, the enlarged still photograph in *Blow-Up* does not spontaneously come to life in clear images of moving figures because to do so might seem absurd in a moving picture. Instead, intrigued by the woman's demand that he turn over the undeveloped roll of film to her, the photographer decides to develop the roll and look closely at each photograph. Something in one of the photographs catches his eye, and through analyzing the successive blowups of the original photograph, the photographer discovers the grainy pattern of a man hiding in the bushes and holding a gun aimed at the couple. The photographer infers that a murder that he did not see or hear was about to take place while he was taking his pictures. Later, he returns to the site, discovers the body of a dead man lying next to the line of trees, and confirms his inference. This substitution is a substantial change in plot required by the move from short story to film, yet it is not a substantial change in theme. As Henry Fernandez points out:

> it seems, if only at first sight, that even the central theme of the film has little to do with the story, that Antonioni has merely taken a basic situation . . . from Cortazar and has created an entirely unrelated film. In my interpretation, the nature of the two media [short story and photograph] and their relation form the theme of Cortazar's story. This is, I believe, also the theme of Antonioni's film. The key word is media, for film and story are different media, and any artist who uses his art as his theme knows enough about his medium to know he cannot copy a different art. The tension between photography and written narrative in Cortazar becomes the tension between photography and cinematography in Antonioni. (165–66)

Fernandez would probably argue that this is not a point-of-departure adaptation because, despite so many narrative changes, the theme is retained. *Blow-Up* is an interesting example of a film that appears to overlap the concentration, interweaving, and point-of-departure strategies. When studying short story adaptations, keep in mind that filmmakers can use several different strategies to address the mismatch between the short story's brevity and the feature film's length.

Summary

The short story is a brief fiction written in prose that includes the same narrative elements found in the novel and the novella. Typically, the short story has fewer scenes and fewer characters than either the novel or the novella. Filmmakers intent on adapting a short story to a feature film face a unique challenge. They must add narrative elements or expand already existing ones to develop and lengthen the story to fit the average running time of the feature film. The filmmaker can expand the story using one or more of the following three strategies:

1. The concentration strategy, in which the filmmakers keep most of the narrative elements from the short story but concentrate them at the beginning, middle, or end of the film and then add a new story.

2. The interweaving strategy, in which the filmmakers keep most of the elements of narrative from the short story, disperse them throughout the film (although not necessarily in their original order), and interweave either new elements or expansions of existing ones.

3. The point-of-departure strategy, in which the filmmakers drop most of the narrative elements from the short story; keep perhaps the plot premise, a character's name, or just the title; and use these elements as a point of departure.

▪▪▪ TOPICS FOR DISCUSSION

1. Choose a short story pairing from the filmography and identify whether the adaptation uses the concentration, interweaving, point-of-departure strategy, or some combination of the three.

2. Choose a short story that has been adapted into a film and define and illustrate the relationship between the two companion pieces. Give some background on the literary text and summarize the plot, characters, point of view, and themes of the story. Introduce the film and then discuss in a systematic way what is kept, dropped, and especially what is added. Identify the important changes made by the adapter and explain the likely reasons behind the changes. Analyze the changes as a way to define a relationship between the text and its adaptation.

3. Reread the section in the chapter on combining strategies. Choose one of the adaptations mentioned and analyze how the narrative elements of two or more short stories by one author are joined to make a feature film.

4. For some readers and viewers, the consequence of adding narrative elements to a short story enriches that story; for others, the consequence of the additions is the superfluous padding of an already completed short story. From the filmography, choose a short story that has been adapted into a film and explain whether you think the additions enrich the story or merely fill it out to feature length.

▪▪▪ WORKS CITED

CHEEVER, JOHN. "The Swimmer." *The Brigadier and the Golf Widow.* New York: Harper & Row, 1964. 61–76.

"Christopher Nolan, Screenwriter/Director." *New York Screenwriter Magazine Online* (2001). 6 March 2002 www.nyscreenwriter.com/article75.htm.

CLARENS, CARLOS. *Crime Movies: An Illustrated History.* New York: W. W. Norton, 1980.

EMMENS, CAROL A. *Short Stories on Film and Video.* 2nd ed. Littleton, Colo.: Libraries Unlimited, 1985.

FERNANDEZ, HENRY. "From Cortazar to Antonioni: Study of an Adaptation." *Focus on Blow-Up.* Ed. Roy Huss. Englewood Cliffs, N.J.: Prentice-Hall, 1971.

HEMINGWAY, ERNEST. "The Killers." *Men Without Women.* New York: Charles Scribner's Sons, 1927. 56–67.

Killers, The. Dir. Richard Siodmak. Perf. Burt Lancaster and Ava Gardner. Universal, 1946.

KITTREDGE, WILLIAM, AND STEVEN M. KRAUZER, ED. *Stories into Film.* New York: Harper & Row, 1979.

KOZIKOWSKI, STANLEY J. "Damned in a Fair Life: Cheever's 'The Swimmer.' " *Studies in Short Fiction* 30 (1993): 367–9.

LAURENCE, FRANK. *Hemingway and the Movies.* Jackson, Miss.: The University of Mississippi, 1981.

NOLAN, JONATHAN. "Memento Mori." *Esquire* March 2001: 186+.

O'HARA, JAMES E. *John Cheever: A Study of the Short Fiction.* Boston: G. K. Hall & Co., 1989.

ROBERTS, CHRIS "Interview with Christopher Nolan." *Virgin.net* 17 Oct. 2000: 1+. 6 March 2002 www.virgin.net/movies/features/feature_6832.html.

Swimmer, The. Dir. Frank Perry. Perf. Burt Lancaster. Columbia, 1968.

WHEELER, DAVID, ED. *No, But I Saw the Movie: The Best Short Stories Ever Made into Film.* New York: Penguin Books, 1989.

SELECTED FILMOGRAPHY OF SHORT STORY ADAPTATIONS

SAMUEL HOPKINS ADAMS. "Night Bus" (1933).
FRANK CAPRA. *It Happened One Night* (1934).

RYUNOSUKE AKUTAGAWA. "Rashômon" and "In a Grove" (1927).
AKIRA KUROSAWA. *Rashômon* (1950).

SHERMAN ALEXIE. "This Is What It Is to Say Phoenix, Arizona" and other short stories from *The Lone Ranger and Tonto Fistfight in Heaven* (1993).
CHRIS EYRE. *Smoke Signals* (1998).

JAMES WARNER BELLAH. "Massacre" (1947).
JOHN FORD. *Fort Apache* (1948).

ROBERT BLOCH. "The Real Bad Friend" (1957).
ALFRED HITCHCOCK. *Psycho* (1960).

RAY BRADBURY. "The Beast from 20,000 Fathoms"(1951).
EUGÈNE LOURIÉ. *The Beast from 20,000 Fathoms* (1953).

HOWARD BRESLIN. "Bad Times at Honda" (1946).
JOHN STURGES. *Bad Day at Black Rock* (1955).

FREDRIC BROWN. "Madman's Holiday" (1943).
IRVING REIS. *Crack-Up* (1946).

THOMAS BURKE. "The Chink and the Child" (1915).
D. W. GRIFFITH. *Broken Blossoms* (1919).

RAYMOND CARVER. Short stories from various collections.
ROBERT ALTMAN. *Short Cuts* (1993).

G. K. CHESTERTON. "The Blue Cross" (1910).
ROBERT HAMER. *Father Brown* aka *The Detective* (UK 1954).

ARTHUR C. CLARKE. "The Sentinel" (1951).
STANLEY KUBRICK. *2001: A Space Odyssey* (1968).

JULIO CORTÁZAR. "Las Babas del Diablo" (1964).
MICHELANGELO ANTONIONI. *Blow-Up* (1966).

JOHN W. CUNNINGHAM. "The Tin Star" (1947).
FRED ZINNEMANN. *High Noon* (1952).

ISAK DINESEN. "Babette's Feast" (1950).
GABRIEL AXEL. *Babette's Feast* (Dan. 1987).

ISAK DINESEN. "The Immortal Story" (1955).
ORSON WELLES. *The Immortal Story* (Fr. 1968).

ANDRE DUBUS. "Killings" (1980).
TODD FIELD. *In the Bedroom* (2001).

DAPHNE DU MAURIER. "The Birds" (1952).
ALFRED HITCHCOCK. *The Birds* (1963).

DAPHNE DU MAURIER. "Don't Look Now" (1966).
NICOLAS ROEG. *Don't Look Now* (1973).

HARLAN ELLISON. "A Boy and His Dog" (1969).
L. Q. JONES. *A Boy and His Dog* (1975).

WILLIAM FAULKNER. "Barn Burning" and "Spotted Horses" (1939).
MARTIN RITT. *The Long, Hot Summer* (1958).

F. SCOTT FITZGERALD. "Babylon Revisited" (1931).
RICHARD BROOKS. *The Last Time I Saw Paris* (1954).

BRUCE JAY FRIEDMAN. "A Change of Plan" (1966).
ELAINE MAY. *The Heartbreak Kid* (1972).

GRAHAM GREENE. "The Basement Room" (1935).
CAROL REED. *The Fallen Idol* (UK 1948).

ERNEST HAYCOX. "Stage to Lordsburg" (1937).
JOHN FORD. *Stagecoach* (1939).

ERNEST HEMINGWAY. "After the Storm" (1938).
GUY FERLAND. *After the Storm* (2001).

ERNEST HEMINGWAY. "Hills Like White Elephants" (1927).
PAIGE CAMERON. *Hills Like White Elephants* (2002).

ERIC HODGINS. "Mr. Blandings Builds His Dream House." (1946).
H. C. POTTER. *Mr. Blandings Builds His Dream House* (1948).

DENIS JOHNSON. *Jesus' Son*, short story collection (1992).
ALISON MACLEAN. *Jesus' Son* (1999).

DOROTHY M. JOHNSON. "A Man Called Horse" (1976).
ELLIOT SILVERSTEIN. *A Man Called Horse* (1970).

DOROTHY M. JOHNSON. "The Man Who Shot Liberty Valance" (1976).
JOHN FORD. *The Man Who Shot Liberty Valance* (1962).

JAMES JOYCE. "The Dead" (1907).
JOHN HUSTON. *The Dead* (1987).

MACKINLAY KANTOR. "Gun Crazy" (1949).
JOSEPH H. LEWIS. *Gun Crazy* (1949).
TAMRA DAVIS. *Gun Crazy* (1992).

DANIEL KEYES. "Flowers for Algernon" (1954).
RALPH NELSON. *Charly* (1968).

GEORGE LANGELAAN. "The Fly" (1957).
KURT NEUMANN. *The Fly* (1958).
DAVID CRONENBERG. *The Fly* (1986).

RING LARDNER. "Champion" (1916).
MARK ROBSON. *Champion* (1949).

W. SOMERSET MAUGHAM "The Vessel
of Wrath" (1931).
ERICH POMME. *The Beachcomber*
(UK 1938).

MARY ORR. "The Wisdom of Eve"
(1946).
JOSEPH L. MANKIEWICZ. *All about Eve*
(1950).

SAMSON RAPHAELSON. "The Day of
Atonement" (1922).
ALAN CROSLAND. *The Jazz Singer* (1927).

TOD ROBBINS. "Spurs" (1917).
TOD BROWNING. *Freaks* (1932).

FRANK ROONEY. "Cyclists' Raid" (1951).
LÁSZLÓ BENEDEK. *The Wild One*
(1953).

DAMON RUNYON. "The Idyll of Miss
Sarah Brown" (1931).
JOSEPH L MANKIEWICZ. *Guys and Dolls*
(1955).

DAMON RUNYON. "The Lemon Drop
Kid" (1934).
SIDNEY LANFIELD. *The Lemon Drop Kid*
(1951).

DAMON RUNYON. "Madame La
Gimp" (1929).
FRANK CAPRA. *Lady for a Day* (1933).
FRANK CAPRA. *Pocketful of Miracles*
(1961).

PHILIP VAN DOREN STERN. "The
Greatest Gift"(1943).
FRANK CAPRA. *It's a Wonderful Life*
(1946).

ROBERT LOUIS STEVENSON. "The Body
Snatcher" (1895).
ROBERT WISE. *The Body Snatcher*
(1945).

SAMUEL W. TAYLOR. "A Situation of
Gravity" (n.d.).
ROBERT STEVENSON. *The Absent-
Minded Professor* (1961).
LES MAYFIELD. *Flubber* (1997).

CORNELL WOOLRICH. "Rear Window"
(1942, 1944).
ALFRED HITCHCOCK. *Rear Window*
(1954).

The short stories written by Robbins,
Adams, Haycox, Rooney, Woolrich,
and Clarke can be found in the anthology *Stories into Film,* edited by William
Kittredge and Steven M. Krauzer. The
short stories written by Orr, Breslin,
du Maurier, Langelaan, Cunningham, Stern, Raphaelson, Hodgins,
and Bloch can be found in the
anthology *No, But I Saw the Movie,*
edited by David Wheeler. Both
anthologies are out of print but can
be purchased on Internet sites. A directory of short stories adapted into
film and video from 1920 to 1984,
Short Stories on Film and Video, com-
piled by Carol A. Emmens, is also out
of print but can be purchased on
Internet sites.

7 THE PLAY

Imagine that a film student named Lisa attends several Broadway plays, falls in love with one, and decides to direct a feature-length adaptation. She obtains the rights, hires the cast, rents the theater, and arranges to film a performance.

Lisa's original seat was fourth row center, so she positions the 35 mm camera to simulate an up-front and near-center seat in the theater. She didn't get up to move around while she watched the performance, so she fixes the camera's position, both in distance and angle from the action. To be sure, the camera will sometimes pan right or left or tilt up or down just as Lisa moved her eyes and head while watching. Lisa saw the main actions on the stage from her seat, so she treats the frame as if it were a *proscenium* stage. The film actors enter and exit exclusively from either right or left and tend to be always facing forward. Now Lisa lets the camera roll until the final curtain.

If Lisa follows these steps, the result will be an accurate photographic record of a live performance of the play. The play was a smashing hit. Will Lisa's film be a success, too?

Unfortunately, Lisa's adaptation is likely to fail no matter how good the performance was the night she filmed. What happens when anyone tries to film a stage play as described above is that the actions appear restricted, the sets unrealistic, the dialogue talky, and the acting "over the top." Lisa recorded a play, but she didn't make a movie.

Let's explain what happened to Lisa's adaptation in another way. As mentioned in Chapter 2, some contemporary theorists claim that a narrative has two parts: a story and a discourse. The story consists of the characters, setting, and chain of events. Adapters focus first on this raw material, the content or the *what* of the narrative. But the story is realized in something larger—a discourse, or the means by which the content is communicated—the *how*. The *what* influences decisions about the *how*—how the film is cast, how it is shot, how it is edited, how it is mixed, and how it is musically scored. For the transposition to be successful, it is important that the adapter understand the means of expression of both discourses—the conventions of the antecedent literary text as well as of cinema itself. Conventions are accepted methods and practices in a specific form that are understood both by the artist and the audience. If the adapter does not take into account the conventions of each form, the result may be something like Lisa's photographed stage play. The theatrical conventions of the antecedent form will cling to the film adaptation and make it seem uncinematic.

One purpose of studying film adaptation is to become more aware of the conventions of literature and film. That awareness offers a finer appreciation of the difficulties filmmakers face in transposing stories from one discourse to another. To that end, the section below describes some conventions shared by fiction, drama, and film and some that belong uniquely to one form or the other. The generalizations about drama refer to conventions found in representational theater and do not address, except in a few cases, the nonrealistic conventions found in experimental and avant garde theater. The discussion is indebted in several ways to Laurence Perrine (see Arp and Johnson 1115–18).

Drama and Fiction

Drama and fiction share many storytelling elements. Both use plot, characters, settings, themes, and figurative language to evoke intellectual and emotional responses. The crucial difference between the two forms, as Perrine suggests, is that *drama is meant to be performed* while *fiction is intended to be read.*

The performance dimension of drama is both a source of strength and of limitation to the storyteller. One opportunity drama offers is the possibility of emotional involvement between the audience and the actors. As Linda Seger points out, people entering a theater "give themselves over to involvement in this special world. They take part in an exchange of energy that happens among the actors, and between the actors and the audience" (35). This dynamic belongs to the theater alone and intensifies the artistic experience. (It is interesting to note that in Bertolt Brecht's revolutionary "epic theater" various effects are designed to create a consciousness of distance between viewer and stage.)

Another advantage drama has over nonperformance works is that truly dazzling performances by talented actors can add meaning and emotion to words. For example, the skilled performances of Stacey Keach in *Cyrano de Bergerac*, Hume Cronyn and Jessica Tandy in *Gin Game*, and Nathan Lane and Matthew Broderick in *The Producers* increased the emotional power of these plays.

An additional feature of dramatic performance is its ability to offer viewers different types of information simultaneously. A novel may describe a character's appearance in one paragraph, how she speaks or acts in a second, and what she utters in a third (Arp 1115). But drama frees these impressions from linear sequence by delivering them to the audience simultaneously. For example, in the famous mad scene in Act 4 of Shakespeare's *Hamlet*, after Ophelia discovers her lover Hamlet has killed her father, she enters the presence of the King and Queen, and from her facial expressions, physical movements, and speech patterns, the audience knows immediately that she is deranged.

Although reading can be viewed as a social activity, there is an undeniable element of isolation to it. As readers we sit alone turning pages. But a stage play is not viewed in isolation. We sit in close proximity with others as part of an audience. Comedy becomes more humorous when we hear others laugh; tragedy becomes sadder when we sense others are moved to tears (Arp 1117). Drama offers a communal experience that intensifies the personal one.

Finally, the experience of drama comes in a darkened theater where constraints are imposed on viewers. Unless outraged at what we see or in desperate need of a restroom, we cannot just walk out. Nor can we stop the performance as we can earmark a page and put down a book until the next convenient moment to resume reading. Thus, the playwright is able to command our undivided attention in a way the fiction writer cannot.

However, according to Perrine, drama's strengths are tied to its limitations. Plays are performed on stages, and the stage restricts what a playwright can portray. Most plays show humans interacting with each other. Except in rare cases, there are no wild animals on stage—lions, tigers, or bears—because of their size and unpredictability. The stage cannot *show* massive things such as space ships landing on the moon, or miniature things such as a drop of blood dripping off a sword. The stage must keep things at a human scale.

Moreover, plays often consist of a limited number of sets or even a single set. The cost and logistics involved in using additional sets discourage frequent changes. It's true that nonrealistic drama can use a bare stage, platforms, lighting, a few props, and cues in the dialogue to exploit the audience's imagination, but it is still not feasible, as it is in fiction, to jump back and forth from here to eternity in the space of a single sentence (Arp 1116). Drama is simply not as spatially mobile as fiction.

A third limit inherent in dramatic storytelling is its lack of flexibility in point of view. The fiction writer has a wide variety of points of view to choose from: first person, omniscient, limited omniscient, objective, and all their variations and combinations. But of the four main points of view employed by the fiction writer, the playwright generally relies on one—the objective or dramatic point of view. This means the playwright shows what can be seen or heard. This restriction makes it difficult for the playwright to offer vast amounts of historical background, to comment directly on the action, or to reveal the characters' inner thoughts. It is true that some stage techniques allow the audience to know what a character is thinking. Arthur Miller in *Death of a Salesman* suggests Biff's inner thoughts through flashback scenes, and Shakespeare sometimes reveals a character's inner thoughts through an aside or a soliloquy. But these devices interrupt the dramatic flow of the play and are used sparingly if at all.

Drama must also tell its story within time limits—usually a two- to three-hour sitting—and that affects the amount that can be told and the way it is told. Many of the world's fictional masterpieces are too lengthy and complex for an evening of theater. As interesting as it might be, a stage production of *Moby-Dick* would be too long for most people to sit through unless the work was seriously abridged. The audience's limited attention span restricts the magnitude of the playwright's material. In short, drama has many advantages in telling a story, but the stage also imposes limitations on the playwright.

Drama and Film

Drama and film are alike in several ways. Both (1) tell a story (2) performed by actors (3) before an audience. In other words, what drama and film have in common (and what distinguishes them from fiction) is that they both tell stories realized in the framework of a public performance.

Although drama and film offer public performances, those performances differ. A play is a performance by live actors on a stage before a live and present audience. A film is a performance by photographed actors projected on a screen before a live audience not present with the actors. The stage performance is given just once, and no two stage performances are exactly the same. The film performance can be shown repeatedly, and, so long as the negative is intact, each performance is the same.

According to Manfred Jahn, "drama and film are artifacts created in a process of collective and collaborative production." Moreover, the reception of this collaborative art involves a social or "collective public experience" in a theater or a cinema. In other words, plays and films are both created collaboratively and received collectively.

Another commonality is that drama and film both begin with scripts. A play script is similar to a film script. However, while plays are often published and studied by a large number of readers in school, film scripts usually remain unpublished, and those that are published are mainly read by an audience of professionals, enthusiasts, and film analysts. In short, plays and films tell stories within the framework of performances that are carefully scripted, collaboratively created, and collectively received.

Though they share some features, plays and films are sharply distinguished by a number of conventions. According to Allardyce Nicoll, "the theatre rejoices in artistic limitation in space" (Marcus 196). Single-set plays are common and accepted by the theater audience. And the backgrounds for these sets are often patently fake—painted backs of books on a wall to suggest a library or painted waves to evoke a sea. On the other hand, the cinema audience does not glory in the limitation of space but expects spatial mobility. And when the camera takes the audience to different locations, the audience demands to be taken *there*—no painted backdrops to suggest mountains or seas. Film audiences expect realism; stage audiences will accept artificial sets and illusion.

Another difference between theater and film involves the audience's assumptions about space. The theater audience has no trouble assuming "that a room with only three walls is actually a room with four walls" (Arp 1160). Meanwhile, the film audience assumes that a two-dimensional film (they are viewing a flat screen, after all) represents a three-dimensional reality (Arp 1163).

Stage acting is usually exaggerated because each actor's voice and movements must project to the furthermost reaches of the theater. If the theater is large, the actor must magnify gestures, overstate facial expressions, and speak distinctly and loudly enough so that viewers in the last row can see and hear him clearly. In film, the problem of the last row does not exist because of the mobility of the camera and the microphone. The viewer of a film can hear an actor even if he or she is talking softly and can see the actor clearly at whatever distance and angle the filmmaker intended. However, there is a problem if an actor uses a theatrical acting style in a film. In film acting, an actor's voice, gestures, facial expressions, and body movements must be modulated in accordance with the actor's distance from the camera. If an actor uses projection techniques in a close-up, the acting will seem exaggerated and "over the top."

Plays tend to depend more on dialogue and less on action to tell their stories. "The film director René Clair once noted that a blind person could still grasp the essentials of most stage plays" (Giannetti 300). However, with films, what is seen is more important than what is heard. "[A] deaf person," Clair continues, "could still grasp most of the essentials of a film" (Giannetti 300).

Perhaps the main difference in audience expectation has to do with movement. The play may show little action for long periods—two actors talking at
length on a single set is not uncommon. But movies are full of movement.
Part of that movement is supplied by human action on shifting sets, but to a
great extent the movement is created by the camera and editing. Even a relatively "static" sequence of two actors talking together on a settee can be
enlivened by varying camera distance, angles, and motion, and by rapid editing between shots.

One more point. We said that drama and film are both narrative and per-
formative genres. Since people tend to think the two forms are closely allied,
they often believe it is easier to adapt a play into film than to adapt a novel,
short story, or novella. However, it is more difficult to adapt a play than it is to
adapt a narrative genre. Why?

Powerful as they are, plays are stage-bound, point-of-view-bound, lan-
guage-bound, and bound to the connection between live actors and a present
audience. These stage conventions aren't easily transposable into a medium
that achieves its storytelling power through conventions that stress visual
images and spatial and temporal mobility. To succeed, most adaptations must
somehow free the story from stage conventions that are often an enormous
source of power for the play. This is a difficult job.

We have highlighted some of the similarities and differences among drama,
fiction, and film as a preliminary discussion to the strategies adapters have
developed to move a story from theatrical to cinematic conventions.

Opening Up a Play

When critics talk about film adaptations of plays, the key term they use is **opening up.** The term refers to a number of strategies developed by adapters to
transpose the story from stage to screen conventions. The photographed stage
play is an example of a play that is *not* opened up, while *A Soldier's Story* (1984),
directed by Norman Jewison, is an example of an adaptation that opens up a
play. The following section considers seven strategies used to open up Charles
Fuller's *A Soldier's Play* (1982).

What do we gain from recognizing the degree to which a play is opened up?

First, identifying the use of the strategies described below reminds us of the
different conventions used in drama and film and makes visible the work of the
adapter in transposing a story from stage to screen.

Second, identifying the degree to which plays are opened up helps us
compare one adaptation to another. For example, one way to relate the adaptations of *Hamlet* directed by Laurence Olivier, Tony Richardson, Franco
Zeffirelli, and Kenneth Branagh is to consider to what degree each opens up
Shakespeare's play.

Third, such a determination offers a generalization about the relationship between play and film that leads to interesting questions. For example, to what degree is the play opened up to cinema space? If stage limitations are respected, why did the filmmakers decide not to exploit the spatial mobility of film? What is lost or gained in opening up a specific play? How is it that a play that is not opened up can be a satisfying work of art?

Identifying the use of the opening-up strategies described below is not an end in itself nor an evaluative measure of an adaptation, but rather a helpful way to begin talking about dramatic and cinematic conventions and the choices filmmakers make in bringing a play to the screen.

A SOLDIER'S PLAY (1982), by Charles Fuller

In a 1982 interview, the African-American playwright Charles Fuller said he saw a shift taking place in the themes that interest black writers. According to Fuller, "We are beginning to turn away from focusing on our problems with whites, to matters involving blacks as human beings." *A Soldier's Play*, Fuller said, was "concerned about how racism affects blacks in their dealings with each other rather than as victims of a larger plot by whites" (Goodman 28).

A Soldier's Play, then, does not concentrate on a confrontation *between* blacks and whites but on a conflict *among* blacks that is fueled and circumscribed by the racism of the white world.

The play concerns a murder and its investigation at Fort Neal, a segregated Army base near Tynin, Louisiana, at the end of World War II. In the opening minutes of the play, Sergeant Vernon Waters, a black noncommissioned officer, is shot dead while returning drunk to the base one night, and the rest of the play is devoted to discovering who killed him. Captain Richard Davenport, a black officer and a lawyer, is appointed by Army officers in Washington to undertake the investigation. Local wisdom suggests the murder is racially motivated and points at the Ku Klux Klan or at white officers. But it is Davenport who keeps asking why Waters was shot, and it is he who eventually uncovers the truth.

It turns out Waters, the leader of an all-black baseball platoon, thinks he can benefit his race by getting rid of what he considers bad examples. "The black race can't afford you no more" (Fuller 72), Waters says to C. J., a man he thinks revels too much in his Southern roots. Waters's persecution of C. J. leads to the latter's suicide and to a backlash from two of the sergeant's men—Private Peterson, who shoots Waters, and Private Smalls, who covers up Peterson's crime. At the end of the play, Davenport bitterly sums up the action and assigns blame:

> Two colored soldiers are dead [Waters and C. J.]—two on their way to prison [Peterson and Smalls]. Four less men to fight with—and none of their reasons—nothing anyone *said*, or *did*, would have been worth a life to men with larger hearts—men less split by the madness of race in America. (Fuller 99)

At first, "the madness of race in America" seems to stand outside the barracks of this closely knit, all-black, baseball-playing platoon, but, just as World War II spreads across the seas, so, too, racism reaches everywhere, stirring conflict and damaging and destroying lives.

In this section we use Fuller's play and its film adaptation to illustrate seven general strategies that filmmakers use to open up drama.

A SOLDIER'S STORY (1984), **Directed by Norman Jewison**

1. Filming Settings Only Suggested in the Drama

Fuller's stage play takes place in and around Fort Neal, but those locations are not represented realistically on stage. Instead, they are suggested by a single set: "a horseshoe-like half circle" surmounted by "several platforms at varying levels" that are connected by "stairs or ramps" (Fuller 7). Props, dialogue cues, and figures stepping in and out of sharply lighted spaces suggest the locations: a military office, barracks, the stockade, the murder scene, and most importantly a courtroom. That single set makes sense for a play. It costs money to build sets for different locations, and it is difficult to shift from one set to another. But the single set does not make sense in a film adaptation since the camera can take a film audience virtually anywhere. So one way to open up a play is to film settings that are only suggested or implied in the drama. Jewison relies heavily on this technique in opening up Fuller's play.

As the play begins, the stage is black, and then a "narrow beam of light" reveals Sergeant Waters on all fours, drunk and mumbling. An unidentifiable figure steps into the light holding a gun and fires. Waters is dead. A second shot is heard and then the stage goes black. Later we are told the murder took place "in a wooded section" by the junction of two roads, "just two hundred yards from the colored N.C.O. club" (Fuller 16).

The film begins just before the opening scene of the play. It adds a visualization of Big Mary's, a substitution for the Non-Commissioned Officers' club, where many black enlisted troops and noncommissioned officers spend time and where Waters gets drunk. As Waters staggers out of the club and begins his woozy walk back to the base, the camera shows a sidewalk crowded with black soldiers and townspeople; a deserted road leading out of Tynin into the woods; and a wooded area, "the woods by the junction" that in the play is represented by a simple beam of light, in which Waters crouches on his hands and knees and talks to someone who stands over him. So the film opens up the beginning of the play by visualizing highly realistic interior and exterior sets.

The realism of the film's settings is no mistake. Most of *A Soldier's Story* was shot at an actual Army base at Fort Chaffee, Arkansas. Exterior shots show the town, areas between town and base, and the Army base itself with its many roads, barracks, offices, training fields, and large parade ground. It is not important here to itemize all the places visualized in the movie. The point is that the film is not confined by the limits of the stage; instead, it moves the play's non-realistic settings into realistic **cinema space.** The film's many locations and the ease and speed with which the camera moves the viewer from one location to another gives the story spatial mobility and variety as well as a realistic depiction of a rural Southern Army base. The film illustrates some of the ways an adapter can open up a confined stage into cinema space.

2. Visualizing Scenes Only Mentioned or Implied in the Drama

Many actions in a play are only mentioned or implied because they could be difficult to perform on stage. Another way to open up a play is to actualize these scenes. The film adds visualizations of two *implied* scenes from the beginning of Fuller's play. We mentioned the scene where Waters walks from the bar toward the murder scene and the reaction shots of people on the street, both black and white, as they notice the drunken black sergeant. Later, we see the arrival by bus of Captain Davenport from Washington, a scene focusing on the reactions of both blacks and whites to his being a black officer. Both implied scenes are difficult to show on the stage for obvious reasons, but both succeed in the film in conveying the pervasive racism that is crucial to all the elements of the story.

A scene simply reported on stage but visualized in the film is the bloody fistfight between Waters and Peterson, which Peterson loses, an event that underlines the hostility between the two men and adds some motivation to Peterson's later act of murder. In the play, we learn that the all-black platoon is drawn from baseball players in the Negro League, but it is only in the film that we see them play a game and witness C. J. hit a game-winning home run. At the end of the play, Captain Taylor tells Davenport in one line that "we all ship out for Europe tomorrow" (100). But in the film, we see the soldiers celebrating the news of their departure and the spectacle of hundreds of black and white troops marching across the parade ground in formation as they prepare to head off to war. The film's actualizations of these implied or mentioned scenes moves the story away from the limitations of the stage.

3. Dramatizing Characters Only Mentioned or Implied in the Drama

Considerations of space and money limit the number of actors performing on stage, but big studio, feature-length films can accommodate and afford large casts. So another way to open up a play is to add characters who are only mentioned or implied in the drama.

One addition to the film is Colonel Nivens—the superior officer, who is often referred to in the play, but who never appears on stage. In the film, Nivens takes on some of the lines and racial attitudes of Captain Taylor, splitting that complicated character into two more simplified ones, each representing a different attitude toward race.

Another addition is Big Mary, played by Patti LaBelle, who gives energetic performances of blues songs at her club. This character is not mentioned in the play, but she is implied by the existence of the N.C.O. club and by the many references to the power and vigor of blues music.

Perhaps the most important additions are the twenty-four named actors in minor parts and the hundreds of actors who represent the soldiers on the base and who march off to war in the final scene. These added characters, impossible to place on stage, are implied in the play and serve to make realistic the portrayal of a fully functioning Army base during World War II.

4. Visualizing Literary Symbols or Motifs

According to Bernard F. Dick, another way of opening up a play is to "[*v*]*isualize symbols so that they cease to be abstract*" (267). In Fuller's play, what is visualized is not so much one symbol—such as the streetcar in Tennessee Williams's *A Streetcar Named Desire*—but a recurring pattern or motif. According to Gary P. Storhoff, "the pattern of reflection" is "an organizing principle that unifies both the play and film thematically, structurally, and ideologically" (21).

An important visualization of the reflection motif occurs in a scene at Big Mary's, in which Waters and Wilkie sit talking at the bar while C. J. plays guitar. Waters turns and gazes into the mirror behind the bar, which also contains C. J.'s reflection. Waters wants to destroy C. J. because he sees him as a bad example of his race. Although Waters has adopted white bigotry, he does not seem aware that this bigotry is aimed at him as well. While Waters verbally distinguishes himself from C. J., the reflection of the mirror undercuts those distinctions by framing their images side by side, making the two men appear

The reflection of Waters (Adolph Caesar), C. J. (Larry Riley), and Wilkie (Art Evans) in the mirror in *A Soldier's Story* (1984).

close together, just as they would seem to a white racist who would notice only the color of their skin. The scene can be interpreted on many levels, and so can other scenes that involve the motif of reflection, but the point here is that an adapter can open up a play by making its symbols or motifs physically present in the film.

5. Using the Camera and Editing to Move the Story into Cinema Time and Space

Using the camera and editing can move the story into **cinema time.** In the naturalistic theater, the action of the play covers a short or long period of time such as a day or a lifetime, but the actors perform each scene in real time. In other words, the length of the scene is equivalent to the time it takes to act it. Elapsed time normally takes place offstage between scenes. In the cinema, the camera is able to slow down time using slow motion, speed it up using fast motion, or even stop it using a freeze frame. Editing may also speed up action by cutting quickly from one shot to another. The direction of time can also be reversed. Generally speaking, theater time moves chronologically forward, but in the cinema flashbacks are common, and sometimes flash forwards are used, too.

In a theater, point of view is limited because the viewer sits through the performance at a certain distance and at a certain angle from the action. Of course, the viewer is free to turn his or her eyes at any time to view anything of interest on stage. In the cinema, point of view is limited in a different way. The camera uses long shots, medium shots, and close-ups to vary the viewer's distance from the action; it uses eye-level, high- or low-angle shots to change the viewer's angle; and it uses panning, tracking, or crane shots to move the viewer in relation to the action. But while the camera can unfix the position of the viewer in relation to the action, it also limits what the viewer sees to what it chooses to show.

Let's look at a specific example of how a film can change stage time and space. Here is the murder scene from Fuller's *A Soldier's Play.* After you read it, study the shot analysis of the corresponding scene in the film adaptation. Notice how the camerawork and editing change the speed of the action and the viewer's position in relation to it.

■ ■ ■

MURDER SCENE FROM FULLER'S *A SOLDIER'S PLAY*

As the play opens, the stage is black. In the background, rising in volume, we hear the song, "Don't Sit under the Apple Tree," sung by the Andrews Sisters. Quite suddenly, in a sharp but narrow beam of light, in limbo, TECH/SERGEANT VERNON C. WATERS, a well-built, light brown-skinned man in a World War II, winter army uniform, is seen down on all fours. He is stinking drunk, trying to stand and mumbling to himself.

WATERS (repeating): They'll still hate you! They still hate you . . . They still hate you!

WATERS is laughing as suddenly someone steps into the light. (We never see this person.) He is holding a .45 caliber pistol. He lifts it swiftly and ominously towards WATERS'S head and fires. WATERS is knocked over backward. He is dead. The music has stopped and there is a strong silence onstage.

VOICE: Le's go!

The man with the gun takes a step, then stops. He points the gun at WATERS again and fires a second time. There is another silence as limbo is plunged into darkness, and the barracks is just as quickly lit. (Fuller 8)

Shot Analysis of Murder Scene
from *A SOLDIER'S STORY*

SHOT	DURATION	PICTURE	SOUND	EDIT
No. 1	9 seconds	Long shot: Landscape: woods Tilt down to close-up of Waters	Night animals Waters: "They still hate you" —Laugh Cock of pistol	Cut
No. 2	5 seconds	Extreme close-up of pistol	Dialogue with laugh	Cut
No. 3	.2 second	Extreme close-up of pistol: back of hammer	Dialogue with laugh	Cut
No. 4	.3 second	Extreme close-up of pistol mouth	Dialogue with laugh	Cut
No. 5	.8 second	Medium shot: Waters being shot Waters flying back into frame	Pistol report	Cut
No. 6	.8 second	Long shot: Landscape: woods	Birds in flight	Cut

No. 7	.5 second	Close-up: Landscape: foliage	Dirt hitting leaf	Cut
No. 8	5 seconds	Long shot: Waters landing dead Slow motion	Music: ominous rhythm and tone	Cut
No. 9	11 seconds	Close-up: Waters's body— dolly forward toward body— close-up Waters's face	Footsteps over music	Cut
No. 10	7 seconds	Long shot: Through branches Shift in focus from branches to moon	Music— second report of pistol	Cut

The film's murder scene consists of ten shots, with a total duration of 39.6 seconds. The average length of a shot is 4 seconds, with ten different cuts. The swift editing back and forth allows the spectator to become involved in two points of action—the unknown killer's and the victim's. Notice how the rapid cutting of the extreme close-ups of the pistol (shots 2, 3, and 4) seem to speed up the action while the slow motion of Waters's fall back into the ditch (shot 8) slows it down. The speeding up of the shooting and the slowing down of the falling body could not be done on the stage. The camera and editing have transposed the real time of theater performance into cinema time. And those manipulations of time allow the filmmakers to suggest both the sudden emotional rashness of the shooting and the slow unfolding consequences of the killing.

Notice also how the camera's point of view is not the same as the stage audience's. After the establishing shot and the tilt down to Waters, much of the time the camera seems to be shooting over the shoulder of a person who is facing Waters but whose back is turned. The extreme close-ups of the pistol seen by the film viewer could not be replicated in the theater. The film moves the stage scene into cinema space by showing the murder scene and its environs from multiple positions, distances, and angles; it moves the stage scene into cinema time through the use of rapid editing and slow motion.

6. Muting or Erasing Act Divisions

Another way that the film adapter often opens up a play is to mute or erase the act divisions, thereby making the film action seem more continuous. Most real-

The killing of Sergeant Waters in *A Soldier's Story*.

istic plays are divided into acts, typically with an intermission in the middle of the performance. Many stage plays have three to five acts, each act working up to its own emotional high point. The act divisions are typically marked in the theater by lights going down and a curtain closing. During this pause, a set can be changed or actors can depart or enter unseen. Filmmakers, practically speaking, do not need these divisions, and so they have the choice of keeping them in some form or making them unnoticeable. Sidney Lumet in *Long Day's Journey into Night* chooses to fade to black as a way to mark act divisions, but in *A Soldier's Story*, the two-act division is erased, giving the illusion of a less interrupted, more continuous action, which better fits the conventions of cinema.

7. Adding Music

One more strategy worth mentioning is that the film adapter can open up a play by adding to the film a musical score that would be difficult to produce in the theater. In a number of scenes in *A Soldier's Play*, C. J. strums a guitar and sings or hums bluesy songs, and the tune "Don't Sit under the Apple Tree," sung by the Andrews Sisters, is heard several times. But in *A Soldier's Story*, the musical score composed by Herbie Hancock is extensive. Patti LaBelle sings several songs, as does C. J., and at the end of the film a marching song is played by a military band. The musical score (both diegetic and nondiegetic) adds interest to scenes, establishes mood, and influences the emotional reactions of the audience to the characters and their situations. Adding an extensive musical score is another way of moving the story away from stage limitations and conventions.

Degrees of Opening Up

A Soldier's Story illustrates seven strategies adapters used to open up a play. In a discussion of other adapted plays, keep in mind the photographed stage play as a kind of benchmark to measure how extensively a play has been opened up. The following discussion includes Eugene O'Neill's *Long Day's Journey into Night*, Tennessee Williams's *A Streetcar Named Desire*, and William Shakespeare's *Macbeth* and their respective adaptations by Sidney Lumet, Elia Kazan, and Akira Kurosawa.

Close to a Filmed Stage Play

Eugene O'Neill's *Long Day's Journey into Night* is set in the living room of a summer home in August 1912. Mary Tyrone has just been released from an institution where she has been apparently cured of morphine addiction. James, her husband, is a once successful but now washed-up actor, whose alcoholism and miserliness have had disastrous effects on the family. Jamie, the eldest son, is also an alcoholic who has tried and failed at acting and is unwilling to find any other work. Edmund, the more sensitive son, has returned home sick and waits for the doctor to confirm that he has consumption.

The major action of the play is the revelation that the mother is not cured of her drug addiction. While the men escape through whiskey, Mary retreats to the past, revealing that after Edmund's birth it was her husband's stinginess that led him to choose a quack doctor for her who prescribed morphine. Jamie blames his brother, Edmund, for his mother's addiction, and Edmund expects his father to send him to the cheapest sanitarium because he is not likely to recover. The play ends with Mary escaping into the past while the other members of the family escape into their own compulsive fantasies.

O'Neill finished the play in 1941, but since it was highly autobiographical, he instructed his publisher Random House in 1945 not to read the play until twenty-five years after his death, and later informed them that he neither wanted the play published nor performed. After the death of his eldest son, presumably the family member he was protecting, O'Neill broached the possibility of the play's production with his wife Carlotta, who, after O'Neill's death in 1953, reacquired the rights and allowed the play to be performed. After watching a TV show called *Play of the Week*, which adapted O'Neill's *The Iceman Cometh*, Carlotta asked its producer Ely Landau to adapt other O'Neill plays, which eventually led to a film version of *Long Day's*. Landau was the eventual creator of the American Film Theater series, which during its brief run from

1974 to 1975 produced fourteen drama adaptations. Landau's motion was to
bring together serious drama and a national audience by adapting a number of
important plays and then showing them several times a week at movie houses
across the country where tickets would be bought in advance by subscription
just as in a theater. Landau, one of *Long Day's* two producers, was interested in
adapting drama to film in ways that would provide a fundamentally theatrical
experience.

Long Day's Journey into Night (1962), directed by Sidney Lumet, is a close
adaptation of O'Neill's play. The three-hour film retains the characters, events,
setting, themes, and almost all of the dialogue. Lumet said:

> On *Long Day's Journey into Night,* I used the text of the play. The only adaptation
> made for the screen was to cut seven pages of a 177-page text during rehearsals.
> And we cut those because I knew I was going to shoot those sections in close-ups.
> The use of close-ups would make those moments clearer sooner. (32)

Although Lumet's film is close to a photographed stage play, it does open up
the work in several ways. First, it visualizes several locations only implied in
the play.

The play begins in the living room of the Tyrones' summer house: "*As the
curtain rises, the family have just finished breakfast. MARY TYRONE and her husband enter together from the back parlor, coming from the dining room*" (O'Neill 12).
The living room is the single set for the entire drama.

However, the film begins with a sustained shot of the burning sun upon
which front credits are superimposed and during which a piano plays. Lumet
explains why he chose an exterior setting: "I moved the first part of Act 1 outdoors and I shot it on a sunny day, so this journey into night could seem even
longer. I wanted more light at the beginning to contrast with the blackness of
the end" (90).

After the credits, we see an exterior shot of the servant girl Cathleen setting out tea on the porch and then crossing the lawn to get the mail by the
house gate. The panning shot reveals that the house fronts a harbor full of
boats. Next we see Mary and Tyrone, who have presumably finished breakfast,
talking outside on the porch. Their two sons join them, and then all four move
to an outdoor table and chairs set in the grass just in front of the house. When
Edmund and his mother walk back into the house, the father and his eldest
son move to the garage where they talk while working on the family car. The
action then moves back into the house, where it pretty much stays for the rest
of the film.

It is not these few added locations of harbor, lawn, and garage, but the
lighting and camerawork that primarily add movement and variety to the
play. The camera enters the living room from the front, back, and sides, points
of view not available to the stage audience. Since most scenes involve two
characters talking, the shot/reverse shot technique is used over and over to
emphasize a character's words and the reaction to what is said. Perhaps the

Jason Robards, Katharine Hepburn, and Dean Stockwell in *A Long Day's Journey into Night* (1962).

most dramatic example of an opening up of the play through the camera occurs in the last shot of the film. Lumet describes it:

> The last shot of the movie is of Katharine Hepburn, Ralph Richardson, Jason Robards, and Dean Stockwell sitting around a table. Each is lost in his or her own addictive fantasy, the men from booze, Mary Tyrone from morphine. A distant lighthouse sweeps its beam across the room every forty-five seconds. The camera pulls back slowly, and the walls of the room gradually disappear. Soon the characters are sitting in a black limbo, getting tinier and tinier as the light sweeps across them. Fade out. (15–16)

Lumet also comments on his use of editing:

> I always shot Katharine Hepburn in long, sustained takes, so that in the editing, the legato feel of her scenes would help us drift into her narcotized world. We would move *with* her, into her past and into her own journey into night. Jason Robards's character was edited in exactly the opposite way. As the picture went on, I tried to cut his scenes in a staccato rhythm. I wanted him to feel erratic, disjointed, uncoordinated. Richardson's and Stockwell's characters were handled for the *picture's* sense of tempo rather than their characters. (162)

Lumet cites both the camera work and the editing as a defense against those who claim the film is too much like a photographed stage play:

A lot of critics condescendingly called it a "photographed stage play." This was easy to say, since I used the play's text. I even faded to black at act endings. The theatrical origin was easily identifiable. No effort was made to disguise it. But the critics were incapable of seeing one of the most complex camera and editing techniques of any picture I've done. (89)

The opening up of the original stage set to other locations and the use of the "complex camera and editing techniques" do not open up the play enough to make viewers forget its "theatrical origin." However, this raises the question of whether an adapted play has to be opened up to be artistically successful. The critical acclaim and awards the film won when it was first released and its continuing reputation as a fine adaptation suggest it does not.

A Few More Degrees Separated from a Filmed Stage Play

More opened up than Lumet's *Long Day's Journey* is Elia Kazan's film version of Tennessee Williams's play *A Streetcar Named Desire* (1951).

In the play, Blanche DuBois, a worn, neurotic schoolteacher, arrives in New Orleans to find her sister, Stella, sharing a shabby two-bedroom apartment with her husband, Stanley Kowalski. Blanche finds Stanley rough, brutish, vulgar, and crude, and Stanley views the fastidious Blanche with dislike and suspicion because she has lost Belle Reve, the family plantation, and caused friction in his marriage. But when Blanche apparently finds love with Mitch, a shy factory worker and one of Stanley's friends, Stanley makes inquiries and learns about Blanche's past as a prostitute. He tells Mitch and ruins Blanche's chance to marry. While his wife is in the hospital having a baby, Stanley comes home drunk and rapes his sister-in-law. At the end of the play, Blanche's mind is disturbed and confused, and a doctor takes her away to an institution, while Stanley reconciles with Stella even though she is aware of what he has done.

Because Williams's play contained some shocking and controversial material for film audiences of the time, its adaptation drew the attention of the Production Code Administration (PCA) and the Legion of Decency. Various censors objected to references to Blanche's homosexual husband, his suicide, and Blanche's prostitution; the bad language, drinking, and gambling; some sexually suggestive lines; Stanley's rape of Blanche; and Stella's decision at the end to stay with Stanley despite the rape.

In discussing the movie, it is helpful to keep in mind two different film versions: the PCA cut, or the version of the film remaining after negotiations concluded between Warner Bros. and the industry censors; and a second version that consists of the PCA's cuts and additional cuts required by the Legion of Decency. This twice-censored film is the one viewers saw in the 1951 theater release of the film. The once-censored or PCA version is what viewers can now see in the 1993 release that restores four minutes of scattered footage ordered removed by the Legion of Decency (Leff 29). The discussion below refers to the 1993 release of the film.

Stella, Stanley, and Blanche from Elia Kazan's *A Streetcar Named Desire* (1951).

Like *Long Day's Journey, Streetcar* is a one-set play. The set consists of "[t]*he exterior of a two-story corner building*" that "*contains two flats, upstairs and down,*" with "*stairs* [that] *ascend to the entrances of both*" (Williams 13). The opening credits of this black-and-white film are displayed over a shot of a similar stage set, but the film begins by visualizing locations only implied or mentioned in the play. We see a train arriving in New Orleans, a street full of taxicabs, passengers disembarking, and then Blanche herself, emerging out of a cloud of steam, boarding an actual streetcar named "Desire." She walks through a rough neighborhood to find the apartment house and then goes to the bowling alley where she meets her sister. Later, we see the delivery of Blanche's trunk, and much later we see Blanche and Mitch at a dance club and hear their conversation on an adjacent waterside dock. We also see the factory where Mitch and Stanley work. Shots of street life, most of which look artificial, are interspersed throughout. But despite these and other visualized locations, most of the action is set in the confined quarters of the apartment house.

There are a few other ways in which the adaptation moves the story away from stage conventions. The film visualizes two implied scenes: Blanche's arrival by train, and Stanley's fight with Mitch at the factory after Stanley tells Mitch about Blanche's unsavory past. All twelve characters from the play are kept except one, and several unnamed minor characters are added, such as a sailor, street vendor, policeman, foreman, and baby. Groups of people and passersby are shown in street scenes and at the train station, bowling alley, dance club, and factory. Perhaps more importantly, the film visualizes an abstract symbol from the play. Heading to Stella's, Blanche boards an actual streetcar, but the streetcar is more than a literal means of transportation. It serves as a symbol of her desire to escape her past and to start life anew. The camera is not used in a way to call attention to itself, but it does add movement through a variety of shots, angles, and motion. However, the film includes some lengthy takes that indirectly suggest the static nature of the play.

Despite the visualization of locations, the addition of characters, the visualized symbol of the streetcar, and the camera work, the film seems close to a stage play because the dialogue is "talky," the pace slow, the street scenes artificial, the limited space claustrophobic, and the attention focused on four characters. Like *Long Day's Journey*, *Streetcar* is not fully opened up to cinematic conventions, yet it is recognized as a classic adaptation.

Far from the Filmed Stage Play

Some argue that Shakespeare is the dramatist whose plays have been adapted to film most successfully. The argument is that Shakespeare did not write single-set plays with only a few characters and limited actions. Instead, his plays offer a variety of settings, a wide range of characters, and plots full of action. Shakespeare's plays give the adapter opportunities to exploit film's freedom in treating time and space.

Adaptations of Shakespeare's plays have been made from early in film history. According to Russell Jackson, "it has been estimated that that during the 'silent' era—before synchronized dialogue complicated the business of adapting poetic drama for the screen—there were more than 400 films on Shakespearean subjects" (2). With the advent of sound films in 1927, filmmakers had to address Shakespeare's Elizabethan language. According to Manvell, the main problem for adapters of Shakespeare has been "the task of making his language . . . as clear and meaningful as possible" (186) to a modern audience. The treatment of Shakespeare's language is one useful way to distinguish among the many film adaptations of his work. For example, in *Romeo and Juliet* (1936), directed by George Cukor, "[v]irtually all the dialogue was retained; even the exposition and purely functional speeches of no particular merit." In this "respectful" film, "the visuals merely illustrate the language," often with "images and dialogue contain[ing] the same information" (Giannetti 300).

Another approach to Shakespeare's language is illustrated by director Franco Zefferelli's period adaptation of the same play in *Romeo and Juliet* (1968).

> Verbal exposition was cut almost completely and replaced (just as effectively) by visual exposition. Single lines were pruned meticulously from some of the speeches where the same information could be conveyed by images. Most of the great poetry was preserved but often with *nonsynchronous* visuals to expand—not duplicate—the language. (Giannetti 300–301)

Baz Luhrmann's *Romeo + Juliet* (1996) illustrates another approach. Exposition and dialogue are severely cut, but the dialogue used is taken directly from Shakespeare. To aid contemporary audiences, that dialogue is reframed in a modern dress production that uses cues from contemporary culture to supplement Shakespeare's lines. The basic situation of star-crossed lovers belonging to feuding families in Renaissance Italy is updated into a kind of gang war waged with guns in the streets of a modern cityscape—Verona Beach, Florida—a stylized, composite location indebted to footage of Mexico City, Miami, and Los Angeles. The characters are updated, too. The Montagues and Capulets are rival corporate dynasties; the Prince of Verona is a police commissioner; Romeo (Leonardo DiCaprio) and Juliet (Claire Danes) are suburban teenagers; Mercutio is a black drag queen; Friar Lawrence is a hip cleric who is into herbals; and the chorus is a well-groomed TV anchorwoman who reads the prologue on the evening news. The important scenes find modern analogues as well. The opening brawl between the two families takes place at a gas station and is shot—fast tracking, slow motion, crash zooms—in the rapid style of an action movie such as *Pulp Fiction* (1994). The famous balcony scene leads Romeo and Juliet into a swimming pool where they say their lines awash in water. Romeo's swordfight with Tybalt is translated into an action movie showdown in which Romeo pumps Tybalt full of lead.

Craig Pearce, co-writer of the screenplay with Luhrmann, explains the strategy.

> The trouble is he [Shakespeare] writes in this obscure language called Elizabethan, and ninety percent of the world can't understand it. We thought the way to help people was to present these very recognizable characters in the modern world. . . . Tybalt when he's presented, you know, you get the image of a big, bad gunslinger, so it says to the audience, even if they can't quite tune their ear into the Shakespearean dialogue at that early stage, they'll say, okay, here's a really scary guy, and he's really good with a gun. Everybody's scared of him. I understand who he is. . . . They just sort of understand his function in the world and in the story.

The audience grasps the gist of Shakespeare's "strange" language (even if the lines are not clearly spoken) because the film is saturated with the familiar: settings, scenes, situations, and songs. These highly recognizable visual and aural cues give the audience a rich context for understanding language written 400 years ago.

One film that has been universally acknowledged as a successful rendering of a Shakespeare play is *Throne of Blood* (Jap. 1957), directed by Akira Kurosawa. This rendering of *Macbeth* offers yet another approach to dealing with Elizabethan language. The film solves its complexities by dispensing with it altogether. The film does not use a single word of Shakespeare in direct translation; in fact, there is not even an attempt at a sketchy translation in the spare dialogue of *Throne*.

Exterior foggy atmosphere and witch from *Throne of Blood* (1957).

Donald Richie suggests that American filmmakers are excellent at showing action; Europeans are excellent at portraying character; and the Japanese are excellent at creating atmosphere (ixx). Kurosawa succeeds in large part because he transposes the mood and atmosphere of Shakespeare's *Macbeth,* set on a heath and in castles in eleventh-century Scotland, to a historical movie (*jidai-geki*), set in a misty forest and in castles in sixteenth-century Japan.

Since *Throne* is a loose adaptation, the comparison between film and play must be in general terms. Except for the addition of a chanting chorus that frames the action and the omission of the Macduff family material, the basic plot is kept. After helping the warlord Tsuzuki (Duncan) put down a rebellion, Washizu (Macbeth) and Miki (Banquo) meet an evil spirit in the forest who predicts their futures (as the witches on the moor predict Macbeth and Banquo's). Washizu will replace Tsuzuki as the chief warlord and ruler of Cobweb Castle, and Miki's son will succeed him. Washizu confides the prediction to his wife Asaji (Lady Macbeth), who encourages him to kill Tsuzuki. After the murder, Washizu takes over Cobweb Castle, but his power and success begin to unravel until his own men kill him.

What links the two works are the atmosphere of the forests, battlefields, and feudal castles; the main characters and their relationships; and the theme that unbridled ambition destroys. "Murdered by ambition," the chorus chants as the film opens. But *Throne* is not as much a direct translation of *Macbeth* from one language, culture, and medium to another as it is a reimagining of *Macbeth*, in which Shakespeare's poetry is transformed into Japanese film images. Some critics think *Throne* is the best adaptation of a Shakespeare play, and a cinematic masterpiece in its own right. But, for the purposes of this chapter, *Throne* is an adaptation that successfully opens up a stage play into film conventions, while sustaining the recognizability of the antecedent story.

The Length of a Play

In previous chapters, we discussed how the length of a genre affects film adaptation. The novel generally requires cutting and condensing existing material, whereas the short story requires adding material. It is hard to generalize about drama because plays vary in length, usually anywhere from one to five acts, with the individual acts also varying in length. Ancient Greek tragedies consisted of five acts, each act roughly reflecting one of the five elements of plot: exposition, rising action, crisis or turning point, falling action, and catastrophe. But since the 1800s, the five-act structure has given way to other forms of division, the three-act play being one of the more common. Except for short or long plays, most can be adapted into the 120-minute feature film without requiring extensive cutting, condensing, or adding. With respect to length, the one-act play challenges the adapter in a way similar to the short story, and the very long play in a way similar to the novel. Adapters of stage plays often use the strategies employed by adapters of other genres to address the issue of length. To illustrate this point, we look at a short play.

The One-Act Play

Leroi Jones/Amiri Baraka's *Dutchman* is a one-act play first performed off-Broadway in 1964. It concerns Clay, a conservative-looking young black man who is riding a New York subway car when Lula, "a tall, slender, beautiful woman with long red hair" (5) enters, looking for trouble. Lula accosts Clay, baiting him into a conversation that involves equal parts sexual invitation and racial insult. After Clay answers Lula's sexual and racial challenges in an explosive speech, he tries to exit the subway car, only to be stabbed by Lula. His corpse is then carried off the train by other passengers who appear to be in conspiracy with her. The play ends with Lula sitting in a subway car about to approach its only other passenger—another twenty-year-old black man who is carrying books.

The film *Dutchman* (1966), directed by Anthony Harvey, was made two years later, at the height of the civil rights unrest in the United States. The adaptation stays close to the play. The dialogue is nearly verbatim, and the film, like the play, uses a subway car as a single set. The few exceptions include the opening shots of a deserted subway platform, Lula waiting, and the train arriving through a tunnel.

Al Freeman, Jr., as Clay and Shirley Knight as Lula in *Dutchman* (1966).

One major substitution occurs in casting. In Baraka's stage directions, there is a clear age difference between "Clay, [a] twenty-year-old Negro" and "Lula, [a] thirty-year-old white woman" (3). Clay is supposed to be a naïve young man who is susceptible to sudden entanglement with a bold, sexy, more experienced woman. In the film version, the age difference between Clay (Al Freeman, Jr., born in 1934), and Lula (Shirley Knight, born in 1936), is muted. Since Freeman was regarded as a fine actor, choosing him for the role is understandable, even though blurring the age difference makes Clay seem less vulnerable and Lula less predatory. At the end, when Baraka's stage directions require another black man of "about twenty," the actor cast in this role is clearly young, indicating that, when possible, Harvey tried to stay close to the play.

Another departure in the film is that Lula's conspiracy with the other passengers on the train is not explicitly stressed. In the play, she stabs Clay and then commands the passengers.

LULA
. . . Get this man off me! Hurry, now!

[*The others come and drag* CLAY'S *body down the aisle*]
Open the door and throw his body out.

[*They throw him off*]
And all of you get off at the next stop. (37)

In the film, Lula yells to passengers, "Get this man off me! Hurry!" but she does not order them to dump the body or to get off the train themselves. Instead, after the murder, the audience sees a brief medium shot of four white men carrying the victim's body that becomes an extreme close-up of the victim's head as they move toward the camera. Next there is a long shot of the train arriving in a station, and then several shots of an empty platform, moving trains, and finally an emptied subway car where Lula prepares to start the same routine with another victim. It is possible the lines of dialogue spelling out the passengers' complicity in the murder were dropped to make the action more plausible, or that the visual scene was intended to replace the lines. Whatever the case—except for a few added subway shots; the clangorous, maniacal percussion score by John Barry used at the beginning, middle, and end of the film; the use of camera shots from different angles and distances on the subway car set; a casting substitution; some dropped lines; and some elements of mise-en-scène such as the addition of subway poster ads—this is essentially a filmed stage play. There are no additions in the dialogue, no added characters or plot elements, no flashbacks, and no filming of incidents in locations other than those mentioned in the play. In most particulars, Harvey decided to stay close to this one-act play. In this case, staying close meant the production of a 55-minute film. Harvey fitted the running time of the film to the length of the one-act play.

Summary

Narratives can be divided into two parts: the "story" and the discourse. The "story" can be regarded as a structure that is independent of its medium and can be transposed from one discourse to another. It is important that adapters take into account the conventions of the antecedent story as well as of cinema itself. Fiction, drama, and film share many conventions, but they also possess distinctive conventions that make adaptation a challenge.

There are at least seven ways for an adapter to open up a play: Visualize (1) sets, (2) scenes, (3) characters, and (4) symbols only mentioned or implied in the play; (5) use the camera to move the story into cinema time and space; (6) erase act divisions; and (7) add a musical score. Film adaptations of stage plays can be identified on a spectrum that measures the degree of separation from stage conventions. At one end is the photographed stage play, and at the other end is a film that is fully opened up to cinematic conventions. However, a play does not have to be fully opened up to be a satisfying work of art.

Plays vary in length, generally from one to five acts, but the modern play does not usually require extensive cutting or adding to fit the constraints of the feature film. Since drama and film both tell stories in the framework of performance, the two forms may seem easy to adapt, but they are not. It is difficult to adapt closely the narrative elements of a play to a film drama because the conventions of the stage do not easily translate into cinematic time and space.

TOPICS FOR DISCUSSION

1. Visit the American Collection at the Masterpiece Theater Web site: www.pbs.org/wgbh/masterpiece/ americancollection/american/ntof. html. Three scenes from Henry James's *The American* are displayed in four different formats. Trace the evolution of one of these scenes from James's novel (1877) to his play (1890) to Michael Hastings's screenplay to the film adaptation (2001) directed by Paul Unwin. What changes are made in each version? Can you explain them in terms of changes in medium?

2. Choose one of the stage play–film pairings from the filmography and identify and illustrate which strategies are used to open up the play. Does the film visualize settings, scenes, characters, or symbols mentioned or implied in the play, use the camera and editing to move the story into cinematic time and space, and erase act divisions?

3. Study two or more film adaptations of stage plays. Using the static qualities of a photographed stage play as a measure, describe to what extent each play is opened up.

4. With the advent of sound films in 1927, filmmakers had to address Shakespeare's Elizabethan language. According to Manvell, the main problem for adapters of Shakespeare has been "the task of making his language . . . as clear and meaningful as possible" to a modern audience. The treatment of Shakespeare's language is one useful way to distinguish among the many film adaptations of his work. Read a passage of dialogue from one of Shakespeare's plays that has been adapted into a film and then view the corresponding scene or sequence from the film. How do the filmmakers translate Shakespeare's Elizabethan English? Do they keep it, revise it into modern English, or drop it altogether and replace it with nonverbal cinematic elements? What is the effect of the filmmakers' decision?

5. Contrast the 1951 and 1993 film releases of Elia Kazan's *A Streetcar Named Desire*. How did the censorship of the film affect the story? Which film version do you prefer?

WORKS CITED

ARP, THOMAS R., AND GREG JOHNSON, EDS. *Perrine's Literature: Structure, Sound and Sense*. 8th ed. New York: Harcourt, 2002.

DICK, BERNARD F. *Anatomy of Film*. 4th ed. Boston: Bedford/St. Martin's, 2002.

Dutchman. Dir. Anthony Harvey. Perf. Shirley Knight and Al Freeman, Jr. Gene Persson, 1967.

FULLER, CHARLES. *A Soldier's Play.* New York: Hill & Wang, 1982.

GIANNETTI, LOUIS. *Understanding Movies.* 9th ed. Upper Saddle River, NJ: Prentice Hall, 2002.

GOODMAN, GEORGE. "Black Theater: Must It Appeal to Whites?" *New York Times* 10 January 1982, late ed.: D1+.

JACKSON, RUSSELL. "Introduction: Shakespeare, Films and the Marketplace." *Shakespeare on Film.* Ed. Russell Jackson. Cambridge: Cambridge University Press, 2000. 1–12.

JAHN, MANFRED. 2002. *Poems, Plays, and Prose: A Guide to the Theory of Literary Genres.* English Department, University of Cologne. Version: 1.6. Date: April 10, 2002. www.uni-koeln.de/~ame02/ppp. htm.

JONES, LEROI. *Dutchman and the Slave.* New York: Apollo Editions, 1964.

LEFF, LEONARD J. "And Transfer to Cemetery: The Streetcars Named Desire." *Film Quarterly* 55 (Spring 2002): 29–38.

Long Day's Journey into Night. Dir. Sidney Lumet. Perf. Katherine Hepburn, Ralph Richardson, Jason Robards, and Dean Stockwell. 1962.

LUMET, SIDNEY. *Making Movies.* New York: Vintage, 1996.

MANVELL, ROGER. *Theater and Film.* Madison, NJ: Farleigh Dickinson Press, 1979.

NICOLL, ALLARDYCE. "Film Reality: The Cinema and the Theatre." *Film and Literature: Contrasts in Media.* Ed. Fred H. Marcus. Scranton: Chandler Publishing, 1971. 190–204.

O'NEILL, EUGENE. *Long Day's Journey into Night.* New Haven: Yale University Press, 1989.

PEARCE, CRAIG. Interview. *William Shakespeare's Romeo + Juliet (Special Edition).* Dir. Baz Luhrmann. Perf. Leonardo DiCaprio and Claire Danes. 1996. DVD. Twentieth Century Fox, 2002.

RICHIE, DONALD. *Japanese Cinema.* New York: Anchor, 1971.

SEGER, LINDA. *The Art of Adaptation: Turning Fact and Fiction into Film.* New York: Henry Holt, 1992.

A Soldier's Story. Dir. Norman Jewison. Perf. Howard E. Rollins, Jr., Adolph Caesar, and Denzel Washington. Columbia, 1984.

STORHOFF, GARY P. "Reflections of Identity in *A Soldier's Story.*" *Film/ Literature Quarterly* 19 (1991): 21–26.

A Streetcar Named Desire. Dir. Elia Kazan. Perf. Vivien Leigh, Marlon Brando, Kim Hunter, and Karl Malden. Warner Bros., 1951.

Throne of Blood. Dir. Akira Kurosawa. Perf. Toshiro Mifune, Isuzo Yamada. Toho, 1957.

WILLIAMS, TENNESSEE. *A Streetcar Named Desire.* New York: NAL, 1974.

■■■ SELECTED FILMOGRAPHY OF DRAMA ADAPTATIONS

EDWARD ALBEE. *Who's Afraid of Virgina Woolf?* (1961–1962).

MIKE NICHOLS. *Who's Afraid of Virgina Woolf?* (1966).

ROBERT ANDERSON. *Tea and Sympathy* (1953).

VINCENT MINNELLI. *Tea and Sympathy* (1956).

ROBERT BOLT. *A Man for All Seasons* (1960).

FRED ZINNEMANN. *A Man for All Seasons* (1966).

ANTON CHEKHOV. *Uncle Vanya* (1896).

LOUIS MALLE. *Vanya on 42nd Street* (1994).

AGATHA CHRISTIE. *Witness for the Prosecution* (1954).

BILLY WILDER. *Witness for the Prosecution* (1957).

MICHAEL FRAYN. *Noises Off* (1982).

PETER BOGDANOVITCH. *Noises Off* (1992).

JOHN GAY. *The Beggar's Opera* (1728).

PETER BROOK. *The Beggar's Opera* (UK 1953).

JEAN GENET. *The Balcony* (1957).

JOSEPH STRICK. *The Balcony* (1963).

LEONARD GERSHE. *Butterflies Are Free* (1969).

MILTON KATSELAS. *Butterflies Are Free* (1972).

WILLIAM GIBSON. *The Miracle Worker* (1957).

ARTHUR PENN. *The Miracle Worker* (1962).

JAMES GOLDMAN. *The Lion in Winter* (1966).

ANTHONY HARVEY. *The Lion in Winter* (UK 1968).

JOHN GUARE. *Six Degrees of Separation* (1990).

FRED SCHEPISI. *Six Degrees of Separation* (1993).

PATRICK HAMILTON. *Gaslight* (1938).

ALFRED HITCHCOCK. *Rope* (1948).

LORRAINE HANSBERRY. *A Raisin in the Sun* (1959).

DANIEL PETRIE. *A Raisin in the Sun* (1961).

RONALD HARWOOD. *The Dresser* (1983).

PETER YATES. *The Dresser* (UK 1983).

BEN HECHT AND CHARLES MACARTHUR. *The Front Page* (1928).

HOWARD HAWKS. *His Girl Friday* (1940).

LILLIAN HELLMAN. *The Children's Hour* (1934).

WILLIAM WYLER. *The Children's Hour* (1961).

LILLIAN HELLMAN. *The Little Foxes* (1939).

WILLIAM WYLER. *The Little Foxes.* (1941).

LILLIAN HELLMAN. *Watch on the Rhine* (1914).

HERMAN SHUMLIN. *Watch on the Rhine* (1943).

BETH HENLEY. *Crimes of the Heart* (1979).

BRUCE BERESFORD. *Crimes of the Heart* (1986).

HENRIK IBSEN. *A Doll's House* (1879).

JOSEPH LOSEY. *A Doll's House* (UK 1973).

WILLIAM INGE. *Picnic* (1952).

JOSHUA LOGAN. *Picnic* (1955).

DAVID MAMET. *Glengarry Glen Ross* (1992).

JAMES FOLEY. *Glengarry Glen Ross* (1992).

DAVID MAMET. *Oleanna* (1992).
DAVID MAMET. *Oleanna* (1994).

W. SOMERSET MAUGHAM. *The Letter* (1927).
WILLIAM WYLER. *The Letter* (1940).

TERRENCE MCNALLY. *Frankie and Johnny* (1987).
GARRY MARSHALL. *Frankie and Johnny* (1991).

ARTHUR MILLER. *The Crucible* (1953).
Nicholas Hyter. *The Crucible* (1996).

ARTHUR MILLER. *Death of a Salesman* (1949).
LÁSZLÓ BENEDEK. *Death of a Salesman* (1951).
VOLKER SCHLÖNDORFF. *Death of a Salesman* (1985).

FERENC MOLNÁR. *One, Two, Three* (1930).
BILLY WILDER. *One, Two, Three* (1961).

MARSHA NORMAN. *'Night, Mother* (1983).
TOM MOORE. *'Night, Mother* (1986).

CLIFFORD ODETS. *The Country Girl* (1950).
GEORGE SEATON. *The Country Girl* (1954).

EUGENE O'NEILL. *The Iceman Cometh* (1939).
JOHN FRANKENHEIMER. *The Iceman Cometh* (1973).

JOHN OSBORNE. *Look Back in Anger* (1956).
TONY RICHARDSON. *Look Back in Anger* (UK 1958).

HAROLD PINTER. *Betrayal* (1978).
DAVID HUGH JONES. *Betrayal* (UK 1983).

DAVID RABE. *Hurlyburly* (1984)
ANTHONY DRAZEN. *Hurlyburly* (1998).

REGINALD ROSE. *Twelve Angry Men* (1957).
SIDNEY LUMET. *Twelve Angry Men* (1957).

EDMUND ROSTAND. *Cyrano de Bergerac* (1950).
JEAN-PAUL RAPPENEAU. *Cyrano de Bergerac* (Fr. 1990).

ANTHONY SHAFFER. *Sleuth* (1953).
JOSEPH L. MANKIEWICZ. *Sleuth* (UK 1972).

PETER SHAFFER. *Amadeus* (1979).
MILOS FORMAN. *Amadeus* (1984).

PETER SHAFFER. *Equus.* (1973)
SIDNEY LUMET. *Equus* (1977).

WILLIAM SHAKESPEARE. *Hamlet* (1600).
LAURENCE OLIVIER. *Hamlet* (UK 1948).
TONY RICHARDSON. *Hamlet* (UK 1969).
FRANCO ZEFFIRELLI. *Hamlet* (1990).
KENNETH BRANAGH. *Hamlet* (UK 1996).
MICHAEL ALMEREYDA. *Hamlet* (2000).

WILLIAM SHAKESPEARE. *Henry V* (1597–1599).
LAURENCE OLIVIER. *Henry V* (UK 1945).
KENNETH BRANAGH. *Henry V* (UK 1989).

WILLIAM SHAKESPEARE. *Julius Caesar* (1599).
JOSEPH L. MANKIEWICZ. *Julius Caesar* (1953).

WILLIAM SHAKESPEARE. *King Lear* (1605).
PETER BROOK. *King Lear* (UK 1971).

WILLIAM SHAKESPEARE. *Macbeth* (1600).
ORSON WELLES. *Macbeth* (1948).
AKIRA KUROSAWA. *Throne of Blood* (Jap. 1957).

WILLIAM SHAKESPEARE. *Much Ado About Nothing* (1598).
KENNETH BRANAGH. *Much Ado About Nothing* (UK 1993).

WILLIAM SHAKESPEARE. *Othello* (1602–1603).
ORSON WELLES. *Othello* (1952).
TIM BLAKE NELSON. *O* (2001).

WILLIAM SHAKESPEARE. *Richard III* (1592–93).
LAURENCE OLIVIER. *Richard III* (UK 1955).
RICHARD LONCRAINE. *Richard III* (UK 1995).

WILLIAM SHAKESPEARE. *Romeo and Juliet* (1594).
FRANCO ZEFFIRELLI. *Romeo and Juliet* (UK 1968).
BAZ LUHRMANN. *Romeo + Juliet* (1996).

WILLIAM SHAKESPEARE. *The Taming of the Shrew* (1593–1594).
FRANCO ZEFFIRELLI. *The Taming of the Shrew* (It. 1967).

WILLIAM SHAKESPEARE. *Titus Andronicus* (1593–1594).
JULIE TAYMOR. *Titus* (1999).

WILLIAM SHAKESPEARE. *Twelfth Night* (1601–1602).
TREVOR NUNN. *Twelfth Night* (UK 1996).

NEIL SIMON. *Barefoot in the Park* (1963).
GENE SAKS. *Barefoot in the Park* (1967).

TOM STOPPARD. *Rosencrantz and Guildenstern Are Dead* (1966).
TOM STOPPARD. *Rosencrantz and Guildenstern Are Dead* (1990).

AUGUST STRINDBERG. *Miss Julie* (1888).
ALF SJÖBERG. *Miss Julie* (Swed., 1951).
MIKE FIGGIS. *Miss Julie* (1999).

ALFRED UHRY. *Driving Miss Daisy* (1987).
BRUCE BERESFORD. *Driving Miss Daisy* (1989).

OSCAR WILDE. *An Ideal Husband* (1895).
ALEXANDER KORDA. *An Ideal Husband* (UK 1947).
OLIVER PARKER. *An Ideal Husband* (1999).

OSCAR WILDE. *The Importance of Being Earnest* (1895).
ANTHONY ASQUITH. *The Importance of Being Earnest* (UK 1952).
OLIVER PARKER. *The Importance of Being Earnest* (UK 2002)

THORNTON WILDER. *Our Town* (1938).
SAM WOOD. *Our Town* (1940).

TENNESSEE WILLIAMS. *Cat on a Hot Tin Roof* (1955).
RICHARD BROOKS. *Cat on a Hot Tin Roof* (1958).

TENNESSEE WILLIAMS. *The Glass Menagerie* (1944).
IRVING RAPPER. *The Glass Menagerie* (1950).
PAUL NEWMAN. *The Glass Menagerie* (1987).

TENNESSEE WILLIAMS. *The Night of the Iguana* (1961).
JOHN HUSTON. *The Night of the Iguana* (1964).

TENNESSEE WILLIAMS. *Suddenly, Last Summer* (1958).
JOSEPH L. MANKIEWICZ. *Suddenly, Last Summer* (1959).

TENNESSEE WILLIAMS. *Sweet Bird of Youth* (1959).
RICHARD BROOKS. *Sweet Bird of Youth* (1962).

8 NONFICTION

The previous three chapters discuss how the novel, novella, short story, and play have been adapted to film. Despite the differences among the three genres, they all share one important element: their stories present imagined rather than actual events and people. That distinction is the primary difference between works of fiction and nonfiction. In this chapter, we present a brief overview of how to analyze the adaptation of nonfiction literature in general.

Nonfiction takes many forms, but filmmakers commonly adapt only a few types: biographies, journalism, and memoirs. Each type presents people, places, and events that, like the elements of fictional stories, can be adapted into narrative film. Biographies that have been adapted include the prose narrative *A Beautiful Mind* and the play *The Miracle Worker*. Journalistic works that have been adapted include *Crime on the Labor Front* (*On the Waterfront*), *Fear and Loathing in Las Vegas*, *The Great Locomotive Chase in Georgia* (*The General*), *In Cold Blood*, and *The Perfect Storm*. Memoirs that have been adapted include *Basketball Diaries; Guadalcanal Diary, Girl, Interrupted; I Know Why the Caged Bird Sings; Elegy for Iris; This Boy's Life;* and *True North.*

The film produced by the adaptation of a nonfiction literary text is neither wholly a **documentary**—a nonfiction film that claims to depict actual people, places, and events that exist in the world beyond the film—nor wholly a fiction film, which portrays imagined characters, settings, and actions. Instead, it is a hybrid of the two. Like a documentary, the film claims to depict actual people, places, and events. Like a fiction film, it is produced with actors rather than actual people, with substituted rather than actual places and things, and with staged events rather than recorded actual events. In addition, imagined characters, places, things, and events can be inserted into the film. Bordwell and Thompson call this hybrid form a **historical film,** and Steve Lipkin calls it a **docudrama.**

Lipkin explains the docudrama:

> Due to the hybrid nature of its form, docudrama demands a particular kind of suspension of disbelief from its audience. . . . We are asked to accept that, in this case, re-creation is a necessary mode of presentation. If we accept the historical substance of pre-filmic events, then we are also asked to grant that these might have happened in much the way we are about to see them depicted. ("Quiz Show" 1, 4)

In order to link the actual and the re-created in docudramas, filmmakers persuade the viewer, as Lipkin says, "of [the film's] connections to actuality [. . . through] one of several possible links between [that] actuality and [its] re-creation" (*Real* 12). Lipkin explains three strategies by which the film makes "connections to actuality." In the **model strategy,** (1) actors are made to resemble the actual people; (2) places and things are made to resemble actual places and things; and (3) the staged events are made to resemble the actual historical events.

The second strategy for linking the actual and the re-created is for footage of events, people, places, and things to be inserted into the film either before or after footage of actors, substituted places and things, and staged events. Lipkin calls this the **sequence strategy.**

The third strategy is for the actual and the re-created to appear simultaneously on the screen, as when an actor is filmed while walking at the actual place where the events occurred. Lipkin calls this approach the **interaction strategy.** Each strategy represents a closing of the gap between the actual and the re-created (*Real* 13).

These three strategies are used in *All the President's Men* (1976), directed by Alan J. Pakula, an adaptation of Carl Bernstein's and Bob Woodward's *All the President's Men* (1974). The book chronicles the efforts of Bernstein and Woodward, both then reporters for the *Washington Post,* to gather information and to write news stories about the Watergate scandal that eventually led to Richard

Carl Bernstein and Bob Woodward, authors of the book *All The President's Men* (1974), at the premiere of the film *All The President's Men,* April 5, 1976.

Nixon's resignation from the presidency. To begin with, the film had to have the same title as the nonfiction work because to do otherwise would jeopardize the film's connection with the widely read, best-selling book—a connection necessary, at least at the time of the film's release, to bring the many readers of the book into the theaters.

Examples of the model strategy can be found in the plot, characters, and setting. The plot of the film follows the chronological narrative of the book because many viewers already knew from the book how Bernstein and Woodward gathered their information and wrote their articles. Dustin Hoffman, Robert Redford, and Jason Robards are made to resemble in physical appearance, costume, makeup, and behavior their real-life counterparts—Bernstein, Woodward, and their executive editor Ben Bradlee—because all three newspapermen had often been pictured. However, actors playing people who were lesser known did not have to resemble their real life counterparts. Although not generally well known and only somewhat described in the book, the set of the *Washington Post* newsroom is built to resemble the actual newsroom, from the florescent lighting to the trash baskets, further authenticating the set and linking the film to an actual place.

Examples of the sequence strategy can be found in the actual TV news footage integrated into the film. For instance, at the beginning of the film, there is an extreme close-up of the typing of a dateline accompanied by the extremely

Robert Redford and
Dustin Hoffman as
Bob Woodward and
Carl Bernstein in the
film *All The President's
Men* (1976) illustrate
Steve Lipkin's model
strategy.

loud sound of the typewriter keys striking a paper surface, then actual TV news
footage of President Richard Nixon arriving by helicopter at night to address a
joint session of Congress, followed by a sequence re-creating the night break-in
at the National Democratic Headquarters inside the Watergate building. Later in
the film, Bernstein, Woodward, Bradlee, and other editors watch on television
actual news footage of Vice President Spiro Agnew denying certain statements
made in a *Washington Post* story written by Bernstein and Woodward.

Examples of the interaction strategy can be found in the use of places
where Bernstein and Woodward work. Hoffman and Redford are shown driving through the streets of Washington, D.C. In a *high-angle shot*, the city's tall
buildings dwarf Woodward's subcompact car. The size contrast between the
car carrying the reporters and the buildings housing the government employees involved in the Watergate affair suggests the immensity of Bernstein and
Woodward's task. Later, they climb up several steps of the Library of Congress.
In the *long shot*, Bernstein bounds up the steps way ahead of Woodward, who
walks slowly and deliberately. The placement of the two figures and their
method of walking in this historical political center suggest their contrary
approaches to the investigation: Bernstein almost recklessly hastens ahead, and
Woodward cautiously lags behind. Taken together the three strategies link the
film to Bernstein and Woodward's chronicle and to the actual people, places,
and events involved in the reporters' investigation of the Watergate scandal.

With Lipkin's definition of docudrama in mind, we will illustrate how filmmakers adapt nonfiction literary texts into docudramas by focusing on (1) Richard
N. Goodwin's short memoir/journalistic/narrative essay, "Investigating the

Quiz Shows," a chapter from his book *Remembering America: A Voice from the Sixties,* and Robert Redford's adaptation *Quiz Show;* and (2) Truman Capote's book-length literary-journalism piece *In Cold Blood* and Richard Brooks's adaptation of the same title. "Investigating the Quiz Shows" and *Quiz Show* concern a congressional investigation and exposure of fraud in 1950s television quiz shows. Note that the discussion is not meant to be comprehensive. You have plenty of room for your own analysis and interpretation.

"INVESTIGATING THE QUIZ SHOWS" (1988), by Richard N. Goodwin

Goodwin's "Investigating the Quiz Shows" combines several categories of nonfiction into one text. First, it is an *essay*—"a moral tale [of fraud and frustration], that, to this day engages the energies of aspiring authors" (44). Second, it is a *memoir,* or a narrative recalling a specific time in the author's life, namely, Goodwin's active involvement in exposing the quiz show scandal. Third, it is a journalistic report of how and why the scandal happened, and of a unique moment in United States history when television was beginning to be successful.

This memoir/journalistic essay is short and, as in a short story, the plot is compact. The characters are few and their personalities undeveloped. The theme emerges from the events described with only brief analysis by the narrator.

The fraud of Goodwin's tale involves the quiz show contestants being "cajoled," "coerced," and "seduced" into cheating by the shows' producers. The frustration is Goodwin's disappointing and embarrassing realization that acting in a politically rational way to protect the reputations of others, such as Charles Van Doren, is not always possible.

Goodwin begins the essay by explaining his position as a lawyer-investigator for the House Subcommittee on Legislative Oversight. He then explains how and why he urged the committee to look into the records of a New York grand jury investigation of fraudulent activities on television quiz shows that had been impounded by Judge Mitchell Schweitzer with "no indictments, no charges of wrongdoing, and no public disclosure of the evidence" (43).

As background to the situation, Goodwin summarizes the origins, formats, sponsorships, and successes of the 1950s quiz shows, especially *The $64,000 Question* and *Twenty-One.* He recounts how he traveled from Washington to New York City in 1959 and, with the help of Assistant District Attorney Joe Stone, easily obtained—to his surprise and satisfaction—the impounded records of the grand jury investigation. In the records, he found enough evidence to suggest to the committee that it launch a congressional investigation into the quiz shows.

The body of the essay narrates this investigation. Goodwin met with Van Doren, Herb Stemple, and other quiz show contestants. He immediately disliked Stemple and liked Van Doren. He tried to protect the latter from having to testify before the congressional committee so as to save his reputation as a well-known professor and cultural commentator. Goodwin suggested to Van Doren that he make no public statements about his involvement in the quiz show. However, forced by NBC to make a statement or lose his job on the *Today Show,* Van Doren publicly denied "he had ever been supplied questions or answers during his appearances on *Twenty-One*" (56). Van Doren's statement forced the committee's hand—it had to subpoena him, and Goodwin delivered the subpoena to Van Doren in person. Like the other contestants on the quiz show, Stemple among them, Van Doren appeared before the committee. He reversed his earlier statement and admitted to fraud.

Goodwin concludes his journalistic report of how and why the fraud happened by relating that eventually producers, representatives of the sponsors, and network executives also appeared before the committee, admitted to knowing little or nothing about the fraud, and fired those involved. Goodwin concludes his essay by suggesting that while the manipulation of the quiz show contestants had not broken the law, it had, in the words of the *Washington Post,* " 'nevertheless robbed people of a kind of faith which is dangerous to destroy in a democracy' " (62). This "robbery," Goodwin observes, "violated our misplaced trust in the guardians of the swelling electronic media, and mocked our libidinous urge to believe in their newly revealed breed of intellectual heroes" (62–3). Goodwin concludes his memoir by stating that his work during the congressional investigation brought him to the attention of those involved in the budding presidential campaign of then Senator John F. Kennedy. He was asked to leave the House Subcommittee on Legislative Oversight and join the Kennedy campaign, which he did.

Goodwin states he liked most but not all of the people whom he met during his involvement in the congressional investigation. For example, Goodwin describes Assistant District Attorney Joe Stone, who helped him obtain the release of the impounded grand jury records from Judge Mitchell Schweitzer, as a model civil servant. He was "diligent, experienced, incorruptible, . . . [without] sign of resentment at my unmasked intrusion, [and with] no hint of . . . condescension" (46). Charles Van Doren is a model aristocratic gentleman, whose "sincerity, honesty, and integrity . . . infused his manner. Courtesy without submission, exposition without resentment. I liked the man; began to doubt my own conviction that he was lying. . . . I wanted to believe Van Doren" (48–9). Herb Stemple, who originally instigated the grand jury investigation into the quiz show in New York City and later was a principal witness in the congressional investigation, is from a "working-class background, a family in the anonymous lower reaches of the social structure, whose otherwise unremarkable history had contained some code of DNA gifting [him] with a remarkable spacious memory" (49). Stemple, according to Goodwin, felt himself much smarter than Van Doren yet had to "lose" to him in a rigged contest in order for the quiz show to present a new winner to its viewing public. "Unable to contain his mounting anger/envy/frustration, Stemple was determined to tell his story, to expose this overprivileged fraud even at the cost of admitting his own. . . . [He was a] disgruntled, disheveled, unstable individual" (50).

Goodwin writes the essay in the first person. He does not pretend to the objectivity associated with expository or argumentative essays, traditional journalism, and some histories. Instead, he appears to be a subjective, discerning sensibility responding to the situation about which he is writing. The reader becomes aware of Goodwin's suspicions concerning Judge Schweitzer's impounding of the grand jury records, his surprise and satisfaction at obtaining the records, his energy in interviewing contestants, his dislike of Stemple, his admiration for Van Doren, his disgust at corporate TV executives, and his pleasure at being asked to join the Kennedy campaign.

The setting in which the congressional hearings are held and in which Goodwin conducts his interviews of contestants and other participating parties in the quiz shows is barely sketched at all. However, two brief mentions of Goodwin's home in relation to both Stemple and Van Doren symbolically indicate Goodwin's attitude toward both men. Goodwin says that Stemple "turned up unexpectedly at my Washington home," while he says that he "invited Van Doren, his wife, Gerry, his father, the Pulitzer Prize–winning poet Mark Van Doren, and Joe Stone to my home for a quiet dinner to go over the details of the next day" (51, 57). According to Goodwin, the working-class stiff barges in, whereas the gentleman and scholar is invited in.

QUIZ SHOW (1994), Directed by Robert Redford

Goodwin's essay is short. Thus, in order for the filmmakers to adapt it, they must add or expand narrative elements to make it fit the average running time of the feature film. They accomplish this by using the interweaving strategy explained in Chapter 6. They keep most of the elements of narrative from the essay, drop a few elements, disperse the kept elements throughout the film (although not necessarily in their original order), and interweave either invented elements or invented expansions on already existing elements.

Most of the narrative elements in Goodwin's essay are kept. The film keeps the people Goodwin meets (except attorney Joe Stone and Dr. Joyce Brothers and her husband); the places in Washington and New York that Goodwin mentions; the basic events of the investigation as reported by Goodwin; Goodwin's varying points of view on the impounding of the grand jury records by Judge Schweitzer, and on Herb Stemple, Charles Van Doren, and corporate executives; the Sputnik reference that claims "American technology and intellectual superiority had fallen into 'the dust bin of history' "; and the notions that contestants on the quiz shows were strongly influenced into committing fraud and that protecting the reputation of others is not always possible.

Ralph Fiennes as Charles Van Doren and Rob Morrow as Dick Goodwin in *Quiz Show* (1994) also illustrate Lipkin's model strategy.

The narrative elements retained by the film assist in linking the congressional investigation of the quiz-show scandal as reported by Goodwin and the reenactment of that investigation in the film. The film persuades the viewer of the correlation through Lipkin's *model strategy,* although it is less extensively used here than in *All the President's Men.* With this strategy, actors, places, and events are made to resemble their actual counterparts in the world beyond the film. For example, the actors Ralph Fiennes and especially John Turturro resemble the contestants Van Doren and Stemple. Fiennes's light hair, tailored suits, and relaxed deportment suggest Van Doren's graceful appearance and calm manner, while Turturro's unkempt hair, blockish eyeglasses, ill-fitting suits, and anxious behavior evoke Stemple's awkward appearance and nervous manner. Sets are constructed to resemble the courtroom where Goodwin appears before Judge Schweitzer, the hearing room where Stemple and Van Doren appear before a congressional committee, and the television sound stage where the quiz show is produced. Judging from actual photographs of the *Twenty-One* stage, the stage in the film seems a convincing replica, from the contestants' sound booths to the moderator's podium.

With the exception of some original TV footage that appears early in the film, the filmmakers do not use Lipkin's sequence strategy. Nor does the film use the interaction strategy in which actors are shown inhabiting the places where the historical events occurred. Instead, actors walk on generic city streets filled with period vehicles that suggest New York in the 1950s. We can infer from this that the filmmakers of *Quiz Show* were not as intent as the makers of *All the President's Men* on persuading viewers of the film's connections to actual historical events. The quiz show scandal happened almost forty years before the film was released, and these events were not as significant as, say, the Kennedy assassination or the Watergate affair, images of which still remain in the national consciousness. The remoteness of both the scandal and its memory gave the filmmakers the freedom not to connect the details of the actuality to its re-creation as fully as some other docudramas do.

Some minor details of the investigation are dropped from the film. These include Charles Van Doren's thank you letter to Richard Goodwin, the role of Dr. Joyce Brothers and her husband, and the NBC cafeteria where Goodwin and Van Doren first met. In the film, the thank you letter is substituted by a friendly nod from Van Doren to Goodwin outside the Capitol building after the congressional hearing in which Van Doren admits to fraud. Brothers did not cheat on *The $64,000 Question,* and Goodwin's interview with her and her husband is pleasant but not informative and does not advance the plot. Goodwin and Van Doren first meet elsewhere, but it really does not matter where.

However, major details of the investigation are also dropped from the film. These include the Greenwich Village cocktail party where Stemple meets the *Twenty-One* producers; Judge Schweitzer's release of the results of the grand jury investigation to Goodwin; Assistant District Attorney Joe Stone; the subject of *The $64,000 Question;* and Mark Van Doren's refusal to believe his son's fraud. Since we do not see how the producers recruit Stemple, we do not learn, according to Goodwin, how he was seduced and manipulated into committing fraud. Since we do not see Judge Schweitzer release the grand jury results and Stone consult with Goodwin, we do not learn, again according to Goodwin, that both of these men cooperate with the congressional investigation. Since we do not see the other quiz show, we do not learn, as Goodwin claims, the extensiveness of the fraud. Since we do not witness Mark Van Doren's refusal to believe his son's fraud, we do not learn, as stated by Goodwin, the depth of family tensions caused by Charles Van Doren's revelations.

Many elements of narrative are added. They include:

Opening sequence of film set in automobile showroom
Dramatization of basic facts explained by Goodwin
Chronological presentation of Stemple's rise and fall and Van Doren's rise and fall
Goodwin's wife
Stemple's triumphant return to Queens after a successful performance on show
Stemple's wife and son at home
Van Doren's interview with Enright and Freedman and their convincing him to appear on the show
Stemple informing his wife that he is to lose to Van Doren by not answering a question
Episode in which Stemple loses and Van Doren wins
Stemple's loss of his winnings from the show and his need for money

Goodwin proposing to the House Subcommittee's chairperson to put
    television on trial
Judge Schweitzer's denying Goodwin's request for the release of the
    results of the grand jury investigation
Goodwin interviewing several of the show's contestants
Dave Garroway interviewing Van Doren on the *Today Show*
Van Doren arriving at Columbia in a limousine
Van Doren snubbing Stemple after Van Doren defeats Stemple on *Twenty-One*
Goodwin contacting Enright
Goodwin interviewing Stemple at Stemple's home
Goodwin visiting Van Doren at Mark Van Doren's birthday party, where
    guests include Edmund Wilson and Thomas Merton
Goodwin interviewing Enright and Freedman in Enright's office, where
    Enright informs Goodwin that he taped Stemple's challenge to him,
    plays the tape for Goodwin, and reveals that NBC paid for Stemple's
    psychiatric treatments
Stemple revealing to Goodman and his wife that he was given the answers
    to the questions before the show and his wife's disgust with him
Goodwin at a card game with Van Doren and others during which
    Goodwin accuses Van Doren of lying about the cards in his hand and
    Van Doren counters that he is bluffing, not lying
Goodwin watching kinescope episode of *Twenty-One* in which Snodgrass
    appears to give correct answer to question, much to Jack Barry's surprise
    and consternation
Van Doren losing on *Twenty-One* and Goodwin, who is in the audience,
    noticing Van Doren's grin of relief and delight
Stemple's self-centered preparations for congressional committee hearing,
    including his insistence that Van Doren knew the questions beforehand
Van Doren confessing to his father that he knew the questions beforehand
Dramatization of Van Doren's prepared statement before the
    congressional committee
Goodwin's final statement that "the committee set out to get television but
    television got us"

These invented elements and expansions on already existing elements are
the filmmakers' contribution to the conversation about the quiz show scandals.
As Lipkin remarks about some of these additions:

The film departs from the general tenor of printed accounts and establishes a more
unique perspective by underlining Stemple's Jewishness and his claims of anti-
Semitism in the rigging of the shows. The film foregrounds Stemple's ethnicity. . . .
Class and ethnic similarities between Stemple, Van Doren, and Goodwin emerge
strongly in subsequent scenes. . . . *Quiz Show* further departs from established
historical accounts by asserting that Van Doren was, in fact, intellectually and visually

comparable to the scandal's primary investigator [Goodwin]. Scenes scrupulously give "Charlie" and "Dick" equal visual weight as they test each other. (*Real* 28–9)

Some of the additions to the film emphasize the ethnic and social differences between Stemple and Van Doren and acknowledge the presence of anti-Semitism in the world of television at that time.

Quiz Show is an adaptation of a nonfiction literary text. Goodwin's essay is based on an actual prior event about which he, other principal participants, and historians have reported. Thus, the film can be compared not only with Goodwin's report but also with other reports to discover what elements are confirmed or contradicted among them. Through such comparisons, readers of the reports and viewers of the film can develop a more comprehensive understanding of the historical events given the inconsistencies of subjective accounts, and they can learn how filmmakers work with such accounts. Crucial to such a comparison are the narrative elements dropped or added to the film, especially the invented or expanded elements.

The second scene of the film, which shows the 1950s television audience's enthusiasm for watching quiz shows such as *Twenty-One,* offers an example of expansion. Goodwin explains that, "[t]he quiz shows were the most extraordinary phenomenon in the history of television. Neither before nor since has any contrivance of the tube so absorbed the fascinated contemplation of the public" (44). The film's scene dramatizes that statement by showing armored-car guards transporting a sealed envelope containing the questions and answers for the *Twenty-One* contestants from a safe-deposit box in a bank vault to the NBC quiz-show studio at 30 Rockefeller Center in New York City. Their trip is interspersed with several glimpses of people rushing along the streets and into bars and apartments to watch the quiz show on television.

An example of an addition not grounded in the essay is Goodwin's attendance at Mark Van Doren's birthday party, and his obvious enthrallment with the Van Doren family and their renowned friends, including Edmund Wilson. Goodwin explains, "I liked the man; began to doubt my own conviction that he was lying. I had accumulated a great deal of evidence that contradicted him. Not conclusively. Not beyond doubt. But very substantial. Yes, damn it, I wanted to believe Van Doren" (48–9). The film's birthday party scene does not correspond to a similar scene in Goodwin's essay, but it does not contradict Goodwin's expression that he "liked the man." The film attempts to dramatize Goodwin's affection and the moral dilemma the friendship creates for him.

Judge Schweitzer's denial of Goodwin's request for the release of the results of the grand jury investigation offers an example of a contradictory addition. In the essay, Goodwin reports that after he formally requested the records of the grand jury investigation, Judge Schweitzer said, "[h]e would accept and consider the motion, meaning, as happened shortly thereafter, they would be released to the committee" (47).

Some of the added narrative elements that do not correspond to Goodwin's essay do correspond to another account of the quiz show scandal. Chapter 43 of

The Fifties, written by David Halberstam, and published in 1993, the year before the release of *Quiz Show,* gives a similar account of the scandal and even mentions Goodwin. For example, Halberstam explains that "[s]ome guests would be put through dry runs only to find that when they appeared on the live shows, the questions were remarkably similar to the ones they had answered correctly in the rehearsal" (648). Such a scene appears in *Quiz Show.* Again, Halberstam writes, "Freedman, sensing that Van Doren's love of teaching was critical to turning him, began to emphasize how much he might help the world of education and the teachers of America by coming on board" (652). Again, such a scene appears in the film. Halberstam mentions that Stemple "squandered . . . his prize money in a series of bad investments" (658). In the film, Stemple tells Enright of these bad investments in the latter's office. Halberstam also mentions that Van Doren told Goodwin about his writing a novel and asking his father, Mark Van Doren, to help him revise and edit it (656). That dialogue appears in the film. In the Works Cited page for Chapter 43, Halberstam refers to author interviews with Enright, Freedman, Goodwin, and to other interviews conducted with Charles Van Doren. Thus, there was more information about the scandal involving *Twenty-One* than Goodwin mentioned in his essay. If Halberstam learned of it, the filmmakers could have also learned of it—independently of Halberstam or with his help.

Yet, while Halberstam's account of the quiz show scandal corresponds to some of the film's added narrative elements, it does not account for all of them, and it does not contradict what film critics and reporters have cited as inaccurate and even fictional events appearing in the film. Richard Zoglin, in his article "Why *Quiz Show* Is a Scandal," in *Time Magazine,* states:

> [t]he film has drawn fire for its historical inaccuracies—and indeed, events spanning nearly three years have been telescoped into a few weeks, while the role of investigator Richard Goodwin has been vastly exaggerated. But the real problem is the easy Hollywood clichés into which history has been transformed. The Van Doren clan is a caricature of effete Waspishness, Goodwin is a garden-variety TV-movie crusader, Herb Stemple . . . is reborn as perhaps the most offensively stereotyped Jew in modern American cinema. To engage the injustice, one has to go back to the actual tapes of Van Doren and Stemple on *Twenty-One.* Van Doren's theatrical groping for answers today looks phony, while Stemple's stolid awkwardness is rather ingratiating. (2)

Desson Howe, in his article "Quiz Show,"which appeared in the *Washington Post,* echoes Zoglin's criticism of the film:

> Redford, who had a controlling hand in the script, has not forgotten what *All the President's Men* did for him. *Quiz Show,* with [Rob] Morrow as the intrepid investigator, is a detective story full of familiar Watergate patterns: the late-night poring over lists of potential sources, the confrontations with tight-lipped witnesses at their front doors, the publicly inaccessible authority that needs toppling. . . .
> In interviews, Redford and company have taken disingenuous refuge behind the poetic-license clause. But when a high-minded movie dips into history to make

implications about America and asks to be taken seriously, it cannot escape certain responsibilities. In a film that takes exception to deception (or dramatic manipulation) in the name of entertainment, it's more than a little ironic that *Quiz Show* . . . pulls the same kind of wool over your eyes. (2)

John Horn, an Associated Press entertainment writer, in his article "*Quiz Show* Gives False Picture of Scandal" written for the *Times-Picayune,* interviews several of the quiz show scandal principals who criticize the accuracy of the film. "From invented dialogue to fabricated court transactions," Horn writes, "*Quiz Show* often takes broad dramatic license. . . . 'As the movie sits,' says Don Enright, son of Dan Enright, 'it is now a half-truth, and a half-truth is the blackest of lies, because it's based on fact and it's impossible to fight.' " Albert Freedman, another Horn interviewee, claims, "[a]ll my conversations (in the movie) were fiction." 'As far as I am concerned, the movie is a farce,' says Judge Joseph Stone, listing a variety of errors, large and small [and stating he] is especially bothered by the film's lionizing of Goodwin, who, Stone says, was a minor player in the scandal and never did half of what he is shown doing." Horn reports that

> Redford and screenwriter Paul Attanasio have said the fictional elements were added to make the story more dramatic and instructive. . . . Attanasio has said he and Redford wanted a "detective story" and had to create one because it wasn't there. Goodwin, similarly, has admitted the film is not "completely accurate." Redford has said he used "dramatic license to make either a moral point or an ethical point and not move too far out of what could possibly have happened." (2–3).

From a historical point of view, there are two main "lies" in the film. One is that Judge Schweitzer did *not* give Goodwin the grand jury proceedings, when, in fact, he did. The second is that Goodwin was a major participant in the quiz show investigation, when, in fact, he wasn't. However, from an artistic point of view, the two "lies" are justified, according to Redford, in order to make a more engaging and dramatic film.

Thus, viewers of *Quiz Show* beware. To return to Lipkin's observation on the credibility of docudrama quoted at the beginning of the chapter:

> Due to the hybrid nature of its form, docudrama demands a particular kind of suspension of disbelief from its audience. . . . We are asked to accept that, in this case, re-creation is a necessary mode of presentation. If we accept the historical substance of pre-filmic events, then we are also asked to grant that these might have happened in much the way we are about to see them depicted. ("Quiz Show" 1, 4)

In *Quiz Show,* viewers are asked to grant credence to apparent historical substance that is actually fiction.

The adaptation of Truman Capote's *In Cold Blood* into the film of the same title (directed by Richard Brooks) presents us not only with another example of the adaptation of nonfiction literature, but also with the rare opportunity to learn of the reactions of an author to the adaptation of his book.

IN COLD BLOOD (1966), by Truman Capote

Truman Capote's *In Cold Blood* combines a report of actual events with the form of the novel. The actual events are the murder of four members of the Clutter family on the night of November 14–15, 1959, in their farmhouse in Holcomb, Kansas, and the eventual capture, trial, and execution of their killers, Richard Hickock and Perry Smith. Like a novel, the plot of this literary journalism includes multitudinous scenes and numerous subplots, a cast of many people, lengthy descriptions of setting, elaborate analysis by the narrator, several symbols, and a number of themes.

The plot parallels the ordinary last day in the lives of the four Clutters with the extraordinary preparations of Hickock and Smith to murder them. The two parallel strands of the story meet when Hickock and Smith enter the Clutter house to rob, terrorize, and murder its inhabitants. The plot then follows the discovery of the bodies and the investigation of evidence and subsequent leads by various police forces. Parallel with the account of the investigation is an account of the flight of the murderers. The two parallel strands of this part of the story meet when Hickock and Smith are arrested in Las Vegas, Nevada. The plot subsequently follows their interrogation in Las Vegas, their extradition to Kansas, their trial in Garden City, their incarceration in the Kansas State Penitentiary for Men in Lansing, Capote's digressive summary of their life stories as told to him by Hickock and Smith, and their execution by hanging on June 22, 1965.

By appropriating the technique of parallel narratives used in narrative fiction, Capote is able to generate a suspense which is not often evoked in traditional journalism—such as the stories that covered the Clutter murder in the newspapers of the day.

The people in the narrative include the Clutter family; Hickock and Smith; the local police and state investigators, especially four from the Kansas Bureau of Investigation, and in particular Alvin Dewey; the townspeople of Holcomb and nearby Garden City, Kansas; a few of the people Hickock and Smith encounter in their flight; the Hickock and Smith families; and a nameless, faceless, seemingly ever-present reporter who, among other reporters, follows the events until a time slightly past the execution of Hickock and Smith.

Of all these people, the murderers Hickock and Smith; their victims, the Clutter family; and their chief interrogator-investigator Alvin Dewey emerge as somewhat *round characters,* having a degree of both depth and complexity. Their depth and complexity suggest to the reader that the murderers, the victims, and the chief interrogator-investigator are people with emotions and ideas, fears and ambitions. Like round characters in novels, these actual people are at once similar to us in their emotions and ideas, yet specifically dissimilar to us in their circumstances. They clearly are not the personality-less names printed in newspaper columns.

The Kansas setting, especially the climate; the geography; the assortment of buildings in Garden City, nearby Holcomb, and the Clutter farm; and the accents, clothes, and ordinary activities of the residents of Garden City and Holcomb are described in vivid detail. The farm is meticulously reconstructed to help the reader follow the details of the crime, and the surrounding region is presented to inform the reader of the conservative moral, intellectual, and social environment of this rural, agricultural world in which the Clutters lived and died.

In Cold Blood is narrated in the past tense, using an *unobtrusive, omniscient* narrator. The story is told in the third person, and the action is not confined to what is seen and heard by any one character. We follow all four Clutters through their last day; we observe Hickock and Smith before, during, and after the murders; we follow Dewey through his investigation of the murder; and we meet various other townspeople through the aftermath of the murders. Capote states that:

> [a]ll the material in this book not derived from my own observations is either taken from official records or is the result of interviews with the persons directly concerned, more often than not numerous interviews conducted over a considerable period of time. ("Acknowledgements")

Through his direct observations and interviews, Capote reports to us what the people think and feel, say and do, and how they look, but not what he thinks and feels about them. In this sense, he merely watches the characters behave, and we watch along with him.

Among the several symbols and themes that Capote develops from the actual details of the murder is the contrast between the stationary Clutters and the mobile Hickock and Smith. The Clutter family put down economic and social roots in Holcomb. They stayed in the small, rural community because they flourished within that community. They abided by the community's norms in part because they endorsed these norms, and in part because the norms gave shape to their successful lives. Capote describes Herbert Clutter as a man "[a]lways certain of what he wanted from the world . . . [who] had in large measure obtained it" (6). He describes Nancy, Clutter's daughter, as "the town darling" (7). In contrast, Hickock and Smith have never put down any sort of roots. They drift from community to community, both urban and rural, and flourish in none of them. They abide by few if any of the community's norms in part because they reject these norms as constricting to their personal freedom.

IN COLD BLOOD (1967), **Directed by Richard Brooks**

In his short memoir of his involvement with the production of Brooks's film, "Ghosts in the Sunlight: the Filming of *In Cold Blood*," Capote remembers and reflects on the artistic choices he made in writing his nonfiction novel, and he comments on the artistic choices Brooks made in writing the screen-play and directing the film. To begin with, Capote explains how he selected details for his nonfiction novel:

> When I was a child I played a pictorial game. I would, for example, observe a landscape: trees and clouds and horses wandering in grass; then select a detail from the overall vision—say, grass bending in the breeze—and frame it with my hands. Now this detail became the essence of the landscape and caught, in prismatic miniature, the true atmosphere of a panorama too sizable to encompass otherwise. Or if I was in a strange room, and wanted to understand the room and the nature of its inhabitants, I let my eye wander selectively until it discovered something—a shaft of light, a decrepit piano, a pattern on the rug—that seemed of itself to contain the secret. All art is composed of selected detail, either imaginary or, as in *In Cold Blood*, a distillation of reality. As with the book, so with the film—except that I had chosen my details from life, while Brooks had distilled his from my book: reality twice transposed, and all the truer for it. (397)

Capote wanted Brooks to direct the film because he respected Brooks's "imag-inative professionalism" (398), and because Brooks concurred with Capote as to how his nonfiction novel should be adapted.

> I wanted the film made in black and white, and I wanted it played by a cast of unknowns—that is actors without public faces. Although Brooks and I have differ-ent sensibilities, we both wanted the film to duplicate reality, to have the actors resemble their prototypes as much as possible, and to have every scene filmed in its real locale: the house of the murdered Clutter family; the same Kansas variety store where Perry and Dick bought the rope and tape used to bind their four victims; and certain courthouses, prisons, filling stations, hotel rooms and highways and city streets—all those places they had seen in the course of their crime and its aftermath. A complicated procedure, but the only possible one by which almost all elements of fantasy could be removed and reality thereby achieve its proper reflection. (398)

Having the actors resemble "their prototypes as much as possible" corre-sponds to Lipkin's first strategy for correlating the actual and the recreated in a docudrama film. Robert Blake especially looks like Perry Smith: short, well muscled through his shoulders and chest, sporting slicked-back black hair, and wearing a short black jacket and boots. However, Paul Stewart, the actor who plays the reporter Jenson, looks and speaks nothing like Truman Capote. Capote was a short, balding, high-voiced, and flamboyantly dressed and mannered man. Stewart is taller, low voiced, and plainly dressed and mannered.

The film's "real locales" correspond to Lipkin's third strategy for correlat-ing the actual and the re-created in a docudrama film. The filmmaker has the actual and the imitation appear simultaneously on screen by, for example, film-ing an actor in the actual place where the event occurred. The "real locales"

Robert Blake as Perry Smith measuring rope inside a variety store in Emporia, Kansas, in the film *In Cold Blood* (1967).

were found and filmed. For example, the then owner of the Clutter farm permitted Brooks to shoot in the house. Capote recalls:

> The rooms looked precisely the same as they had when I examined them in December, 1959—that is soon after the crime was discovered. Mr. Clutter's Stetson hanging on a wall hat rack. Nancy's sheet music opened at the piano. Her brother's spectacles resting on a bureau, the lens shimmering in the sunlight. . . . Thus reality, via an object, extends itself into art; and that is what is original and disturbing about this film: reality and art are intertwined to the point that there is no identifiable area of demarcation. (399)

Capote became sick with the flu, left the Kansas filming location, and returned to New York. Six months later, he went to California to view a rough cut of the film with Brooks. When Capote saw him, Brooks seemed strained, and when Capote asked him why, Brooks replied, "Of course, I'm nervous. . . . Why shouldn't I be? It's *your* book—and suppose you don't like it?" (402)

After the first few sequences of the film had been run by him, Capote became

> increasingly gripped by a sense of loss; and a ring forms around my heart, like the frosty haze around a harvest moon. Not because of what is on the screen, which is fine, but because of what isn't. Why has such-and-such been omitted? Where is Bobby Rupp [Nancy Clutter's boyfriend who was the last to see the family alive]? Susan Kidwell [Nancy's best friend]? The postmistress and her mother? (403)

Capote seemed to be concerned about the problem all filmmakers face when they adapt a novel to a feature film 80 to 120 minutes long: they have to contend with the novel's many characters, multitudinous scenes, numerous subplots, elaborate analysis by the narrator, lengthy descriptions of setting, and many symbols. Thus, they are faced with the necessity and the challenge of dropping substantial elements of narrative from the novel in order to make it fit the running time of the feature film. Even a relatively short novel of 140 pages is just too long a narrative to be wholly contained within a feature film. Filmmakers have no choice but to cut, combine, condense, and truncate elements of narrative. True, Capote's book is not a novel but rather a work of nonfiction; however, the nonfiction content is shaped like a novel, so Brooks had to drop substantial elements of narrative from the text to simplify and shorten it to fit the running time of his feature film. That meant dropping Bobby Rupp and Susan Kidwell. Brooks considers them solely as characters and chooses to drop them. However, Capote considered Rupp and Kidwell as actual people who played significant roles in Nancy Clutter's life and death, so dropping them seemed to Capote to profoundly alter Nancy's life and death and his own experience in re-creating that life and death.

Capote eventually realized Brooks's situation and came to terms with it:

> I managed to resolve the quarrel I was having with myself. Look, an inner voice said, you're being unrealistic, unfair. This picture is two hours long, and that is as long as it can reasonably be. If Brooks included everything you would like to have shown, every nuance you're grieving over, it would last nine hours. So stop worrying. Watch it for what it is: judge from that. (403)

Capote watched and judged. He became inundated by the reality portrayed in the film. When the film and the emotional experience of watching it were over, he noticed "[a] man sitting near me. Who was he, and why did he look at me so intently, as if expecting me to say something? Ah, Brooks. Finally, I said, 'By the way, thank you' " (404). Capote's judgment, it seems, was positive. Despite Brooks's drops and additions, which Capote does not mention in his memoir, the author of the nonfiction novel ultimately assents to the filmmaker's adaptation of it.

Summary

There are many forms of nonfiction, but filmmakers usually adapt only a few types: biographies, journalism, and memoirs. Each of these three types presents an account of events, people, and conversations that can be adapted and dramatically presented in narrative film.

The film produced by the adaptation of a nonfiction literary text is neither wholly a fiction film—which portrays imagined characters, settings, and actions—nor wholly a nonfiction film, or documentary—which claims to depict actual people, places, things, and events that belong to the world beyond the film—but rather a hybrid of the two, or what Steve Lipkin calls a docudrama. Like a fiction film, it is produced with actors rather than with actual people, and with re-created or staged places, things, and events. Like a documentary, the film claims to depict actual people, places, things, and events.

Due to the hybrid nature of its form, docudrama demands a particular kind of suspension of disbelief from its audience. Viewers are asked to accept that, in this case, re-creation is a necessary mode of presentation. In order to link the actual and the re-created in docudrama films, filmmakers use several approaches. In the model strategy, actors, places, and events are made to resemble closely their actual counterparts in the world beyond the film. In the sequence strategy, footage of actual events, people, and places are inserted into the film. In the interaction strategy, the actual and the re-created are made to appear simultaneously on the screen.

The nonfiction literary text is based on an actual prior event about which the author and others report. Aside from being an adaptation of a text, the docudrama is also a report of an actual event. Inevitably, comparisons will be made among the docudrama, the nonfiction literary text, and other relevant nonfiction texts in order to discover the contradictions among them. Crucial to such comparisons are the narrative elements dropped or added in the film, especially the invented additions or expansions on already existing elements.

■■■ TOPICS FOR DISCUSSION

1. Robert Redford said that in *Quiz Show* he used "dramatic license to make either a moral point or an ethical point and [did] not move too far out of what could possibly have happened." To what extent do you believe filmmakers are at liberty to make factual changes in generally agreed-upon historical accounts of important national or world events?

2. Truman Capote said of the film *In Cold Blood*, "I wanted it played by a cast of unknowns—that is actors without public faces." Consider if the film had featured a cast of known actors. Would their "public faces" have altered the audience's reaction to the film, even if their public faces were made up to resemble the actual faces of the people dramatized in the film?

3. Select a docudrama from the filmography and explain whether it uses Lipkin's (1) model, (2) sequence, or (3) interaction strategies, or some combination in linking the film to the literary text on which it is based and, if you can determine, to actual events to which both the literary text and the docudrama refer.

4. Describe how a specific docudrama departs from the adapted text and from the historical events on which both text and film are based. Read newspaper, magazine, and journal articles and other nonfiction texts to achieve a grasp of the historical events. Do you feel the film's changes are justified by dramatic license, or do they alter or deform the factual story to the point of historical misrepresentation?

WORKS CITED

All the President's Men. Dir. Alan J. Pakula. Perf. Robert Redford, Dustin Hoffman, and Jason Robards. Warner Bros., 1976.

BERNSTEIN, CARL, AND BOB WOODWARD. *All the President's Men.* New York: Simon and Schuster, 1974.

BORDWELL, DAVID, AND KRISTIN THOMPSON. *Film Art: An Introduction.* 5th ed. New York: McGraw-Hill, 1997.

CAPOTE, TRUMAN. *In Cold Blood.* New York: Random House, 1966.

————. "Ghosts in the Sunlight: The Filming of *In Cold Blood.*" *The Dogs Bark: Public People and Private Places.* New York: Random House, 1973. 393–404.

GOODWIN, RICHARD. "Investigating the Quiz Shows." *Remembering America.* Boston: Little, Brown, 1988. 43–65.

HALBERSTAM, DAVID. "Chapter 43." *The Fifties.* New York: Villard Books, 1993. 643–666, 775.

HORN, JOHN. "*Quiz Show* Gives False Picture of Scandal." *Times-Picayune* 23 Sept. 1994: A3+.

HOWE, DESSON. "*Quiz Show.*" *Washington Post* 16 Sept. 1994 <http://www.washingtonpost.com/wp->.

In Cold Blood. Dir. Richard Brooks. Perf. Robert Blake and Scott Wilson. Columbia, 1967.

LIPKIN, STEVEN N. "*Quiz Show* as Persuasive Docudrama." *Images Journal.* 6 June 2002 <http://www.imagesjournal.com/issue01/features/quiz.htm>.

————. *Real Emotional Logic: Film and Television Docudrama as Persuasive Practice.* Carbondale: Southern Illinois Univ. Press, 2002.

Quiz Show. Dir. Robert Redford. Perf. John Turturro, Rob Morrow, and Ralph Fiennes. Hollywood Pictures, 1994.

ZOGLIN, RICHARD. "Why *Quiz Show* Is a Scandal." *Time* 10 October 1994 <www.time.com/time/magazine/archive/1994/941010/941010.television.html>.

SELECTED FILMOGRAPHY OF NONFICTION ADAPTATIONS

MAYA ANGELOU. *I Know Why the Caged Bird Sings* (1970).
FIEDLER COOK. *I Know Why the Caged Bird Sings* (1979).

JOHN BAYLEY. *An Elegy for Iris* (1999).
RICHARD EYRE. *Iris* (2001).

MARK BOWDEN. *Black Hawk Down* (1999).
RIDLEY SCOTT. *Black Hawk Down* (2001).

CHRISTY BROWN. *My Left Foot* (1982).
JIM SHERIDAN. *My Left Foot* (1989).

WILLIAM GIBSON. *The Miracle Worker* (1960).
ARTHUR PENN. *The Miracle Worker* (1962).

LAURA HILLENBRAND. *Seabiscuit* (2001).
GARY ROSS. *Seabiscuit* (2003).

MALCOLM JOHNSON. *Crime on the Labor Front* (1950).
ELIA KAZAN. *On the Waterfront* (1954).

SABASTIAN JUNGER. *The Perfect Storm* (1997).
WOLFGANG PETERSEN. *The Perfect Storm* (2000).

SUSANNA KAYSEN. *Girl, Interrupted* (1993).
JAMES MANGOLD. *Girl, Interrupted* (1999).

WALTER LORD. *A Night to Remember* (1955).
ROY WARD BAKER. *A Night to Remember* (1958).

PETER MAAS. *Serpico* (1973).
SIDNEY LUMET. *Serpico* (1973).

MALCOLM X AS TOLD TO ALEX HALEY. *The Autobiography of Malcolm X* (1964).
SPIKE LEE. *Malcolm X* (1992).

SYLVIA NASAR. *A Beautiful Mind* (1998).
RON HOWARD. *A Beautiful Mind* (2001).

JOSEPH D. PISTONE. *Donnie Brasco* (1996).
MIKE NEWELL. *Donnie Brasco* (1997).

WILLIAM PITTENGER. *The Great Locomotive Chase* (1862).
BUSTER KEATON AND CLYDE BRUCKMAN. *The General* (1927).
FRANCIS D. LYON. *The Great Locomotive Chase* (1956).

BRUCE PORTER. *Blow* (1993).
TED DEMME. *Blow* (2001).

ERNIE PYLE. *The Reports of Ernie Pyle* (1941, 1943, 1944).
WILLIAM A. WELLMAN. *The Story of G.I. Joe* (1945).

DORE SCHARY. *Sunrise at Campobello* (1958).
VINCENT J. DONEHUE. *Sunrise at Campobello* (1960).

PETER SHAFFER. *Amadeus* (1979).
MILOS FORMAN. *Amadeus* (1984).

HUNTER S. THOMPSON. *Fear and Loathing in Las Vegas* (1971).
TERRY GILLIAM. *Fear and Loathing in Las Vegas* (1998).

RICHARD TREGASKIS. *Guadalcanal Diary* (1943).
LEWIS SEILER. *Guadalcanal Diary* (1943).

TOBIAS WOLFF. *This Boy's Life* (1989).
MICHAEL CATON-JONES. *This Boy's Life* (1993).

9 ANIMATION

Not many critics have given animation adaptations much thought. As Paul Wells observes, "most of this writing [on adaptation] relates to how a novel, play or short story has become a *live-action film,* while comparatively little attention has been given to the literary adaptations in animation" (199). Reasons for the scant attention devoted to animation adaptations can be found in Imelda Whelehan's remark that "animation remains very much the 'second cousin to mainstream cinema' . . . associated primarily with a children's audience and assumed to be therefore less structurally or thematically rich" (215).

The situation is regrettable since animated films have a long history of adapting works of literature. The chronological list that follows suggests an elementary historical timeline of animation adaptations and the wide range of literary genres from which animation filmmakers have successfully drawn their inspiration.

> *The Adventures of Prince Achmed* (1926), from the folk tale "The Enchanted Horse" and "Aladdin and His

Enchanted Lamp" from *The Thousand and One Nights* (fourteenth century)

Snow White and the Seven Dwarfs (1937), anonymous

Song of the South (1946), from the stories of Joel Chandler Harris

The Adventures of Ichabod (1949), from the short story "The Legend of Sleepy Hollow" by Washington Irving (1820)

Animal Farm (UK 1954), from the novel of the same name by George Orwell (1946)

Rikki-Tikki-Tavi (1975), from the short story of the same name by Rudyard Kipling (1888)

Watership Down (UK 1978), from the novel of the same name by Richard Adams

The Little Prince (1979), from the novella of the same name by Antoine de Saint-Exupéry (1943)

"The Raven" (1989), from the poem of the same name by Edgar Allan Poe (1845)

Aladdin (1992), from the folk tale "Aladdin and the Magic Lamp" from *The Thousand and One Nights* (fourteenth century)

James and the Giant Peach (UK 1996), from the novella of the same name by Roald Dahl (1961)

Shrek (2001), from the illustrated short story by William Steig (1990)

In this chapter we present a brief overview of how to analyze animation adaptation of literature in general. Like live-action filmmakers, animation film-makers keep, drop, and add elements of narrative to create close, loose, or intermediate adaptations. Depending on the literary genre and the length of the film, animation filmmakers use many of the adaptation strategies explained in earlier chapters. In addition, animation contributes to adaptation in a way live-action films cannot, except for, perhaps, computer-generated images that enhance live action. The different types of animation, their exaggerated and embellished forms, their intensified colors, and their distorted sounds create a fantastic, magical world that transforms a literary text in a way not seen in live-action films.

Some Fundamentals of Animation

Animation comes in four basic types: (1) drawings or etchings on individual sheets of paper or most often on individual sheets of celluloid or *cels* (*The Adventures of Ichabod*); (2) *cutout silhouettes* (*The Adventures of Prince Achmed*); (3) *computer-generated images* (*Shrek*); and (4) three-dimensional objects.

The last category consists of six types: (1) *clay or plasticine models* (*The Little Prince*); (2) *handheld or string-pulled puppets* (*Hanzel and Gretel*); (3) actual objects (*Dreams of Toyland*); (4) live actors who freeze their movements (*The Secret*

Adventures of Tom Thumb); (5) the combination of live action and *stop-motion models* (*Alice*); and (6) fluid materials such as ink or sand on glass (*The Metamorphosis of Mr. Samsa*). Whichever type of animation is used, the figure is positioned, often against a stationary background; a single frame is shot, usually with a *multiplane camera* that gives two-dimensional drawings a three-dimensional effect; the figure is then repositioned; another frame is shot; and so on until the figure has completed an action recorded on film or video. Projected, these recorded images produce an apparent motion and depth similar to the apparent motion and depth produced in live-action films.

Animation starts with a human, animal, or inanimate form and then typically exaggerates that form to create a comic, idealized, or grotesque figure. The unusual features or peculiar personalities of human or animal characters are often deliberately exaggerated to produce clear, instantly recognizable comic figures, or *caricatures*, that amuse audiences. For example, in the photograph of the cel-animated character Ichabod Crane, his whole body—most noticeably his ears, nose, arms, and feet—is elongated. When he walks, his movements imitate the ungraceful-graceful walk of his bird namesake. The purpose of his appearance serves not only a comic effect, but also serves to contrast Ichabod with the pretty and graceful Katrina, with whom he is in love, and the handsome and athletic Brom Bones, with whom he competes for Katrina's affections.

Although many of animation's exaggerations are comic, not all are. The features and personalities of human or other forms are sometimes exaggerated to produce idealized figures that please audiences. For example, in the photograph of the cutout-silhouette animated character from *The Adventures of Prince Achmed*, the delicate details of the character's feathers and of the palm fronds and the fine sinuous lines of the character's tail and legs and of the tree trunks, all set in high contrast with the smooth, glassy, bright water, to create a figure perfectly suited to the romanticized landscape of the scene.

Sometimes human or animal forms are exaggerated to produce grotesque figures designed to disgust or scare other characters and the audience. For example, the puppet-animated character from *Alice* has ugly facial features and a misshapen body that repels the shrunken Alice, yet because she is trapped in his "wonderland" world, she must tolerate him despite her revulsion.

Exaggeration is not confined to human or animal forms. Inanimate places and things are also given conscious life and exaggerated into caricatures, idealizations, or grotesques. Thus, an old-fashioned, red-painted, clapboard, one-room schoolhouse, topped with a small bell tower and narrow chimney, full of impatient children unable to wait much longer for the recess bell, begins to pulsate, its walls and roof expanding and contracting rhythmically and forcefully. Even the red, orange, and yellow flowers and the green-leafed trees surrounding the schoolhouse, as well as the white, puffy clouds in the blue sky above, dance to the same beat, reflecting the children's anticipation of liberation. The sound track plays an instrumental dance song. Finally, the school bell rings loudly, its clapper wagging like a huge tongue, and the children stream through the doors, climb out of the windows, and run away in all directions, laughing and screaming. At last, relieved of its burden, the schoolhouse collapses, exhausted, the shutters on its front windows change into drooping eyelids, and the smoke from its chimney is exhaled forcibly. The flowers and trees stop their dancing and also droop from exhaustion, while the clouds roll over and rest on their backs in the shapes of humans lying in bed.

Hand in hand with animation's exaggeration of human, animal, or inanimate forms are its exaggerations of color and sound. The colors, or *hues*, can be more **saturated,** or intensified, and thereby made more brilliant than in the replicated world of live-action films. The **pitch, loudness,** and **timbre** of music, sounds and voices can also be distorted and made stranger, odder, more peculiar, and more outlandish than in live-action films. These special effects of color and sound are coordinated with the animated forms to create whatever comic, idealized, or grotesque tone, mood, and atmosphere the animator wishes to convey. Such exaggeration can result in agist, ethnic, gender, or racial slur.

The types of animation, their exaggerated and embellished forms, their intensified colors, and their distorted sounds can create a type of **magic realism** similar to that found in some twentieth-century prose fiction. Magic realism is seen principally as a Latin American movement; its major proponent is Gabriel García Márquez, especially in his novel *One Hundred Years of Solitude.* Other practitioners include John Barth, Jorge Luis Borges, Italo Calvino, Umberto Eco, John Fowles, Günter Grass, and Salman Rushdie. These writers, like animators, seamlessly blend commonplace events of daily life with fantastic elements derived from dreams, fairy tales, and myths. Like animated films, magic realism creates a fictional place where the distinctions between logic and irrationality, waking and dreaming, and the possible and impossible are denied.

Here is a passage from Gabriel García Márquez's short story "A Very Old Man with Enormous Wings."

> Sea and sky were a single ash-gray thing and the sands of the beach, which on March nights glimmered like powdered light, had become a stew of mud and rotten shellfish. The light was so weak at noon that when Pelayo was coming back to the house after throwing away the crabs, it was hard for him to see what it was that was moving and groaning in the rear of the courtyard. He had to go very close to see that it was an old man, a very old man, lying face down in the mud, who, in spite of his tremendous efforts, couldn't get up, impeded by his enormous wings. . . .
>
> "He's an angel," [their neighbor] told them. "He must have been coming for the child, but the poor fellow is so old that the rain knocked him down." (237)

The story combines the mundane, even squalid details of daily life in a fishing village with fantastic events—the discovery of an old man with angel-like wings and, later, a woman who is metamorphosed into a spider because she disobeys her parents.

In her book *Shadow Puppets, Shadow Theaters and Shadow Films,* the director and silhouette animator Lotte Reiniger advises animation students to choose fables, fairy tales, fantastic poems and plays, and myths for their "shadow plays," as she calls them, because these stories cannot be presented with real actors but only with animated figures (124). She adds, "the *Arabian Nights Tales,* with their rich Oriental fantasy, are also very well worth study" (124). That piece of advice comes from her own experience. She adapted "The Enchanted Horse" and "Aladdin and His Enchanted Lamp" into the silent, cutout-silhouette, animated film *The Adventures of Prince Achmed.*

In commenting on animation in general, Paul Wells connects it with the magical:

> "metamorphosis" is about changes in character or situation that may be termed "magical" or impossible within the concept of a real world served by physiological, gravitational, or functionalist norms. Virtually all animated films play out this definition of metamorphosis as a technical and narrational orthodoxy, thus rendering the adaptation of a fairy tale on this basis, a matter of relative ease. (201)

In commenting on the work of the director and animator Jan Svankmajer, Frantisek Dryje also connects animation with the fantastic and notices a possibly deliberate, unresolved dramatic tension between reality and fantasy:

> [t]he dream does not rule over reality, nor the reality over the dream; their relationship is dialectical. . . . At the end of [*Alice,* Svankmajer's animated adaptation of Lewis Carroll's *Alice in Wonderland*], Alice wakes up in the nursery from which the White Rabbit has enticed her. He is a stuffed museum piece, who has found his way here by pure chance, come alive, and broken a glass case. . . . Was everything just a dream then? Alice's glance wanders around the room and suddenly falls on some actual fragments of broken glass. . . . So, was everything mere reality? And why should the answer not be paradoxical? (132)

Our point is that the literary movement of magic realism is similar to animation in that both blend details from everyday life with the fantastic. The departure from the real into the impossible is not seen as a departure at all but as a convention of animation that is understood and even expected by the audience of animated films.

The audience of animated films consists mainly of children and teenagers. Animation's magic realism attracts, engages, and holds the attention of younger audiences just by being beautifully, mysteriously, and thrillingly different from the actual world of our day-to-day lives. Adult audiences, however, are not excluded. Some animated films—*Alice,* for example—are primarily aimed at adults. In earlier decades, film packages at local theaters included short animated films, such as those featuring Bugs Bunny, Mickey Mouse, Popeye, Tom and Jerry, and Woody Woodpecker, along with coming attractions, newsreels, and short live-action films. Adults sat through the short animated films as they waited for the featured live-action films to begin.

Thus, many animated films include elements intended to entertain more mature sensibilities.

Some literary texts express serious themes, but when animators adapt these texts, the serious intellectual meaning is often not carried over. It appears that if the ideas or thematic elements cannot be visualized by the animators in an exaggerated, embellished, intensified, or distorted way, and enjoyed as such by a younger audience, then those elements are simply dropped from the animated adaptation or are tugged so out of shape as to be recognized only as a parody of the original. This feature of animated adaptations may not be a limitation of the medium but simply the product of choices made by filmmakers who aim at a younger audience.

Although animation films are primarily associated with younger audiences and tend to be less thematically rich than either serious live-action films or literature, we do not regard film animation as a second-class form. Animation seems virtually boundless in its *potential* to adapt literary narratives since the conventions of the medium allow the filmmaker to blend so seamlessly representations of persons, places, and things with the fantastic.

Some of the typical features of an animated film become clear when comparing Edgar Allan Poe's poem "The Raven" (1845) to its animated adaptation "The Raven," directed by David Silverman for "The Treehouse of Horror" episode of *The Simpsons* (1989). Later in the chapter we will compare Washington Irving's "The Legend of Sleepy Hollow" (1820) to its animated adaptation *The Adventures of Ichabod* (1949) directed by Jack Kinney.

▪ ▪ ▪

"THE RAVEN" (1845)

by Edgar Allan Poe

Once upon a midnight dreary, while I pondered, weak and weary,
Over many a quaint and curious volume of forgotten lore,
While I nodded, nearly napping, suddenly there came a tapping,
As of some one gently rapping, rapping at my chamber door.
" 'Tis some visitor," I muttered, "tapping at my chamber door;   5

Only this and nothing more."

Ah, distinctly I remember it was in the bleak December
And each separate dying ember wrought its ghost upon the floor.
Eagerly I wished the morrow;—vainly I had sought to borrow

From my books surcease of sorrow—sorrow for the lost Lenore,   10
For the rare and radiant maiden whom the angels name Lenore:

   Nameless *here* for evermore.

And the silken sad uncertain rustling of each purple curtain
Thrilled me—filled me with fantastic terrors never felt before;
So that now, to still the beating of my heart, I stood repeating,   15
" 'Tis some visitor entreating entrance at my chamber door,
Some late visitor entreating entrance at my chamber door:

   This it is and nothing more."

Presently my soul grew stronger; hesitating then no longer,
"Sir," said I, "or Madam, truly your forgiveness I implore;   20
But the fact is I was napping, and so gently you came rapping,
And so faintly you came tapping, tapping at my chamber door,
That I scarce was sure I heard you"—here I opened wide the door:

   Darkness there and nothing more.

Deep into that darkness peering, long I stood there wondering, fearing,   25
Doubting, dreaming dreams no mortal ever dared to dream before;
But the silence was unbroken, and the stillness gave no token,
And the only word there spoken was the whispered word, "Lenore!"
This I whispered, and an echo murmured back the word, "Lenore!"

   Merely this and nothing more.   30

Back into the chamber turning, all my soul within me burning,
Soon again I heard a tapping somewhat louder than before.
"Surely," said I, "surely that is something at my window lattice;
Let me see, then, what thereat is, and this mystery explore—
Let my heart be still a moment and this mystery explore;   35

   'Tis the wind and nothing more!"

Open here I flung the shutter, when, with many a flirt and flutter,
In there stepped a stately Raven of the saintly days of yore.

Not the least obeisance made he; not a minute stopped or stayed he;
But, with mien of lord or lady, perched above my chamber door—   40
Perched upon a bust of Pallas just above my chamber door—

   Perched, and sat, and nothing more.

Then this ebony bird beguiling my sad fancy into smiling,
By the grave and stern decorum of the countenance it wore,
"Though thy crest be shorn and shaven, thou," I said, "art sure no craven, 45
Ghastly grim and ancient Raven wandering from the Nightly shore—
Tell me what thy lordly name is on the Night's Plutonian shore!"

   Quoth the Raven, "Nevermore."

Much I marvelled this ungainly fowl to hear discourse so plainly,
Though its answer little meaning—little relevancy bore;   50
For we cannot help agreeing that no living human being
Ever yet was blessed with seeing bird above his chamber door—
Bird or beast upon the sculptured bust above his chamber door,

   With such name as "Nevermore."

But the Raven, sitting lonely on the placid bust, spoke only   55
That one word, as if his soul in that one word he did outpour.
Nothing further then he uttered—not a feather then he fluttered—
Till I scarcely more than muttered—"Other friends have flown before—
On the morrow *he* will leave me, as my hopes have flown before."

   Then the bird said, "Nevermore."   60

Startled at the stillness broken by reply so aptly spoken,
"Doubtless," said I, "what it utters is its only stock and store
Caught from some unhappy master whom unmerciful Disaster
Followed fast and followed faster till his songs one burden bore—
Till the dirges of his Hope that melancholy burden bore   65

   Of 'Never—nevermore.' "

But the Raven still beguiling all my fancy into smiling,
Straight I wheeled a cushioned seat in front of bird and bust and door;

Then, upon the velvet sinking, I betook myself to linking
Fancy unto fancy, thinking what this ominous bird of yore,   70
What this grim, ungainly, ghastly, gaunt, and ominous bird of yore

   Meant in croaking "Nevermore."

This I sat engaged in guessing, but no syllable expressing
To the fowl whose fiery eyes now burned into my bosom's core;
This and more I sat divining, with my head at ease reclining   75
On the cushion's velvet lining that the lamplight gloated o'er,
But whose velvet violet lining with the lamplight gloating o'er

   She shall press, ah, nevermore!

Then, methought, the air grew denser, perfumed from an unseen censer
Swung by Seraphim whose foot-falls tinkled on the tufted floor.   80
"Wretch," I cried, "thy God hath lent thee—by these angels he hath sent thee
Respite—respite and nepenthe from thy memories of Lenore;
Quaff, oh quaff this kind nepenthe, and forget this lost Lenore!"

   Quoth the Raven, "Nevermore."

"Prophet!" said I, "thing of evil! prophet still, if bird or devil!—   85
Whether Tempter sent, or whether tempest tossed thee here ashore,
Desolate yet all undaunted, on this desert land enchanted—
On this home by Horror haunted—tell me truly, I implore—
Is there—*is* there balm in Gilead?—tell me—tell me, I implore!"

   Quoth the Raven, "Nevermore."   90

"Prophet!" said I, "thing of evil!—prophet still, if bird or devil!
By that Heaven that bends above us—by that God we both adore—
Tell this soul with sorrow laden if, within the distant Aidenn,
It shall clasp a sainted maiden whom the angels name Lenore—
Clasp a rare and radiant maiden whom the angels name Lenore."   95

   Quoth the Raven, "Nevermore."

"Be that word our sign of parting, bird or fiend!" I shrieked, upstarting—
"Get thee back into the tempest and the Night's Plutonian shore!

Leave no black plume as a token of that lie thy soul hath spoken!
Leave my loneliness unbroken! quit the bust above my door!   100
Take thy beak from out my heart, and take thy form from off my door!"

  Quoth the Raven, "Nevermore."

And the Raven, never flitting, still is sitting, *still* is sitting
On the pallid bust of Pallas just above my chamber door;
And his eyes have all the seeming of a demon's that is dreaming,   105
And the lamp-light o'er him streaming throws his shadow on the floor;
And my soul from out that shadow that lies floating on the floor

  Shall be lifted—nevermore!

In Poe's poem, an exhausted scholar is visited in his room one stormy evening by a Raven that speaks just one word: "Nevermore." Grief-stricken by the death of his beloved Lenore, the scholar asks the bird if he will ever reunite with her in the afterlife. The bird repeats its one word. Driven mad by the repetition, the scholar makes increasingly unreasonable demands on the bird until the Raven sits silent in the melancholy atmosphere.

The Raven may signify the scholar's inner fears and thwarted longings. Night black, thick feathered, and harsh voiced, the Raven appears "emblematical of *Mournful and Never-ending Remembrance*," as Poe states in "The Philosophy of Composition," his account of writing "The Raven" (17). The bird's invasion and subsequent occupation of the scholar's room suggests that this condition of mournful sadness has penetrated into the innermost chamber of his exhausted, grieving consciousness.

The scholar has been pursuing knowledge, one aspect of wisdom, to bring his grief to an end. Instead, his pursuit has brought him exhaustion. The Raven arrives with its message of never-ending sadness. Finding succor through knowledge is a fruitless endeavor, the Raven appears to say, as it takes a dominant position in the room, perching atop the bust of Pallas, the Greek goddess of wisdom.

"THE RAVEN," from "TREEHOUSE OF HORROR" Episode of *THE SIMPSONS* (1990), Directed by David Silverman

Annually, the *Simpsons* series presents a Halloween episode that includes three short *skits*, or comic dramatic sketches, related by subject matter and theme to the October 31 celebration of trick or treat. In their first Halloween special, the third skit was an adaptation of Poe's "The Raven," with Homer in the role of the Scholar, Bart as the Raven, Marge as Lenore, Lisa and Maggie as angels, and the voice of James Earl Jones as the Narrator who takes over some of the lines from the speaker in the poem.

Emotional pain and loss, treated as serious business in the poem, are mocked in the film. The shift in tone from the serious to the comic is reflected in many narrative and cinematic elements of the animation.

The Simpsons' dramatic reenactment of the poem is framed by an introduction and conclusion that is set in the "real" world of the Simpsons. Before the beginning of the poem, Bart and Lisa quibble over reading a book on Halloween. During the poem, Bart occasionally interjects his reaction to the poem. At the end of the poem, the whole family gets ready for bed.

In the introduction and conclusion, the framing is conventional: the angle is straight and level; the height is eye-level; and the characters and objects appear in medium-long, medium, medium close-up, and close-up. These elements of framing do not call attention to themselves, and we should hardly notice them. Yet once Lisa announces the title of the poem and its reenactment begins, the framing changes. It becomes unconventional and busy with multiple angles, ranging from overhead to practically underfoot, with much **canting** (dropping one side of the frame to tilt the people and things in the frame), with multiple heights from the ceiling to the floor, and with the characters appearing in drawings ranging from extreme long to extreme close-up. The busy movements coupled with many short duration shots and rapid cutting suggest the Scholar's agitated mood. In this way, the framing and editing emphasize an important emotional point in the poem: The Scholar is upset at losing his lover and at hearing the Raven's sad pronouncement. In the film, the excessive movement exaggerates the Scholar's distress to the point of hysteria.

As we mentioned earlier, color in animated films is saturated, or intensified, and thereby made more brilliant than in live-action films. The predominate colors of the fire-lit chamber vary. However, except for the bookcases, which are out of the direct light of the fire, the fireplace, furniture, rugs, and characters' costumes are lurid. This garish color scheme replaces the poem's somber atmosphere with a sensational one.

Sound effects and characters' voices in animated films often deviate from the usual. Here's an example of a sound described in the poem:

> *Back into the chamber turning, all my soul within me burning,*
> *Soon again I heard a tapping something louder than before.*
> *"Surely," said I, "surely that is something at my window lattice;*
> *Let me see, then, what thereat is, and this mystery explore—" (31–34)*

The "tapping something louder than before" (7) is represented in the film as a loud banging whose force shakes the frame and disturbs the delicate assonance in the Scholar's lines.

Homer Simpson as the Scholar and Bart Simpson as the Raven in "Treehouse of Horror" (1990), not looking like what we might have expected.

Humor is common in animation and is often inserted in adaptations whether there is humor in the adapted literary text or not. Consider the following segment from the film in which Homer asks the Raven its name:

HOMER

Ghastly grim and ancient Raven wandering from the Nightly shore——

Tell me what thy lordly name is on the Night's Plutonian shore!

NARRATOR

Quoth the Raven——

BART/RAVEN

Eat my shorts!

Lisa tells Bart that the Raven says "Nevermore" and nothing else. Bart reluctantly gives in.

Bart interrupts the reenactment of the poem with a characteristically impulsive and flippant outburst. Lisa chastises him for intruding on the text, disrupting the reading, and making a mockery of the poem. Reluctantly, he agrees not to interrupt again. However, Bart's signature phrase—"Eat my shorts!"—is a comic rephrasing of the Raven's response to the Speaker's questions, or, at least, a comic rephrasing of the tone of that response.

We do not know what the Scholar or Lenore look like. Because the poem is set in a library, we imagine the Scholar to be bookish and sensitive and his beloved Lenore to be young and beautiful. Obviously, the Simpsons do not look like what we might have expected the poem's characters to look like. Casting the insensitive, balding, fat, and flat-voiced Homer as the grieving Scholar; the puerile, vindictive, piercing-voiced Bart as the Raven; and the older and plainer Marge as a beauty, both amuses and jars us.

Meanwhile, the Simpsons characters bring their own comic conflict into the story. Superimposed on the conflict between the Scholar and the Raven is the typical conflict between Homer and Bart Simpson. Homer usually asks Bart to do or say something, Bart ignores or refuses Homer, and Homer threatens Bart. Eventually, Homer chases Bart and sometimes assaults him. Bart either surrenders or escapes, taunting Homer all the more. As they unfold in the animated adaptation, the stages of this typical, comical, active-aggressive conflict contrast with and supercede the melancholy, passive-aggressive Raven-Scholar conflict in the poem.

Visual puns are typical comic fare in animated films. In this adaptation, when we are introduced to the scholarly figure played by Homer, we see he has fallen asleep over—and drooled on—a tome entitled *Forgotten Lore II*. Later, during the chase scene, the Raven/Bart tosses down on Homer books with the titles of Poe's short stories. The first visual pun is an anti-intellectual jibe aimed at the Scholar's learning; he's an advanced student of pointless knowledge—*Forgotten Lore II* (and how could it be published if it's forgotten?). The second jibe is aimed at Poe himself, with Bart turning the author's works against one of his own creations.

The odd angles, the lurid colors, the loud sounds, and the insertion of humor support the filmmakers' choice to superimpose a contemporary, thoughtless, dysfunctional, lower-middle-class family from an animated situation comedy onto the story of a poem expressing the terror and despair of a thoughtful, distraught, Romantic man grieving over his dead love.

By their superimposition of *The Simpsons* on "The Raven," the filmmakers create a *parody* of Poe's poem. Parody is a form of criticism. It retains enough of the elements of content, form, and style in a work to be recognizable, but it treats the text's serious subject in a humorously undignified manner, thus trivializing the subject and the work. As criticism, it often highlights a weakness in the literary work.

The *Simpsons* parody of "The Raven" puts a finger on its weakness. Daniel Hoffman asks, "[a]re we supposed, supinely, to admit the plausibility of a raven knocking on the door of a lonely chamber on a stormy night . . . and forever croaking 'Nevermore'? Are we expected to believe that the youth in his chamber actually would address the errant bird as 'Prophet'? . . . And we're not supposed to laugh when 'Quoth the Raven, "Nevermore." ' " (74–75)

Moreover, Hoffman asks, are we to accept that the Scholar times and frames his questions "so that they occupy the regularly spaced interstices between the bird's cacophonous utterances" and fit their sense? The plausibility of the situation is sustained

> as long as we willingly sink into the intellectual stupor which Edgarpoe's [sic] pounding rhythms and clanging rhymes are intended to produce in us. Just let your mind fight back, just a little, against the maniacal regularity, the hypnotic fanfare in which the same combinations of rhyme occur with the inexorability of a Chinese water torture—just resist the spell a little bit, and the whole contraption suddenly comes apart at the seams. (74)

The filmmakers had to understand the poem in order to parody its implausible premise. The parody employs all the commonly associated elements of animation, including exaggerated forms, intense colors, and distorted sounds. Thus, *The Simpsons'* "The Raven" is an intermediate-to-loose adaptation that recreates some of the elements of Poe's "The Raven," so that it can, as Hoffman advises, resist its spell and comically critique it.

The Simpsons' skit may treat Poe's serious subject in a less dignified way, but it also treats the Simpsons with more dignity than they usually are given. Casting Homer as the Scholar, Bart as the Raven, and Marge as a beauty amuse us, but the casting also confers on Homer a seriousness and sensitivity his character seldom projects in the situation comedy series. Deep down in his animated heart, Homer depends on and loves Marge and, in the event of her death, he would truly pine for her and be at a loss as to what to do. The casting also confers on Marge an importance she deserves but that seldom seems to be recognized by her family. She finally is the object of her husband's love and not merely his matter-of-fact and sometimes annoyed acceptance. The casting confers on Bart a symbolic dominance over his father that is rarely his privilege.

"THE LEGEND OF SLEEPY HOLLOW" (1820), by Washington Irving

"The Legend of Sleepy Hollow" tells the story of Ichabod Crane, the schoolmaster of Sleepy Hollow, a village in southeastern New York, near Tarrytown. Crane desires Katrina Van Tassel, the daughter of a rich farmer. His rival for Katrina's affections is Brom Bones, a local, wild champion of the young men in the area. Bones plays pranks on Ichabod in hopes of discouraging him from wooing Katrina. After an autumn-night party at Van Tassel's, the legendary Headless Horseman chases Ichabod through a forest, and Ichabod is never seen again in Sleepy Hollow. Bones marries Katrina.

In one sense, the narrator of the story presents Ichabod as a creature of scorn. He is physically unattractive, bookish, courtly, and tyrannical in the classroom. In contrast, Bones possesses several admirable qualities. He is physically attractive, natural, and full of vital energy. He is neither bright nor erudite and lacks social graces, but he has native ingenuity and daredevil courage. Katrina is presented as a coquette, who flirts with both men and pits one suitor against the other.

The story abounds with historical references. It makes a point of emphasizing the earthy Dutch backgrounds of the local characters. It talks a good deal about the Revolutionary War, especially the battles that occurred in the area and the superstitions attached to figures from that war. Among those superstitions is the Headless Horseman, a Hessian mercenary hired by the British to fight against the Colonists. He lost his head to a cannonball in battle and now, like the war itself, haunts the land. This haunting may suggest the difficulty experienced by these new democratic citizens in freeing themselves from the colonial past and establishing a tradition of their own.

The newly arrived Ichabod is an outsider in this rural community. Although he is an American of New England origin, his role as schoolteacher, his bookish knowledge, and his courtly manners link him to a more cultivated world. In contrast to Ichabod is Bones, a native insider, who is a rough, brash, natural American. Their prize is Katrina, who is connected—as future inheritor of her father's farm—with the land and all its bounty and promise. In this romantic battle between two men over the affections of a woman, we see a larger cultural war over the future of America. Bones wins both the romantic battle and the war by finding a way to exploit the outsider's fears. He uses what haunts the local people against the outsider and drives Ichabod out of the county and away from Katrina. Bones is then free to marry her, inherit the land, and endow it with his own rough, natural qualities. The romantic triangle dramatizes the conflict between Ichabod's mannered European etiquette and Bones's naturalness and spontaneity. The two styles compete for the American dream of rural abundance and simple contentedness, and it is the natural man who wins the hand of the American Dream.

THE ADVENTURES OF ICHABOD (1949), Directed by Jack Kinney

This short, animated film was originally released as *The Adventures of Ichabod and Mr. Toad*. The *Mr. Toad* part of the title refers to another short, animated adaptation, also directed by Kinney, of Kenneth Grahame's novel *The Wind in the Willows*. The two parts are linked only by a brief voiceover transition. Since their original release by Walt Disney, the films have sometimes been shown separately both in theaters and on television, and have also been sold separately. We focus exclusively on the Ichabod film.

Irving's short story opens with a densely detailed description of the setting:

> In the bosom of one of those spacious coves which indent the eastern shore of the Hudson, at that broad expansion of the river denominated by the ancient Dutch navigators the Tappan Zee, and where they always prudently shortened sail, and implored the protection of St. Nicholas when they crossed, there lies a small markettown or rural port, which by some is called Greensburgh, but which is more generally and properly known by the name of Tarry Town. This name was given, we are told, in former days, by the good housewives of the adjacent county, from the inveterate propensity of their husbands to linger about the village tavern on market days. (1058)

In this passage and in several like it, the descriptive details emphasize the rural locale, Dutch customs, and Revolutionary War references. These details are dropped from the animated film. In terms of practical considerations, the references to Dutch history and to the Revolutionary War are difficult to bring up without clumsy digressions that would slow the fast pace of the narrative. Moreover, the Dutch and Revolutionary War history is too remote and unfamiliar for most 1949—let alone twenty-first century—audiences, adult and adolescent. The cultural implications of these references are intangible, so concrete equivalents for them cannot be substituted.

With the cutting of historical references and associations, the film loses the larger historical context for the battle between Ichabod and Bones. All the film has left is the small, local context of a specific romantic competition between two men, both poor, over a rich woman. This situation, in turn, is simplified into essentially a two-guys-and-a-girl caper full of narrative-related sight gags that humorously exaggerate Katrina's influence on both men. For instance, the first time Ichabod sees Katrina, while on a picnic, he absentmindedly places a whole chicken on his head and takes a bite out of the brim of his hat. While these fantastic comic bits are not in the short story, they are not exactly new additions to the narrative. They plausibly follow from the short story's plot and are the filmmakers' animated comic amplifications of Irving's literary text.

The physical characteristics of all of Irving's characters are kept and then exaggerated into impossibly humorous or handsome figures. Ichabod has the thin face, the lanky posture, and the ungraceful-graceful walk of the crane. Bones is a square-jawed, broad-shouldered, thick-calfed beach athlete out of a 1940s muscle-building magazine, the typical look of Disney's animated heroes. Katrina is pretty, petite, and pert, like a hummingbird flitting from flower to flower, and is typical of Disney heroines.

This contrast of the humorous grotesqueness of Ichabod and the idealized cuteness of Bones and Katrina identifies a symbolic difference between the characters. As Imelda Whelehan points out, "Typical of Disney . . . the binary opposition of good and evil seems to be mirrored by the delineation of grace set against the grotesque" (219). Although Ichabod is not evil *per se*, he is a newcomer to the area and disruptive of the already established romance between Bones and Katrina. Consequently, he must be eliminated from their company, as evil would be eliminated from a society, so that they can continue their courtship.

The love triangle is resolved the same way as in Irving's story. Bones wins the romantic battle by finding a way to exploit Ichabod's fears. He uses the legend of the Headless Horseman against Ichabod and drives the schoolteacher out of the county and away from Katrina. Bones then is free to marry her, inherit her father's land, and endow it with his own rough qualities.

In the film, the triumph of the earthy Bones over the more cultivated Ichabod is dramatized by the tone of the narrator's (Bing Crosby) low-pitched voice. Crosby is cool, laid back, and informal; he doesn't take anything too seriously. This jazz singer's cool is in line with Bones's cool and is a vocal demonstration—more than 150 years later—of Bones's physical and social victory over the nervous, worried, formal, serious, and affected Ichabod.

Animated dances and songs are interwoven throughout the film. Like the sight gags, the dances and songs are amplifications of the comical and comically grotesque elements of Irving's narrative. One example is the light and airy *signature song* associated with and even congratulatory of Katrina's fair appearance and coquettish behavior. Another example is the comic, energetic, foot-stomping, barn-dance *ballad* associated with the boisterous Bones's rollicking tale of his encounter with the Headless Horseman. Chief among the dances is the exquisitely choreographed, subtly detailed chase sequence in which the Headless Horseman pursues Ichabod through the woods.

The film sequence begins with the night woods. Ichabod enters them, becomes increasingly frightened by the nocturnal sights and sounds surrounding him, encounters the Headless Horseman, is pursued, escapes across the bridge, and is hit by a fiery pumpkin thrown by the Headless Horseman as a parting shot.

The color scheme of the eerie woods is dominated by shades of blue and black. In the first shot of the sequence, the moon is seen as a pale white disk with a pale yellow corona. Later in the sequence, it is all pale yellow. The clouds in front of the moon are light- and medium-blue striations that later curve into fingers that close in on the moon. Bathed in whatever moonlight is available, the woods below are medium to dark blue with black trees.

Through the woods Ichabod rides on Gunpowder, a plodding, swayback, light-gray mare, whose color might be a pun on the old song, "The Old Gray Mare." Ichabod himself is dressed in light-colored clothes. His big eyes, ears, and nose are large enough to discern the sights, sounds, and scents of any phantom beside him, including the demonic presence and laugh of the Headless Horseman. Mounted on a black steed with fire-red eyes, the Headless Horseman is dressed all in black with a vermilion cape flying behind him.

Up until Ichabod meets the Headless Horseman, the pace of the sequence is slow, as if keeping pace with the plodding progress of Gunpowder. The narrator briefly sets the eerie scene and comments occasionally on Ichabod's growing anxiety. Silences punctuate Ichabod's unhurried whistling in the dark; the tune he manages to follow is Katrina's signature song. Natural sounds such as crickets' chirps and frogs' croaks seem to call his name, crows seem to caw "beware," and the wind blows shrilly through broken reeds and loudly beats the pods of bulrushes against a fallen hollow tree trunk with the rhythm of galloping hooves.

We know the sounds Ichabod hears are natural because we are shown not ghosts and goblins but crickets, frogs, and crows in silhouette making their noises. The noises are formed carefully to suggest simultaneously their chirps, croaks, and caws and the human English words "Ichabod" and "beware." Because the crickets and frogs are shown at ground level as Ichabod passes by them mounted on Gunpowder, it is difficult to determine if he, too, is aware of the sources of these sounds.

By the time he hears the wind beating the pods of the bulrushes against the tree trunk, he has been driven mad with fear. Once he discovers the beating sound is not galloping hooves but hard pods drumming against a hollow trunk, he laughs hysterically. The laughter is catching as Gunpowder eventually joins in with a calmer horse laugh. Ichabod's high-pitched shrieking and Gunpowder's lower pitched chortle are suddenly interrupted by the loud, low-pitched laugh of the Headless Horseman.

With the Headless Horseman's appearance, the chase-dance begins. Gunpowder erupts into a gallop with Ichabod holding on for dear life, alternately striking the old horse with his riding crop and looking over his shoulder at the perpetually gaining, sword-swinging, demonically laughing Headless Horseman.

In a highly acrobatic chase, the two horses and their riders fly along the road, soar over each other, tumble down banks, swim underwater, and, in the case of Ichabod, even change mounts. Through all this, the Headless Horseman remains firmly mounted on his steed, while Ichabod is all over Gunpowder from neck to rump. These flexible stunts are accompanied by blaring, pulsating horns. The sequence is brought to a crescendo by a close-up of the fiery pumpkin hurling across the bridge at Ichabod's head.

On the whole, the film keeps most of the significant elements of the story, such as the romantic rivalry between Ichabod Crane and Brom Bones over Katrina Van Tassel, the lower Hudson Valley setting, and some of the dialogue. The film also substitutes another, more optimistic ending for Ichabod. On the one hand, the film drops the descriptive details that emphasize the rural locale, the Dutch customs, and the Revolutionary War; the absence of these details, in turn, diminish the context for the symbolic battle for Katrina. On the other hand, the film adds narrative-related sight gags that humorously exaggerate Katrina's influence on both men and narrative-related dances and songs that amplify the comical and comically grotesque elements of Irving's narrative. The result is an intermediate-to-close adaptation of the short story.

A frightened Ichabod Crane riding Gunpowder through the dark and spooky woods in *The Adventures of Ichabod* (1949).

The filmmakers add no new substantial elements of narrative to lengthen the story to fit the running time of a feature film because the running time is adjusted down from the average two hours to 26 minutes. Thus, while the film drops most of the historical material, it amplifies the comic mood, so that the dropped elements and the amplified elements offset each other in both significance and running time.

Summary

Animated films have a long history of adapting a wide range of literary genres. Animation comes in four basic types: drawings, cutouts, computer images, and three-dimensional objects. The different types produce an apparent motion and depth similar to that produced in live-action films. Animation starts with a human, animal, or inanimate form and then exaggerates or embellishes the form to create a comic, idealized, or grotesque figure. Combined with animation's exaggeration of forms is its exaggeration and embellishment of color and sound. Animation creates a world similar to magic realism, where the divisions between the possible and impossible are erased. Animated films are aimed primarily at younger audiences, although adults are not excluded. Animations tend to drop abstract yet important thematic elements of the literary texts from which they are adapted, although this may be due more to a filmmaker's choice than to a limitation of the medium.

■■■ TOPICS FOR DISCUSSION

1. Choose several lines from Poe's "The Raven" that are kept in the *Simpsons* adaptation. Analyze the shots in which the lines are spoken. What type of framing is used? What is the predominate color? What sound effects are used? How do the framing, color, and sound change the emotional pitch of the lines?

2. *The Adventures of Ichabod* uses cel animation. What would be the effect of telling the story in another animation format, such as cutout silhouettes, computer-generated images, or three-dimensional objects? For example, what effects would be lost in the sequence showing Ichabod's ride through the dark forest and his encounter with the Headless Horseman if another format were substituted for cel animation? What

effects might be added in the same sequence if it were shown in another format?

3. Take a descriptive passage from a literary text that has been adapted into a feature animation film. Read the passage and then view the corresponding scene or sequence from the film. Explain how caricature, sound, and color or other characteristics of animation change the literary story.

4. Choose an animated adaptation from the filmography and identify the major human, animal, or inanimate forms. Are these forms portrayed as comic, grotesque, or idealized figures? How do these characterizations relate to the text's portrayal of characters?

■■■ WORKS CITED

Adventures of Ichabod, The. Dir. Jack Kinney. Perf. Bing Crosby. Walt Disney, 1949.

DRYJE, FRANTISEK. "The Force of Imagination." *Dark Alchemy: The Films of Jan Svankmajer.* Ed. Peter Hames. Westport, Conn.: Greenwood Press, 1995.

HOFFMAN, DANIEL. *Poe, Poe, Poe, Poe, Poe, Poe, Poe.* New York: Doubleday, 1973.

IRVING, WASHINGTON. "The Legend of Sleepy Hollow." *Histories, Tales, and Sketches.* New York: Library Classics of the United States, 1983. 1058–88.

MÁRQUEZ, GABRIEL GARCÍA. "A Very Old Man with Enormous Wings." *Perrine's Literature: Structure, Sound, and Sense.* Ed. Thomas R. Arp and Greg Johnson. 8th ed. New York: Harcourt, 2002. 329–35.

POE, EDGAR ALLAN. "The Philosophy of Composition." *Edgar Allan Poe: Essays and Reviews.* New York: Library Classics of the United States, 1984. 13–26.

———. "The Raven." *Edgar Allan Poe; Poetry and Tales.* New York: Library Classics of the United States, 1984. 467–71.

——— and Sam Simon. "The Raven." "Treehouse of Horror." *The Simpsons.*

<http://www.snpp.com/episodes/7f04.html>.

"Raven, The." "Treehouse of Horror." *The Simpsons.* Dir. David Silverman. Perf. Dan Castellaneta and James Earl Jones. Twentieth-Century Fox, October 25, 1990.

REINIGER, LOTTE. *Shadow Puppets, Shadow Theaters, and Shadow Films.* Boston: Plays, Inc., 1970.

WELLS, PAUL. " 'Thou Art Translated': Analyzing Animated Adaptations." *Adaptations: From Text to Screen, Screen to Text.* Ed. Deborah Cartmell and Imelda Whelehan. New York: Routledge, 1999. 199–213.

WHELEHAN, IMELDA. " 'A Doggy Fairy Tale': The Film Metamorphosis of *The Hundred and One Dalmatians.*"*Adaptations: From Text to Screen, Screen to Text.* Ed. Deborah Cartmell and Imelda Whelehan. New York: Routledge, 1999. 214–225.

SELECTED FILMOGRAPHY OF ANIMATION ADAPTATIONS ■■■

RICHARD ADAMS. *Watership Down* (1972).
MARTIN ROSEN. *Watership Down* (1978).

ANONYMOUS. "The Enchanted Horse" and "Aladdin and His Enchanted Lamp" from *The Thousand and One Nights* (fourteenth century).
LOTTE REINIGER. *The Adventures of Prince Achmed* (German, 1926).

ANONYMOUS. "Snow White and the Seven Dwarfs" (n.d.).
BEN SHARPSTEEN. *Snow White and the Seven Dwarfs* (1937).

J. M. BARRIE. *Peter Pan* (1904).
HAMILTON LUSKE. *Peter Pan* (1953).

LEWIS CARROLL. *Alice in Wonderland* (1865).
HAMILTON LUSKE. *Alice in Wonderland* (1951).
JAN SVANKMAJER. *Alice* (1988).

LEWIS CARROLL. *Nonsense Poems* (1876).
MICHAEL SPORN. *The Hunting of the Snark* (1989).

KENNETH GRAHAME. *The Wind in the Willows* (1908).
JACK KINNEY. "The Adventures of Mr. Toad" (1949).
DAVE UNWIN. *The Wind in the Willows* (1995).

JOEL CHANDLER HARRIS. *Uncle Remus: His Songs and His Sayings* (1881).
WILFRED JACKSON (ANIMATION) AND HARVE FOSTER (LIVE-ACTION). *Song of the South* (1946).

WASHINGTON IRVING. "The Legend of Sleepy Hollow" (1826).
UB IWERKS. "The Headless Horseman" (1934).
JACK KINNEY. "The Adventures of Ichabod" (1949).
SHANE WILLIAMS. *The Night of the Headless Horseman* (1999).

RUDYARD KIPLING. *The Jungle Book* (1894).
WOLFGANG REITHERMAN. *The Jungle Book* (1967).

RUDYARD KIPLING. "Rikki-Tikki-Tavi" (1888).
CHUCK JONES. *Rikki-Tikki-Tavi* (1975).

GEORGE ORWELL. *Animal Farm* (1946).
JOHN HALAS. *Animal Farm* (1954).
JOHN STEPHENSON. *Animal Farm* (1999).

EDGAR ALLAN POE. "The Raven" (1845).
DAVID SILVERMAN. "The Raven." "Treehouse of Horror." *The Simpsons.* (October 25, 1990).

ANTOINE DE SAINT-EXUPÉRY. *The Little Prince* (1942).
WILL VINTON. *The Little Prince* (1979).

WILLIAM STEIG. *Shrek* (1990).
ANDREW ADAMSON AND VICKY JENSEN. *Shrek* (2001).

JONATHAN SWIFT. *Gulliver's Travels* (1726).
DAVID FLEISCHER. *Gulliver's Travels* (1939).

10 THE FAILED ADAPTATION

Why do adaptations fail?

Well, you might ask, what do we mean by failure?

Most people recognize two kinds: a commercial failure and a critical failure. Here are our stipulative definitions of each. A film fails commercially when it does not make back its budget at the box office on domestic release. *Heaven's Gate* (1980), *Ishtar* (1987), and *Waterworld* (1995), although not adaptations, are notorious examples of commercial flops.

A film fails critically when contemporary reviewers using various standards *agree* that it doesn't succeed as a movie. Added to that measure can be the film's lack of nominations or awards in any of the categories in annual film competitions—anything from the People's Choice to the Academy Awards. (Of course, a film may be heavily criticized at the time of its release, receive no awards, but years later be acknowledged as a landmark.)

Commercial and critical failures are different but can come together. For example, Roland Joffé's *The Scarlet Letter* (1995), despite an all-star cast of Robert Duvall, Gary Oldman, and Demi Moore, lost $50 million at the box office and was heavily criticized in newspapers, magazines, and film and literary reviews.[1] Likewise, Brian De Palma's *The Bonfire of the Vanities* (1990) lost about $35 million at the box office and was labeled by *Variety* as "a misfire of a thousand inanities" (Qtd. in Salamon 403). *Eyes Wide Shut* (1999), directed by Stanley Kubrick, an adaptation of Arthur Schnitzler's *Dream Novel*, costing $65 million to make, grossed only $55 million in its three-month domestic run and received uneven reviews. *The Perfect Storm* (2000) lost more than $60 million, and *Stuart Little 2* (2002), which cost $120 million to make, lost $54 million in domestic release. Both were critical failures. *The Shipping News* (2001), based on E. Annie Proulx's Pulitzer Prize–winning novel and starring Kevin Spacey, Julianne Moore, and Judi Dench, garnered lackluster reviews and lost $24 million. Other movies adapted from texts—such as *The Rules of Attraction* (2002), *White Oleander* (2002), *The Importance of Being Earnest* (2002), and *The Emperor's Club* (2002)—received mixed reviews and did poorly or broke even at the box office.

Of course, film adaptations can succeed critically but not financially. *Glengarry Glen Ross* (1992), based on David Mamet's Pulitzer Prize–winning play of the same name, is acknowledged by critics as a memorable movie with an almost unparalleled cast of stars: Al Pacino, Jack Lemmon, Alec Baldwin, Alan Arkin, Ed Harris, and Kevin Spacey. Although it was a low-budget film that cost just $12.5 million to make, it lost almost $2 million at the box office.

Many may argue with our shorthand criteria for failure, objecting to the idea that a film's success rests on its domestic earnings or on the reviews immediately following its release. So let's approach the subject another way by attempting to define what makes a good movie. One measure used by reviewers is a film's overall coherence. A good film synthesizes the contributions made by a strong script, a fine director, excellent actors, and high production values. Each cinematic element (the mise-en-scène, camera work, sound, and editing) needs to work with the narrative structure (cause and effect motivation, point of view, and other story elements) for the film to cohere. In other words, cinematic elements need to be synchronized with a script's narrative logic so that a film achieves coherence on many different levels. When filmmakers are able to coordinate the technical, stylistic, and narrative options at their disposal, the film achieves a higher level of aural and visual meaning than could be achieved by the sum of its parts.

---

[1] Box office amounts come from www.boxofficeguru.com and www.the-numbers.com. Figures may not always be accurate since they depend on budget amounts provided by studios that sometimes inflate or deflate the cost of making a film. The film budgets used do not include the cost of advertising and promotion. The earnings are based on domestic ticket sales and do not take into account profits from worldwide release, video, DVD, laserdisc, cable and network TV, soundtrack albums, or commercial tie-ins, which today often account for the bulk of a film's revenue.

Negative box office returns, weak reviews, and a lack of coherence are common measures of film failure, but what interests us more are the decisions made in the process of adaptation that lead to the making of a less than successful movie. The following generalizations about failure may not apply to all adaptations in all times and places, but they supply a starting point for classroom discussion as well as a review of some of the general principles of adaptation discussed earlier.

Uncinematic Texts

Our general view is that film adaptations fail because (1) the text isn't cinematic enough to begin with and/or (2) because of what the adapter decides to do in transferring the text to the film medium.

Let's begin with the notion of a cinematic text. What kind of text is relatively easy to adapt and what kind of text is not? C. Kenneth Pellow offers a formula for the novel.

> Probably the ideal transformation would start with a novel composed of a good plot, a few compelling characters, and one central theme. The novel would preferably be short—fewer than 300 pages, say—or would have some quantity of material that could be excised, as not being germane to the central plot or the one theme. The quality should not be too reliant upon fine prose, or the development of characters by interior monologue or to great depth, or on any complex use of narrative point-of-view. (303)

Notice that Pellow offers both a positive and negative definition of a cinematic text. There are some things it should have and some things it shouldn't.

Narrative texts that lend themselves to adaptation should have a manageable length. Ideally, the text is not a one-million-word novel like Samuel Richardson's *Clarissa* or a 60-paragraph short story like William Faulkner's "A Rose for Emily." If the text runs between 60 to 120 pages, then the adapter is not required to add or cut substantial material to fit the time parameters of the feature film. If the text is longer than a short novel, it should contain material that can be cut without harming the plot or the central theme of the story.

The cinematic text must have a good plot. Ideally, the text has causally connected and clearly motivated actions that are developed through a structure with a beginning, middle, and end. If the actions are conceived in scenes, then the text is even more cinematic. The text should also have a few multidimensional characters who are interesting and sympathetic and at least one of whom is capable of some kind of development or change.

A narrative text that is relatively easy to adapt should *not* depend for its power on the author's prose style, authorial comments or reflections, or tone (such as irony or sarcasm). *Nor* should it make extensive use of historical detail, literary allusions, philosophical ideas, abstract meditations, or symbolism. Finally, the text should *not* use the first-person point of view or some complex combination of points of view.

One example of an uncinematic text is Cervantes' novel *Don Quixote*. According to Philip French, "the history of cinema is marked by the bleached bones of unmade or unfinished versions of *Don Quixote*, stretching from Sergei Eisenstein's in the 1920s to Orson Welles's in the 1950s. It's as if some curse were transferred from its mad, idealistic hero to those attracted to bringing him to the screen." Clearly, part of *Quixote*'s "curse" is that it runs 1,000 pages, requiring huge cuts to shrink it to modern screenplay size.

Of course, all these rules about what texts are cinematic belong to the broadest kind of generalization. Many successful films are based on uncinematic works. *Adaptation* (2002), directed by Spike Jonze, is an example. In 1995, Susan Orlean published a think piece for *The New Yorker* about several thefts of orchids in Florida. Orlean later expanded that article into a book that added the character of the orchid thief John Laroche. Orlean sold the film rights, and Charlie Kaufman was signed to write the screenplay. But this nonfiction book was more a rumination on orchids and orchid thievery than a narrative with a beginning, middle, and end that could lend itself to a Hollywood storyline. To fix the problem, Kaufman devised a whole new story—the story of Kaufman himself struggling to adapt this "great, sprawling *New Yorker* stuff"—and inserted it into a screenplay that attempted to remain "faithful" to Orlean's material. The insertion included the screenwriter himself; an invented twin brother, Donald Kaufman; Susan Orlean, the author of *The Orchid Thief*; the director of the film; and Kaufman's agent. *Adaptation*, then, has two main matters: the story of John Laroche, the orchid thief, derived from the book; and the story of Kaufman's own struggle to adapt the book. The problem for both the actual and portrayed screenwriter is that Orlean's nonfiction book on orchids lacks dimensional characters and a strong plot. These had to be added to make a movie.

So one reason adaptations fail is that the anterior text is uncinematic either because it contains narrative features that are difficult to carry over to film (such as the length of *Don Quixote*) or lacks strong narrative features (such as plot and characters in *The Orchid Thief*). As useful as the notion of uncinematic text is, it is important to keep in mind that whatever the inherent difficulties of an original text, its story can be transferred to film given a flexible approach, a strong script, fine acting, and good direction.

Cinematic Misjudgments

Let's assume that an adapter chooses a text that lends itself to adaptation. There is still a mountain of decisions that stands between the text on one side and a successful film on the other. Where do things go wrong?

1. Keeping Too Closely to the Text

According to a recent estimate, the average Hollywood feature film today costs in excess of $100 million (including publicity and promotion) to make. Since the investment is daunting, it helps studio executives decide to go ahead with a film if its story is "pre-kissed" by popular success. Ted Tally, who wrote the screenplay for *The Silence of the Lambs* (1991), explains in an interview: "Somebody already published this book, so it must have something—at least, that's what they [the studios and producers] figure. Even if they haven't read it, they assume there must be something to it; there are at least existing stories and characters" (Engel 127).

It is no accident that many films are based on best sellers written by authors with huge readerships. Think of Stephen King, John Grisham, Michael Crichton, and James W. Patterson. These authors and their books bring with them built-in audiences that promise at least a modest return at the box office. But to ensure the audience doesn't turn against the film, the studios must make sure the adaptation stays relatively close to the popular text. In general, the more familiar readers are with the details of the work, the closer the adaptation has to be. But sometimes the desire to stay close backfires, and the result is a filmed book that is unsatisfying.

One case of a film staying too close to its antecedent is *Harry Potter and the Sorcerer's Stone* (2001), directed by Chris Columbus. J. K. Rowling, the best-selling author of the Harry Potter series, knew that she had a loyal following, and so in selling the film rights, she required that the film stay close to the Potter text, even insisting on her approval of the director and actors and other elements of film production. When the film was released, it delighted many loyal readers because of its fidelity, but it also disappointed some reviewers who complained that it did not work as a film. "As a movie, *Harry Potter and the Sorcerer's Stone* has no inner life—no pulse—of its own: It's secondhand," writes David Edelstein in *Slate*. "Solid but uninspired, *Harry* lacks brio. It's respectable and a bit dull," echoes J. Hoberman in the *Village Voice*. Although reviews were mixed, a common complaint emerged that the adaptation stayed too close to the text at the expense of a dramatic movie. The second Harry Potter—*The Chamber of Secrets* (2002)—was more successful perhaps because it was a bit less obsessed with fidelity. Likewise, *The Lord of the Rings: The Fellowship of the Ring* (2001), directed by Peter Jackson, was more flexible in its approach than *Harry Potter I* and received high praise and won many awards. In short, one reason an adaptation can falter is that it stays too close to a text.

Film has long been regarded as a teaching medium that can instruct a nation about its cultural heritage. This is especially the case in England, where it is common to adapt and readapt works produced by such national literary eminences as Shakespeare, Austen, the Brontës, Dickens, Hardy, and so on. Often the problem with these adaptations is that they pay homage to the literary masterpiece through a literal translation rather than by exploiting the resources of film to tell the story. John C. Tibbetts complains about such over-reverent adaptations in a review essay of adaptations produced during the '90s:

> it should be remembered that more literary adaptations than ever before have displayed a faithfulness bordering on obsession. . . . Michael Winterbottom's *Jude* (1996), Bille August's *Les Misérables* (1998), Claude Berri's *Germinal* (1993), and Claude Chabrol's *Madame Bovary* (1991)—to cite just a few—have displayed such respect for the text of Thomas Hardy, Victor Hugo, Émile Zola, and Gustave Flaubert, respectively, that the results fairly choked on their own literary bile. (30)

Critical judgments about the films Tibbetts mentions can vary, but the point is that an over-reverent approach to a classic text can mean the adaptation doesn't work as a movie.

Whether it is profit-minded studio executives trying not to turn off the loyal audience of a best seller or respectful adapters trying to preserve a literary masterpiece for a new generation, adaptating a text without fully using the film medium to tell the story is not a formula for success. The question the adapter must ask is not, "Is this being true or untrue to the original?" but rather, "Does this make for a coherent and persuasive narrative in its own right?" (McFarlane 2).

2. Adding the Wrong Elements

We discussed above how screenwriter Charlie Kaufman added characters and a storyline to Susan Orlean's nonfiction book in order to adapt an uncinematic text into a film that won high praise from critics. Although the addition of melodramatic mayhem and death in the last twenty minutes of the movie is pure Hollywood, the addition works because it mocks the typical cliché-ridden Hollywood ending, thus fitting the ironic tone established in the beginning of the movie. But sometimes additions do not fit as organically.

For example, Richard Siodmak's *The Killers* (1946) closely adapts Hemingway's story of the same name in the first twelve minutes of the film. The rest of the movie is a 91-minute tack-on that develops another plot, introduces new characters and settings, and brings in a new theme. This massive addition serves to make the Hemingway story the introductory finale to "a caper story about a meticulously planned holdup" (Clarens 199). For some, Siodmak's addition is considered a necessary padding of a short story in order to make a feature-length film. Others believe the adaptation changes one kind of gangster story that skillfully undercuts a reader's expectations into another kind of gangster story that too predictably fulfills them. The addition submerges Hemingway's sophisticated literary story into an unsophisticated popular one.

3. Cutting Something Essential

John Huston's film version of *Moby Dick* (1956) keeps the major characters, some dialogue, and the realistic narrative parts of the novel, especially the whaling scenes where the action almost races out of control. But the film drops page after page of scientific, historical, philosophical, political, and religious digression, as well as the many chapters devoted to cetacean classifications, which Melville uses to magnify the subject of whaling. What is left is the narrative spine of the novel without the pattern of symbolic detail that gives this whaling voyage its ability to raise questions about the nature of God and the universe. In short, the weighty metaphysics were cut in favor of a fishing tale, leaving the viewer without a sense of the qualities that generation after generation of readers have found most valuable.

4. Going Hollywood

In general, the more a text is historically removed from its readers, the more the adapter can depart from it without fear of losing an audience. Most members of a film audience today have never read Thomas Malory's *Morte d'Arthur,* so they are unlikely to recognize the massive liberties Hollywood takes in retelling the Arthurian legends. (Certainly, different versions of the Arthurian story draw not only on Malory but also on other English and French texts, so it is hard to determine whether a departure from *Morte d'Arthur* is the screenwriter's decision or whether it was derived from another source.) Even fewer viewers have read the anonymous fifteenth-century ballad romance *The Geste of Robin Hood,* the original source of Robin Hood stories, in which Maid Marian, a staple of Hollywood adaptations, never even appears, and in which Robin robs not only from the rich but also from the clergy, whom he beats, ties, and leaves by the roadside. In both cases, modern filmmakers may not be adapting specific texts but legends that have come down through the centuries in many forms, including other movies. The point is that playing fast and loose with remote story material in order to bring it in line with Hollywood conventions will not turn viewers off, but applying the same Hollywood treatment to a more well-known classic can backfire.

Take, for example, Nathaniel Hawthorne's *The Scarlet Letter,* a novel most Americans read in high school or college. The novel begins with Hester Prynne being guided out of prison by a Puritan jail-warden, wearing a scarlet A on her bosom while holding her newborn infant Pearl—both symbols of her adultery. On a scaffold in the public square in front of the Puritan community, the hypocritical Reverend Arthur Dimmesdale admonishes Hester to give up the name of her fellow adulterer. Meanwhile, her long-lost husband Roger Chillingworth arrives, hides his identity, and sets out to find Hester's partner in sin. At the end, Dimmesdale confesses that he is the adulterer and dies. Hester takes Pearl to Europe, and, once her daughter is grown and well married, Hester, for reasons Hawthorne never fully explains, returns to Boston to take up the scarlet letter once again. After many years, Hester dies and is buried next to Arthur under the same tombstone.

The Scarlet Letter poses a challenge to any adapter because there is very little action except in the minds of the characters. "Confined as they are by their

Gary Oldman as the
Reverend Arthur
Dimmesdale and
Demi Moore as
Hester Prynne in a
sex scene never
described in
Hawthorne's *The
Scarlet Letter.*

Puritan setting, Hawthorne's characters think and feel; love, hate, interpret, and speculate, but they rarely *do* anything" (Bercovitch 3). The novel's most intriguing action by modern standards is the seductive entanglement that initially led Hester and Arthur to the sexual act, but this is never described by Hawthorne. Hollywood fixes that in the 1995 version of *The Scarlet Letter,* directed by Roland Joffé. In this loose adaptation, Hester first sees Arthur skinny-dipping and then fantasizes about him in her own nude bathing scene, which is watched through a keyhole by Hester's indentured servant,

Mituba. Hawthorne's never-described sex scene between Dimmesdale and Hester takes place in a barn and is again observed by the ubiquitous Mituba. Besides nudity, sex, and voyeurism—all photographed in a soft pornographic haze—Joffé adds graphic violence to the story: torture, self-mutilation, an attempted rape, a murder, a suicide, a scalping, an interrupted execution, an Indian attack, and a fire. The character of Dimmesdale is changed from a guilt-wracked, hypocritical wimp to a romantic tormented by his longings for Hester. Hester herself is transformed into a free-spirited feminist who is sexually liberated and who opposes male chauvinism wherever she finds it. Finally, in place of Hawthorne's ambiguous conclusion, there is the Hollywood upbeat ending. Dimmesdale does not die but instead joins Pearl and Hester as *she* drives a buckboard out of Boston, heading toward a new life. The movie ends with Dimmesdale and Hester's long kiss, and a voiceover in Pearl's mature voice explaining that "[m]y parents shared a love like no other."

Another text given the Hollywood treatment is Richard Connell's short story "The Most Dangerous Game," which has become a standard in high school and college textbooks and has served as the basis for at least nine films. The story concerns Rainsford, a famous big game hunter, who, shipwrecked on a Caribbean island, meets General Zaroff, an aristocratic madman who shares his passion for the sport but who prefers to hunt human beings. When he becomes Zaroff's prey, Rainsford uses his knowledge of hunting lore to evade Zaroff and eventually to kill him.

Ernest B. Schoedsack and Irving Pichel's adaptation of this story in *The Most Dangerous Game* (1932) goes Hollywood by adding Eve Trowbridge, a damsel in distress, played by Fay Wray of *King Kong* fame, who draws Zaroff's lust and Rainsford's protection. Although the premise of two men hunting each other is kept, Eve accompanies Rainsford in his escape through the island jungle. After giving Zaroff a final beating, Rainsford motors off with Eve as the injured Zaroff falls from a high window to his death. Hollywood's addition of a romantic angle was no doubt intended to make a movie of male competition and violence into a story that held some appeal for women. However, the image of Fay Wray, predecessor of Marilyn Monroe and other Hollywood sex goddesses, running through the jungle in high heels and a low-cut dress undermines the plausibility of the story.

Such Hollywoodizing of adaptations is not unusual. Mark Axelrod claims that a text chosen for adaptation must naturally fit the Hollywood formula or be given the Hollywood treatment. "No matter how the text starts out, inevitably what becomes adapted in a Hollywood film is a story line with rounded characters and linear story development" (206). Works that do not fit this formula may not be adapted, but if they are, their adaptation will seem like a greater divergence than other adapted works that contain a linear storyline and developed characters. The Hollywood film industry adapts material in a way that imposes its formulas and reduces or "undermines the effusive nature of a work of fiction" (201).

5. Miscasting

Miscasting means choosing an actor who does not fit the role. In Chapter 3, we talked about how Humphrey Bogart does not fit the physical description of Sam Spade, a character drawn from Dashiell Hammett's novel *The Maltese Falcon*. Bogart, however, is a reasonable substitution because he projects a kind of menace under control in a similar way to Hammett's Spade. Earlier, we said that fidelity is no measure of an adaptation's quality; both close and loose adaptations can succeed or fail. Applying this principle to casting, we believe that choosing actors to fit closely the physical and personal details of characters adapted from a text is not essential. What is important, though, is to choose actors who fit the literary character well enough so that they do not create a new emphasis that undermines the coherence of the story.

Many film stories are character driven. The character's desires and ambitions lead him or her to take one action and then another and then another. But sometimes an actor is cast whose age, looks, build, prior roles, or public reputation "rewrites" the part. Then the problem is that the "rewritten" character may not fit the motivations attributed to him or her. As a result, the actions that are supposed to flow from the character's motivations may seem implausible.

For example, in Stephen Crane's *The Red Badge of Courage,* the protagonist Henry Fleming is portrayed as a young, untried foot soldier who deserts the field during a battle in the Civil War. The novel describes Fleming's fear of being a coward and his eventual success in controlling his fear. For the Fleming role, John Huston decided to cast soldier-turned-actor Audie Murphy, who was the most decorated enlisted man in World War II. How does the story of an untried youth struggling to overcome his fear work when the actor himself was known to contemporary audiences for his courage? It is equivalent to casting the most profligate young actor in Hollywood as Jesus Christ or Mahatma Gandhi. Fleming's subsequent displays of courage in Huston's *Red Badge* (1951) seem inevitable in a way they are not in the book simply because few viewers in that era could have imagined Audie Murphy turning out to be a coward.

Sometimes the miscasting has to do with an actor's age. For example, in Hemingway's *A Farewell to Arms,* Lieutenant Frederick Henry is a young ambulance driver who comes of age during World War I. The novel draws on Hemingway's own experiences at age 18 as an American serving as an officer in the Italian army. Although Henry's age is never specified in the novel, we get the idea he is young, probably about Hemingway's age at the time of the action. However, in the 1957 adaptation, Henry is played by a 32-year-old Rock Hudson. Hudson appears too mature and experienced to portray Henry as an innocent young man undergoing an initiation into love, war, and skepticism. A similar miscasting occurs in another Hemingway adaptation, *The Sun Also Rises* (1957), in which Jake Barnes is played by Tyrone Power (age 44), Robert Cohn by Mel Ferrer (40), Bill Gorton by Eddie Albert (49), and Mike Campbell by Errol Flynn (48), who looks wizened and wasted. They all seem too old to play the thirty-something characters represented in the novel.

Sometimes an actor is hired for a part he or she does not fit. The adapter may then decide to change the character derived from the text to fit the actor. For example, in a rehearsal for *The Bonfire of the Vanities* (1990), an adaptation of Tom Wolfe's best-selling novel of the same name, director Brian De Palma discovered he needed a rewrite.

> [Bruce] Willis didn't have the skill or the self-confidence of someone like [F. Murray] Abraham, or Tom Hanks. . . . Hanks was diligent and uncomplaining—and he had talent. Willis wasn't without talent, it just fell within a narrow range. When De Palma and Michael Christofer [the screenwriter] watched Willis in rehearsal, it became clear to them that they would have to rethink the part of Peter Fallow. The journalist has been written as a despicable sellout. Willis, however, couldn't shake his persona. He wasn't an actor who could easily slip into someone else's skin. He was a movie star more than anything else. The characters he played tended to become the same likable rogue. (Salamon 119–20)

Willis's limited acting range meant the character drawn from Wolfe's *Vanities* needed to be revised. The actor caused the rewriting of the role.

Several reviewers criticize the casting in *The Human Stain* (2003), directed by Robert Benton and adapted from Phillip Roth's novel. The central figure in the film is Coleman Silk, a dean and a professor who teaches classics at a small New England college. Silk appears to be Jewish, but he is actually the son of black parents whose pale skin allows him to "pass" for white. The actor chosen to play Silk is Anthony Hopkins, so what we are asked to accept, as Anthony Lane points out, is "the unique spectacle of a Welshman playing a black American playing a white American Jew" (105). It is hard to believe. Similarly, Silk has an unlikely love affair with Faunia Farley, ostensibly an illiterate, coarse, and unkempt janitor/farmhand, who is played by Nicole Kidman. One can imagine Faunia, who is perceived in the novel as white trash, acting the way she does but not the glamorous Kidman. The casting affects the viewer's suspension of disbelief and the story's plausibility.

A role can be reduced or eliminated because of casting. This happens sometimes when an actor in a secondary role upstages a star and threatens to steal the movie. The leading actor complains to the director, and in order to placate the star, the role is reduced or even eliminated. This is unfortunate because the reduction or elimination of a secondary role can sometimes weaken the plot and even the overall success of the film. For example, Doris Dowling in *The Blue Dahlia* (1946), based on a screenplay written by Raymond Chandler, upstaged Veronica Lake and, as a consequence, had her role reduced. A variation on this theme occurred in Howard Hawks's *Red River* (1948), adapted from Borden Chase's short story "The Chisholm Trail." Cherry Valance, played by John Ireland, figures prominently as an important minor character in the first third of the movie, but then suddenly disappears. John Wayne, star of the movie, explained later that Ireland and Hawks were chasing the same girl, and, as a result, Ireland's role was reduced. Miscasting, role rewriting, and role reduction can happen for any number of reasons, but it is important to keep in mind that casting choices can alter narrative emphases in a way that affects the coherence and plausibility of the story.

6. Focusing Too Much on Reproducing the Period

One temptation for some adapters of classic literary works is to lavish a great deal of attention on recreating the details of the time and place of the story. There is nothing wrong with this **period emphasis** approach as long as the attention to historical detail does not result in an elaborate period piece that fails to convey the story's emotional drama. Producer Ismail Merchant, director James Ivory, and screenwriter Ruth Prawer Jhabvala are famous for their film productions of classic works. These include adaptations of Henry James's work in *The Europeans* (1979), *The Bostonians* (1984), and *The Golden Bowl* (2000); adaptations of E. M. Forster's in *A Room with a View* (1985), *Maurice* (1987), and *Howard's End* (1992); and of Kazuo Ishiguro's in *The Remains of the Day* (1993). Although these adaptations succeed in varying degrees, critics complain that some of them stress the visual splendor of costumes, houses, furnishings, and grand settings at the expense of drama. The films are accused of having wooden characters, conventional storytelling, a want of emotion, and a lack of verve. The exceptions are *A Room with a View, Howard's End*, and *The Remains of the Day*, which are quite good at using period detail to show characters rooted in their historical time and place, characterizations that wouldn't be conveyed in any other way.

7. Having Problems with Outside Factors

Many factors in filmmaking that have nothing to do with a text can contribute to a failed adaptation. In *preproduction*, for example, a film may have problems with financing, script revision, casting, or location scouting; in *production*, there can be problems with actor availability, principal photography, second unit work, costumes, or lighting; and in *postproduction*, there can be problems with editing, sound mixing, scoring, previews, reediting, advertising, and promotion. Keith Fulton and Louis Pepe show several ways a film can go wrong in preproduction and production phases in their documentary *Lost in La Mancha* (2002). The documentary follows the making of *The Man Who Killed Don Quixote*, an adaptation of Cervantes's novel, directed by Terry Gilliam. Backed by European investors, the film was underfunded from the start; its production stage in Madrid was too small and had poor acoustics; and scenes shot on location in the desert were interrupted by roaring jets, rain, and a flash flood that changed the terrain. A lead actress signed late, and the actor who played Quixote had such serious back problems he was forced to leave the set for an extended period. Aware of shooting delays, the completion guarantors and insurance adjustors arrived to see if the film could be finished and decided to shut it down. The problems with inadequate funding, inhospitable locations, bad weather,

Jean Rochefort and Terry Gilliam from *Lost in La Mancha* (2002), a documentary.

actor availability, illness, and investor interference came together with a tight shooting schedule that didn't allow for mishap. This fascinating case may not fit our chapter. After all, Gilliam's adaptation was never made, so it "failed" in another sense than we have been using. But the case reminds us of the many factors having nothing to do with a text that influence what is brought to the screen.

8. Lacking a Cinematic Equivalent for an Author's Point of View

An easy-to-adapt text most likely does not depend for its power on the author's use of the first-person point of view. However, many first-person texts are so attractive as stories that they appeal to adapters despite the problem of point of view. Avron Fleischman calculates that one out of six fiction films since 1927 have used first-person techniques enough to be categorized as narrated films (22). Not all of these narrated films are adaptations, but Fleischman's figure gives an indication of the widespread use of first-person techniques in film.

We discussed the problems of point of view in film in Chapters 2 and 5, but let's look at one specific passage and imagine the difficulty of transposing its first-person point of view to film. This is the opening of J. D. Salinger's *The Catcher in the Rye:*

> If you really want to hear about it, the first thing you'll probably want to know is where I was born, and what my lousy childhood was like, and how my parents

were occupied and all before they had me, and all that David Copperfield kind of crap, but I don't feel like going into it, if you want to know the truth. (1)

Holden Caulfield, the narrator here, has a distinctive voice that reveals through direct commentary and word choices his judgments about characters and his attitudes as he relates the story. Much of the power of the text depends on the subtlety of Holden's voice as he ponders his own experience. However, in film, the camera has difficulty conveying the judgments of a first-person narrative voice and sustaining the illusion that all events are filtered through a central consciousness. Despite the use of voiceover and other techniques, the audience tends to identify with the camera, which serves as a third-person (limited or omniscient) point of view. Film adaptations of narrated works run the risk of losing an important dimension to the story, as we will see in the following discussion of an adaptation of Fitzgerald's *The Great Gatsby*.

THE GREAT GATSBY (1974), Directed by Jack Clayton

Now that we have looked at some areas where adaptations can stumble, let's look at a specific adaptation that in our opinion failed: *The Great Gatsby* (1974), directed by Jack Clayton. The film was not a commercial success. It cost $13 million to make, a considerable amount in 1974 considering that six years later, in 1980, the average cost of making a film was $9.4 million. The film was so heavily promoted in the summer of 1974 that it has gone down as one of the most overhyped movies in film history. Despite the promotion, *Gatsby* barely broke even at the box office. The film's faults fall into five of the areas discussed above: (1) first-person narration, (2) miscasting, (3) cutting, (4) adding, and (5) period emphasis.

The story of F. Scott Fitzgerald's novel *The Great Gatsby* is told in the first person by Nick Carraway, a young Midwesterner, who comes East to make his fortune selling bonds on Wall Street during the 1920s. Nick rents a house in West Egg, Long Island, just across from a mansion owned by a mysterious neighbor, Jay Gatsby, whose extravagant parties are financed by bootlegging and swindling activities. Nick discovers that as a penniless Army lieutenant, Gatsby fell in love with Nick's cousin Daisy. When Gatsby goes off to fight in World War I, Daisy does not wait for him as promised, but instead marries Tom Buchanan, a wealthy man who turns out to be a brutish philanderer. At the Buchanan estate in East Egg, Nick renews his acquaintance with Daisy and Tom and meets Daisy's friend Jordan Baker, who becomes his love interest. Meanwhile, Nick arranges for Gatsby to meet Daisy again, and Gatsby's long devotion and new wealth both touch and impress her.

While Gatsby and Daisy have an affair, her husband continues his own with the sensuous Myrtle Wilson, the wife of George, a local garage mechanic.

When the husband catches on, he locks Myrtle in her room, but she escapes, running out in the middle of the road to wave down a car she mistakenly believes belongs to Tom. Myrtle is accidentally killed by the car, which is driven by Daisy. Gatsby tries to protect Daisy from the authorities, but by this time she has reconciled with Tom, who tells Wilson it was Gatsby driving the car. Wilson kills Gatsby and then himself. Gatsby never achieves his dream of possessing Daisy, and after the bloodbath, Tom and Daisy retreat into their wealth. After ending his relationship with Jordan, Nick returns to the Midwest, disillusioned by what he has observed, and resolved to live a moral life.

First-Person Narration

In discussing the novel, we often ask students who the main character is. Sometimes the answer is Nick Carraway, even though Gatsby is named in the title. The reason students choose Nick is that he plays a dual role. He is the narrator of the story—everything described is seen retrospectively through his eyes—and he is a character involved in the action who is changed by what he sees.

The filmmaker intent on a close adaptation of *The Great Gatsby* may not have much trouble with Nick as a character since he can be portrayed like Tom or Daisy or Myrtle or anyone else, but the adapter needs to address Nick's role as narrator. We discussed the problem of transferring the first-person point of view from text to film. How is Nick's narration brought over?

Clayton addresses the problem in two ways. First, he uses voiceover narration extensively at the beginning of the film. Starting from the film title and excepting one scene, the voiceover continues through the first 16 minutes of the film. The soundtrack narration begins as Nick inexpertly guides a small motorboat over the courtesy bay to visit the Buchanans in their glittering white palace in East Egg. While Nick clumsily dodges sailboats, his voiceover quotes verbatim the first two paragraphs of the novel.

> In my younger and more vulnerable years my father gave me some advice that I've been turning over in my mind ever since.
>
> "Whenever you feel like criticizing any one," he told me, "just remember that all the people in this world haven't had the advantages you've had." (1)

The voiceover skips a sentence, and then Nick declares, "In consequence, I'm inclined to reserve all judgments" (1). Francis Ford Coppola's screenplay follows Fitzgerald in making clear that Nick's judgments are careful, measured, and important. In Nick's next voiceover, he introduces his cousin Daisy and her husband, Tom Buchanan, two of the three important characters to be judged.

After Nick's opening narration introduces the place, time, and characters, the voiceover soundtrack temporarily disappears; however, the camera follows Nick's point of view into the next scene. After disembarking, Nick greets Tom and is driven a short distance to the mansion where he eats dinner and converses with the couple and Jordan Baker. Although a **subjective camera** is not used and a few reaction shots show Nick's face, the point of view pretty much stays with Nick in that there is nothing the viewer sees that Nick does not. As Nick departs on his boat, seen off by the Buchanans, the voiceover returns, and this time Nick mentions Gatsby, the third subject to be judged, and even offers his final word on him—"For Gatsby turned out alright in the end"—the judgment he will render months in the future, thus signaling the retrospective nature of the narration.

The next morning, Nick is shown rising while his voiceover describes the elaborate preparations made for Gatsby's Saturday night parties. Later as Nick eats dinner on his porch, the voiceover describes the party visibly going on next door. In the next scene, the voiceover describes the Valley of Ashes, to which Nick is driven in Tom's car. Except for the dialogue in the dinner scene at the Buchanans, the first 16 minutes of action has been accompanied by Nick's voiceover narration, quoting selected parts of the novel's first and second chapters. After the first 16 minutes, the voiceover appears twice for a sentence or two each time, and then one final time at the very end of the film. The use of voiceover is heavily frontloaded.

The film's second method of transferring the novel's first-person point of view is to translate some of Nick's exposition into dialogue. For example, Jordan tells Nick about Daisy's wedding. In the novel, this long description is presented as an extended paraphrase without quotation marks.

> In June she married Tom Buchanan of Chicago with more pomp and circumstance than Louisville ever knew before. He came down with a hundred people in four private cars, and hired a whole floor of the Muhlbach Hotel, and the day before the wedding he gave her a string of pearls valued at three hundred and fifty thousand dollars. (77)

The film puts part of Nick's second-hand report into dialogue between Daisy and Gatsby.

> GATSBY
> Why did you marry him?
>
> DAISY
> Mr. Tom Buchanan, son of Mr. Tom Buchanan of Chicago, Illinois, blew into my life with more pomp and circumstance than Louisville ever knew before. He came down with a hundred people in four private railroad cars. He hired a whole floor of the Muhlbach Hotel. He just blinded me with excitement.
>
> GATSBY
> He gave you a string of pearls valued at three hundred and fifty thousand dollars.

Similarly, Nick's lengthy catalogue of guests who came to Gatsby's parties is recounted in part by Tom as he enters his first Gatsby party and recognizes different faces. "Oh, look, darling, over there. Cecil Roebuck." At the very end of the book, Henry C. Gatz, Gatsby's father, shows Nick a copy of *Hopalong Cassidy* in which Nick reads Gatsby's "General Resolves." In the film, the father, riding in a car with Nick to the cemetery, reads aloud what his son wrote as a boy.

Despite the voiceovers, the translation of narratorial exposition and analysis into dialogue, and the use of Nick as the focal character, the film fails to transfer the first-person point of view to the screen. After the first 16 minutes of the film, it is fair to say that Nick virtually drops out as narrator, and for one long stretch of the movie he drops out altogether. The camera replaces Nick as the central observer, and we forget we are seeing events through his eyes, events that change him as a character.

Nick's dropping out in the middle of the film creates a logical problem, too. In the book, readers know only what Nick sees directly or is told about or what he reasons from what he knows. But the film audience views scenes involving Daisy and Gatsby's reunion, Tom and Myrtle's affair, and Wilson and Myrtle's domestic disputes where Nick is not present and which, given their private nature, it is unlikely he would be told about. At the end, filmgoers know things *beyond* the logical limits of Nick's first-person perspective.

Miscasting

Another problem with Clayton's adaptation is miscasting. The actors do not fit the characters in the book to the extent that their casting disturbs the story's logical coherence. Let's start with Fitzgerald's complex portrayal of Jay Gatsby. He is described as an "elegant young roughneck," a tough, even thuggish man, involved in illegal activities with Meyer Wolfsheim, the gambler who fixed the 1919 World Series. The rumor that he killed a man is readily believed, perhaps because he has a hoodlum's hard edge. Despite his fabulous wealth, those who belong to the upper class (such as Tom, Sloan, and a pretty woman who visit him on horseback) see instantly that he does not belong; he does not have the manners or the pedigree to be a member of the secret club of the very rich.

In his portrayal of Gatsby, Robert Redford appears too urbane and has trouble showing Gatsby's hard edge. Despite himself, Redford exudes a kind of refinement. As Vincent Canby writes in his review, "he looks so Ivy League it's difficult to believe that he didn't prep at Choate." Coppola cut the scene where the group on horseback rejects Gatsby, but it is hard to imagine that scene working visually because Redford appears smoother than his social betters. Redford's Gatsby does not seem much different from Tom or Nick, who both went to Yale, and does not allow the viewers to see through him as a phony, as someone putting up a front.

The novel reveals another side to Gatsby, one that attracts Nick and forms the basis for their bond of sympathy.

Elegant Robert Redford as Gatsby in *The Great Gatsby* (1974).

> He smiled understandingly—much more than understandingly. It was one of those rare smiles with a quality of eternal reassurance in it, that you may come across four or five times in life. It faced—or seemed to face—the whole external world for an instant, and then concentrated on *you* with an irresistible prejudice in your favor. It understood you just as far as you wanted to be understood, believed in you as you would like to believe in yourself, and assured you that it had precisely the impression of you that, at your best, you hoped to convey. Precisely at that point it vanished—and I was looking at an elegant young rough-neck, a year or two over thirty, whose elaborate formality of speech just missed being absurd. (48)

What Nick finds most engaging in Gatsby is not his wealth nor his mystery, but what he describes as his "heightened sensitivity to the promises of life," his "extraordinary gift for hope, a romantic readiness such as I have never found in any other person." There is a youthful romantic ardor that belongs to Gatsby and that attracts Nick because he shares it to a lesser degree.

If Redford's portrayal of Gatsby lacks hardness, it also lacks flashes of that romantic ardor that drive him over the years to recapture Daisy, his dream princess. Redford seems wooden and overcontrolled. He speaks Gatsby's lines, but we do not sense Gatsby's "romantic readiness" or his underlying passion. Redford succeeds neither as a roughneck nor as a romantic.

Tom Buchanan, Gatsby's rival for Daisy, is described as arrogant and smug, an athlete—"one of the most powerful ends that ever played at New Haven" (6)—a "hulking" man of great physical superiority, who is a wealthy and weak-minded social snob.

> Now he [Tom] was a sturdy straw-haired man of thirty with a rather hard mouth and a supercilious manner. Two shining arrogant eyes had established dominance over his face and gave him the appearance of always leaning aggressively forward. Not even the effeminate swank of his riding clothes could hide the enormous power of that body—he seemed to fill those glistening boots until he strained the top lacing, and you could see a great pack of muscle shifting when his shoulder moved under his thin coat. It was a body capable of enormous leverage—a cruel body. (7)

Bruce Dern captures Tom's arrogance and his sexist and racist blockheaded-ness, but he is physically miscast. Dern does not possess a "cruel body" of "enormous power" or "enormous leverage" with "a great pack of muscle shift-ing" beneath his coat. Sometimes appearing weak or confused, Dern's Tom fails to fit the picture of the handsome, manly, physically powerful All-American. Without those traits, Tom does not seem to be the embodiment of the American Dream, and therefore his portrayal as a decadent philanderer and hypocritical prig does not make as sharp or surprising a contrast.

Fitzgerald's Daisy is beautiful, interesting, and exciting. She's one of Fitzgerald's femme fatales, a woman who mesmerizes men with a promise of excitement and a "voice full of money." Gatsby, Tom, and even Nick see Daisy as a woman to be pursued—the beautiful princess high in a white castle.

In one scene, Nick and Gatsby talk about her.

> "She's got an indiscreet voice," I remarked. "It's full of—" I hesitated.
> "Her voice is full of money," he said suddenly.
> That was it. I'd never understood before. It was full of money—that was the inexhaustible charm that rose and fell in it, the jingle of it, the cymbals' song of it. . . . High in a white palace the king's daughter, the golden girl. (120)

Mia Farrow does not seem to fit the role of Fitzgerald's femme fatale. Farrow plays a vague, odd Daisy who does not seem to know Daisy's secret of charm-ing men. Farrow's sometimes shrill voice suggests neither money nor excite-ment, and her Southern accent sounds fake. Fitzgerald's Daisy is the prize that motivates both Gatsby's exertions to recapture her and Tom's fight to retain her, but Farrow's portrayal of Daisy does not make her seem extraordinary enough to be the cause of all that trouble.

Mia Farrow as Daisy and Robert Redford as Gatsby in *The Great Gatsby.*

Nick describes seeing Myrtle, Tom's mistress, for the first time:

> Then I heard footsteps on a stairs, and in a moment the thickish figure of a woman blocked out the light from the office door. She was in the middle thirties, and faintly stout, but she carried her surplus flesh sensuously as some women can. Her face, above a spotted dress of dark blue crêpe-de-chine, contained no facet or gleam of beauty, but there was an immediately perceptible vitality about her as if the nerves of her body were continually smouldering. (25)

Karen Black is fashionably thin, not a "thickish figure," and has none of Myrtle's "surplus flesh"; she looks younger than Myrtle's mid-thirties; and her face, rather than "contain[ing] no facet or gleam of beauty," is full of it, as the camera makes clear in a number of tight close-ups. Her sexuality is not "smouldering" but overt. She seems a little wired, crazy, flaky. In the novel, Myrtle serves as Daisy's foil. Myrtle is sexually vital, sensuous, and coarse, the woman Tom resorts to in the bleak Valley of the Ashes even though he has the top girl at home. With this casting choice, the film loses the strong contrast between Daisy and Myrtle and the resulting implications about Tom's character.

With all these casting choices, the problem is not that the actors are not faithful to the novel's characterizations, but that the actors' portrayals reshape the roles and disrupt the architecture of the original story.

Cutting and Adding

Other problems with this adaptation have to do with what was cut from and added to the text. The adapter of a long novel is under pressure to cut, but *The Great Gatsby* is a short novel of 182 pages with a clear beginning, middle, and end. However, Coppola's screenplay makes a substantial addition to the story in the form of invented romantic scenes between Daisy and Gatsby inserted between their initial reunion and Gatsby's appearance at the Buchanans' house for luncheon. Perhaps Coppola was merely filling a hole he recognized in the novel.

As Canby writes:

> The novel is so cleverly constructed that one doesn't become overly conscious of everything that's in it, nor of the things left out. Fitzgerald himself acknowledged "a BIG FAULT" of the book. In a letter to Edmund Wilson he wrote:
>
> "I gave no account (and had no feeling or knowledge of) the emotional relations between Gatsby and Daisy from the time of their reunion until the catastrophe."
>
> This hole in the book is filled by exposition in which Nick tells us about Gatsby's early years and about his brief, intense affair with Daisy in Louisville when he was in the Army and about to go overseas. The movie, instead, treats us to shots of Gatsby and Daisy picnicking, holding hands, and behaving like models in soft-focus hair dye commercial. ("They've")

The love sequences, shot in soft focus and inserted in the middle of the film, do provide an answer to what Fitzgerald identified as the novel's "BIG FAULT," but these invented scenes are slow paced, repetitive, conventional, and sentimental. The addition requires cutting some of the biography of Gatsby that is intended to show his social rise from son of shiftless parents to fabulous millionaire. And it also cuts short the portrayal of Nick and Jordan's love affair, reducing the importance of Nick's parallel celebration of the romantic dream and his subsequent disillusionment with it.

Period Emphasis

Fitzgerald was known as the poet of the Jazz Age, and this novel is often praised for its ability to capture the roaring twenties. Likewise, the 1974 adaptation does a superb job of recreating the atmosphere of the mid-1920s with evening gowns and tuxedos, automobiles, wild parties, bootleg gin, flappers doing the Charleston, and popular '20s songs such as "What'll I Do?" or "Every Morning, Every Evening." The film's success in recreating the period visually and musically was recognized when it won its only Oscars for Theoni Aldridge's costume design and Nelson Riddle's nostalgic musical score. However, the adaptation falls among those films mentioned earlier that overemphasize period at the expense of emotion. As Canby writes, "The sets and costumes . . . are exceptionally good, but the movie itself is as lifeless as a body that's been too long at the bottom of a swimming pool" (Review).

Critique of the American Dream

To paraphrase Lionel Trilling, one of our teachers, America is the only country with a dream named after it. And *The Great Gatsby*, as Marius Bewley points out, offers "the most damaging criticism of it in American literature" (287). Fitzgerald evokes and celebrates the American Dream, but he also depicts the social forces that work against it. His theme is disillusionment, but wonderful disillusionment, based on the kind of ecstasy worth losing the world for.

The novel portrays the beauty of Gatsby's incorruptible dream and its inadequacy because it does not take into account human limitations. The dream has enabled Gatsby to make great material progress in life, advancing from poverty to extraordinary wealth, but Gatsby mistakenly believes that same progress can be applied to other areas of life. For example, he believes he and Daisy can repeat the past (even though she has a daughter), that she can honestly deny all the love she ever had for her husband, and that the secret club of the very rich will accept him and his ill-gotten wealth. Gatsby defies limits, and those limits slowly and viciously destroy his dream.

Gatsby's dream is paralleled by others in the novel. The Valley of Ashes, occupied by George and Myrtle Wilson, is the flip side of the American Dream; it is the place where dreams come from. George hopes to buy Tom's car to make a profit and move west to find a better life. Myrtle's dream of grandeur led her to marry George in the first place because she thought he was a gentleman. Ironically, the place everyone is striving to arrive at is already occupied by Tom and Daisy at East Egg, but Fitzgerald shows only unhappiness, corruption, and careless disregard there. Tom, who has everything, hangs out in the Valley of Ashes. And Nick himself is an American dreamer.

> I began to like New York, the racy, adventurous feel of it at night. . . . I liked to walk up Fifth Avenue and pick out romantic women from the crowd and imagine that in a few minutes I was going to enter into their lives. . . . Sometimes, in my mind, I followed them to their apartments on the corners of hidden streets, and they turned and smiled back at me before they faded through a door into warm darkness. At the enchanted metropolitan twilight I felt a haunting loneliness sometimes. (57)

Nick's romantic impulse can be seen in his affair with Jordan Baker, a woman, like Daisy, of beauty and social class.

The critique of the dream comes from the color and subtlety of Nick's musings and judgments on Gatsby's experience and his own. But in mostly eliminating those musings, the movie does not seem able to find any equivalent cinematic way to offer a severe criticism of the dream. Further, the addition of the invented scenes in the middle of the film shifts the Gatsby material toward a standard love story, whereas in the novel that part of the relationship is only suggested, and the emphasis stays focused on the contest between Gatsby's dream and social reality. The reduction of the Carraway-Baker subplot weakens Nick's story as a dreamer who reaches a disillusionment parallel to Gatsby's but lives to grow beyond it. The film is unable to show Redford's urbane

Gatsby as unacceptable to the highest social levels, and both Daisy and Tom do not seem to fit the idealizations of the American Dream well enough to make their corruption such a vivid point.

Clayton, Coppola, and others attempt to make a close-to-intermediate adaptation of Fitzgerald's story, but choices concerning first-person narration, casting, period emphasis, and cutting/adding of narrative elements and thematic interests affect the transposition. In our view, Coppola does not give us Fitzgerald's story, nor does he come up with a coherent narrative on his own.

Summary

Films can fail commercially as well as critically. Film adaptations of literary texts often fail because the text is not cinematic enough to begin with, and/or because of what the adapter decides to do. A cinematic text can be defined as one whose size does not mandate large cuts or additions to fit the feature film, that has a clear storyline, and a few dimensional characters, at least one of whom draws the audience's sympathy and is capable of change. An easy-to-adapt text should not depend for its power on the author's prose style or tone; make extensive use of historical detail, literary allusions, philosophical ideas, abstract meditations, or symbolism; or use the first person or a complex point of view.

An adaptation can falter because it stays too close to the text; distorts the coherence of the literary story through adds, drops, misguided casting, or Hollywoodizing without offering a coherent story of its own; reproduces the historical period at the expense of drama; or fails to find satisfactory equivalents for uncinematic elements such as an authorial presence in the text.

TOPICS FOR DISCUSSION ▪▪▪

1. Choose a literary text you are familiar with and discuss its cinematic possibilities. Explain which parts of the story would be easy to adapt and which would resist translation. What are some of the social, economic, technical, or spectatorial challenges a filmmaker might encounter in adapting the text?

2. Discuss how the casting of star actors in the central roles in a film adaptation may lead to new narrative emphases in the story.

3. Choosing a narrated film, evaluate the extent to which the camera is able to act as a substitute for the first-person narrator of the original material.

4. The critical response to Stanley Kubrick's adaptation *Eyes Wide Shut* was divided. At Metacritics.com, read a sampling of positive and negative reviews and state the main points of the controversy. Explain which side you find most convincing and why.

■■■ WORKS CITED

Axelrod, Mark. "Once Upon a Time in Hollywood; or, The Commodification of Form in the Adaptation of Fictional Texts to the Hollywood Cinema." *Literature/Film Quarterly* 24 (1996): 201–8.

Bercovitch, Sacvan. "*The Scarlet Letter*: A Twice-Told Tale." *Nathaniel Hawthorne Review* 22 (Fall 1996): 1–20.

Bewley, Marius. *The Eccentric Design: Form in the Classic American Novel.* New York: Columbia Univ. Press, 1963.

Canby, Vincent. Review of *The Great Gatsby*, dir. Jack Clayton. *New York Times* 28 March 1974: 32.

———. "They've Turned 'Gatsby' to Goo." Rev. of *The Great Gatsby*, dir. Jack Clayton. *New York Times* 31 March 1974: 11.

Clarens, Carlos. *Crime Movies: An Illustrated History.* New York: W. W. Norton, 1980.

Edelstein, David. "Flat Magic." Rev. of *Harry Potter and the Sorcerer's Stone*, dir. Chris Columbus. *Slate.* 16 November 2001 <http://slate.msn.com/?id=2058739>.

Engel, Joel. *Screenwriters on Screenwriting.* New York: MJF Books, 1995.

Fitzgerald, F. Scott. *The Great Gatsby.* New York: Scribner's, 1925.

Fleischman, Avron. *Narrated Films: Storytelling Situations in Cinema History.* Baltimore: Johns Hopkins University Press, 1992.

French, Philip. "Down the Shoot." Rev. of *Lost in La Mancha*, dir. Keith Fulton and Louis Pepe. *Guardian Unlimited.* 4 August 2002 <http://film.guardian.co.uk/News_Story/Critic_Review/Observer_Film_of_the_week/0,4267,768840,00.html>.

Great Gatsby, The. Dir. Jack Clayton. Perf. Robert Redford, Mia Farrow, and Sam Waterston. Paramount, 1974.

Hoberman, J. "Slack Magic." Rev. of *Harry Potter and the Sorcerer's Stone*, dir. Chris Columbus. *Village Voice* 9 November 2001 <http://www.villagevoice.com/issues/0146/hoberman.php>.

Lane, Anthony. "Deceived: 'Shattered Glass' and 'The Human Stain.' " *New Yorker* 3 November 2003: 104–105.

McFarlane, Brian. *Words and Images: Australian Novels into Film.* Victoria, Australia: Heinemann Publishers, 1983.

Pellow, C. Kenneth. *Films as Critiques of Novels: Transformational Criticism.* Lewiston, New York: Mellen Press, 1994.

Salamon, Julie. *The Devil's Candy: The Anatomy of a Hollywood Fiasco.* Cambridge: Da Capo Press, 2002.

Tibbetts, John C. "So Much Is Lost in Translation: Literary Adaptations in the 1990s." *Film Genre 2000: New Critical Essays.* Ed. Wheeler Winston Dixon. Albany: State University of New York Press, 2000. 29–44.

SELECTED FILMOGRAPHY OF "FAILED" ADAPTATIONS

Any list of "failed" adaptations is highly subjective, so feel free to disagree with the choices below. All the adaptations received mixed to poor reviews at the time of their release. They are offered here as starting points for discussion and writing.

BRIAN ALDISS. "Supertoys Last All Summer Long" (1969).
STEVEN SPIELBERG. *Artificial Intelligence: AI* (2001).

J. M. BARRIE. *Peter Pan* (1904).
STEVEN SPIELBERG. *Hook* (1991).

DAVID BRIN. *The Postman* (1985).
KEVIN COSTNER. *The Postman* (1997).

WILLIAM S. BURROUGHS. *Naked Lunch* (1959).
DAVID CRONENBERG. *Naked Lunch* (1991).

JOSEPH CONRAD. *Heart of Darkness* (1902).
NICOLAS ROEG. *Heart of Darkness* (1994).

MICHAEL CRICHTON. *Congo* (1980).
FRANK MARSHALL. *Congo* (1995).

F. SCOTT FITZGERALD. *The Last Tycoon* (1941).
ELIA KAZAN. *The Last Tycoon* (1976).

JOHN GRISHAM. *Runaway Jury* (1996).
GARY FLEDER. *Runaway Jury* (2003).

MARK HANDLEY. *Idioglossia* (n.d.).
MICHAEL APTED. *Nell* (1994).

NATHANIEL HAWTHORNE. *The Scarlet Letter* (1850).

ROLAND JOFFÉ. *The Scarlet Letter* (1995).

L. RON HUBBARD. *Battlefield Earth: A Saga of the Year 3000* (1982).
ROGER CHRISTIAN. *Battlefield Earth: A Saga of the Year 3000* (2000).

SEBASTIAN JUNGER. *The Perfect Storm* (1997).
WOLFGANG PETERSEN. *The Perfect Storm* (2000).

FRANCES MAYES. *Under the Tuscan Sun* (1996).
AUDREY WELLS. *Under the Tuscan Sun* (2003).

E. ANNIE PROULX. *The Shipping News* (1993).
LASSE HALLSTRÖM. *The Shipping News* (2001).

MARIO PUZO. *The Godfather* (1969).
FRANCIS FORD COPPOLA. *The Godfather: Part III* (1990).

DAVID RABE. *Hurlyburly* (1984).
ANTHONY DRAZEN. *Hurlyburly* (1998).

TIM RICE. *Evita* (1978).
ALAN PARKER. *Evita* (1996).

DR. SEUSS. *The Cat in the Hat* (1957).
BO WELCH. *The Cat in the Hat* (2003).

JEFF SHAARA. *Gods and Generals* (1996).
RONALD F. MAXWELL. *Gods and Generals* (2003).

WILLIAM SHAKESPEARE. *Love's Labour's Lost* (1594).
KENNETH BRANAGH. *Love's Labour's Lost* (UK 2000).

WILLIAM SHAKESPEARE. *The Taming of the Shrew* (1593).

GIL JUNGER. *10 Things I Hate About You* (1999).

JANE SMILEY. *A Thousand Acres* (1991).

JOCELYN MOORHOUSE. *A Thousand Acres* (1997).

BRAM STOKER. *Dracula* (1897).

FRANCIS FORD COPPOLA. *Bram Stoker's Dracula* (1992).

HUNTER S. THOMPSON. *Fear and Loathing in Las Vegas* (1971).

TERRY GILLIAM. *Fear and Loathing in Las Vegas* (1998).

H. G. WELLS. *The Island of Dr. Moreau* (1896).

JOHN FRANKENHEIMER AND RICHARD STANLEY. *The Island of Dr. Moreau* (1996).

TOM WOLFE. *The Bonfire of the Vanities* (1987).

BRIAN DE PALMA. *The Bonfire of the Vanities* (1990).

GLOSSARY

actualités A type of early silent film that captures scenes of everyday life, such as workers leaving a factory; an early term for nonfiction films.

adaptation The transfer of a printed text in a literary genre to film.

added elements Those narrative and cinematic elements not in a work of literature but included in a film adaptation.

ambient sound The background noises in a scene.

animation A type of film in which a figure is positioned, often against a stationary background; a single frame is shot; the figure is then repositioned; another frame is shot; and so on until the figure has completed an action recorded on film or video. Projected, these recorded images produce an apparent motion and depth similar to the apparent motion and depth produced in live-action films.

antagonist A character with whom the main character, called the **protagonist,** is in a major conflict.

auteur The French word for "author." The term refers to the director, who is seen as the main creative force behind a film and who imprints the material with his or her own unique personal style, vision, and thematic preoccupations.

backstory The necessary background exposition for a plot.

camera angle The camera's position in relation to the subject being photographed. There are three main angles: **high angle,** in which the camera looks down on the subject; **straight-on** or **eye-level,** in which the camera looks straight ahead at the subject; and **low angle,** in which the camera looks up at the subject.

camera movement Any motion of the camera that changes the camera's perspective on the subject. Common camera movements include **tilting,** in which the camera head moves upward or downward, thereby scanning the scene vertically; **panning,** in which the camera head moves left or right, thereby scanning the scene horizontally; traveling or **tracking,** in which the camera moves forwards, backwards, or laterally, or moves toward, away, or with the subject; craning, in which the camera is mounted high on a crane and moves in any direction, but often with an ascending or descending motion; canting, or dropping either the left or right side of the frame to make the people and things in the frame appear tilted.

catastrophe See **plot.**

character A personality on paper or in film. The reader or viewer comes to know a character through what she or he looks like, does, says, and thinks, and through the opinions of other characters and/or the narrator. Characters can be

round, possessing the multi-dimensional qualities of actual people, or **flat,** possessing a one-dimensional quality and known by a single idea. Characters can also be divided into **static characters,** who do not change, and **developing characters,** who do.

cinema space Film space is different from the actual space we observe around us in that the camera allows us to see the same subject in the same place from different points of view. The camera can use **long, medium,** and **close-up shots** to vary the viewer's distance; it can use **eye-level, high-angle,** or **low-angle shots** to change the viewer's position; and it can use **tilting, panning,** traveling, or **crane shots** to move the viewer in relation to the action.

cinema time Film time is different from the actual time we experience in that the camera can slow down time using slow motion, speed it up using fast motion, or even stop it using a freeze frame. Editing can also speed up action by cutting quickly from one shot to another. The direction of time can also be changed.

climax See **plot.**

close adaptation When most of the story elements in a work of literature are kept in the film, few elements are dropped, and not many are added. A close adaptation conforms to the literary text.

close-up See **shot.**

comic plot See **plot.**

concentration strategy In this approach, most of the narrative elements from the short story are concentrated either at the beginning, middle, or end of the film and new elements are added to the rest of the film.

condensing A strategy in which a filmmaker compresses or combines story elements in adapting a text.

continuity and coherence A character's action may grow out of a character trait, but if the scene emphasizing that trait is eliminated, then the action may seem unmotivated. After cutting, transitional material may be needed to make the film coherent to the viewer.

continuity editing The assembly of **graphic matches** (two similar shots joined together by the film editor) in such a way as to relate a story clearly, concisely, and with unity and cohesion. Various strategies of editing include **crosscutting,** using alternating shots of at least two strands of action happening in different places at the same time; **establishing shots,** that show in long shots and extreme long shots the characters and the objects in spatial relation to one another within the setting; **eyeline matches,** in which a character in one shot is shown looking in a direction and in the next shot the space toward which the character is looking is shown; **match on action,** in which one shot of an action is replaced by another shot of the same action in the same moment but from a different view, so there appears to be no interruption to the action; and **shot/reverse shot,** in which at least two shots joined together show first one character and then another character talking to each other.

conventions Established ways of doing things in a specific form that are understood by the artist and the audience. For example, a convention in traditional theater is to have the lights go down and the curtain close to signal the end of an act.

costuming The clothing worn by actors. The clothes can be historical or contemporary, suggest the time and place of the action, indicate a character's social status, and contribute to the color scheme of the film.

crane shot See **camera movement.**

crosscutting See **continuity editing.**

cut See **editing.**

cutting A strategy by which a filmmaker eliminates plot elements or characters in adapting a novel.

dead track The total absence of sound in a scene.

denouement See **plot.**

developing character See **character.**

dialogue or **speech** In film, character discourse, spoken by the actors on screen or spoken by the actors off screen. Dialogue conveys background information; expresses the thoughts and feelings of the characters about actions, the behavior of other characters, or features of the setting; and distinguishes each character by language idiom.

diegetic sound Sound that is produced within the screen space.

discourse The expression, the means by which the content of a narrative is communicated.

disjunctive editing A transition device the film editor uses to create a relationship of discontinuity, as opposed to continuity, between two shots in terms of their photographic elements. If the two shots are different, the film editor has created a graphic variance, or disjunction, between the two shots.

dissolve See **editing.**

docudrama or **historical film** Neither a **documentary** nor a fiction film, but a hybrid of these two types. Like a documentary, the film is based on actual people, places, things, and events. Like a fiction film, it is produced with actors rather than actual people, with substituted rather than actual places and things, and with staged rather than actual events. In addition, imaginary characters, places, things, and events can be inserted into the film.

documentary A nonfiction film that shows actual people, places, things, and events. It presents historical and social subjects in a factual and informative way. Some reenactments of the actual events may be shown.

drama Prose or poetic narrative intended to be performed by actors before an audience.

dropped elements Those elements in a work of literature not included in a film adaptation.

editing The twofold job of first choosing the best camera shots taken and then joining these shots together to build a scene, a sequence, and ultimately a completed movie. These joins, or transitions, can take the form of a **fade-in,** in which the beginning of a shot goes gradually from dark to light; a **fade-out,** in which the end of a shot goes gradually from light to dark; a **dissolve,** in which the end of one shot is for a moment superimposed with the beginning of the next shot; a **wipe,** in which the end of one shot appears to be pushed aside by the beginning of the next shot; a **cut,** in which the end of one shot is simply spliced to the beginning of the next shot that immediately replaces it on the screen; or a **jump cut,**

in which one shot is replaced abruptly with another shot that is mismatched in a way that calls attention to the cut and jars the viewer.

episodic plot   See **plot.**

establishing shots   See **continuity editing.**

eye-level   See **camera angle.**

eyeline matches   See **continuity editing.**

exposition   See **plot.**

fade-in   See **editing.**

fade-out   See **editing.**

falling action   See **plot.**

fidelity   The degree to which the film is "faithful" to the text.

film history   Takes as its subject the technological, economic, social, and artistic development of the cinema over time.

film noir   The French words for "black film." The term refers to a specific style of film made in Hollywood during the 1940s and '50s. This style features a sinister, vicious, and violent urban world of vice and crime, populated by base and neurotic characters and emphasizing dreary settings, dark shadows, and high contrasts of light and dark.

first-person point of view   See **point of view.**

flat character   See **character.**

framed narrative   A film that begins in a narrative present, stops, and then backs up to a past narrative that eventually catches up to the narrative present and moves beyond it.

graphic match   See **continuity editing.**

high angle   See **camera angle.**

high-key lighting   See **lighting.**

historical film   See **docudrama.**

interaction strategy   In order to correlate the actual and the re-created in **docudrama** films, filmmakers persuade the viewer of the film's connec-

tions to actuality through one of several possible links between that actuality and its re-creation. One link is for the actual and the recreated to appear simultaneously on screen, as when an actor is filmed while walking at the actual place where the event occurred.

intermediate adaptation   Some narrative elements from the work of literature are kept, others are dropped, and still others are added to the film. An intermediate adaptation neither closely conforms to the literary text nor entirely departs from it.

intertextuality   The view that texts are always related to and dependent upon other texts. Intertextuality calls attention to the fact that texts refer to or cite other texts. Film adaptations are by definition intertextual since they refer to an antecedent text.

interweaving strategy   An approach in which most of the elements of narrative from the short story are retained, dispersed throughout the film although not necessarily in their original order, and new elements or expansions of existing elements are interweaved.

jump cut   See **editing.**

kept elements   Those elements of narrative in a work of literature included in a film **adaptation.**

language of fidelity   Any words used to indicate whether a film adaptation is "faithful" or "unfaithful" to the text.

lighting   The illumination of actors and sets in the production of a film. A lighting director decides whether the light is natural or artificial, the direction it should take, and its intensity. Lighting can direct attention toward major areas of interest. Lighting can be **high key,** in which a scene is brightly lit with shadows kept at a minimum in order to create a buoyant and joyful mood often used in comedies and musicals, or **low key,** in which a scene is dimly lit with a good deal of shadow in order to create a dark, harsh, and somber mood often used in serious drama, mystery, and horror films.

limited-omniscient point of view See **point of view.**

long shot See **shot.**

loose adaptation When most if not all of the narrative elements in the work of literature are dropped from the film, and most elements in the film are added. A loose adaptation uses the literary text as a point of departure.

loudness The volume of sound in a film.

low angle See **camera angle.**

low-key lighting See **lighting.**

macrocosmic application A form of adaptation study in which the whole literary text and the whole film are investigated. It weighs the uneven adapted passages and sequences and determines if the general trend of the adaptation is **close, loose,** or **intermediate.**

magic realism A literary style that seamlessly blends commonplace events of daily life with fantastic elements often derived from dreams, fairy tales, and myths.

makeup The use of cosmetics to enhance or change an actor's natural appearance in a way appropriate to the role she or he is playing. Makeup emphasizes the mobile—and thus meaningful and representative—elements of the actor's face.

match on action See **continuity editing.**

medium shot See **shot.**

microcosmic application A form of adaptation study in which a passage from the literary text and the corresponding sequence from the film are investigated. It determines if the adaptation is **close, loose,** or **intermediate.**

miscasting In the context of adaptation, this means the film actors chosen do not fit the characters in the text to the point of disturbing the story's plausibility and coherence.

mise-en-scéne Basically refers to all elements placed before the camera. These elements include **sets, costumes, lighting, makeup, props,** placement of objects and people, and actors' gestures and movements.

model strategy In this **docudrama** strategy, a film's connections to actuality is established by having actors resemble closely actual people, substituted places and things resemble actual places and things, and staged events resemble actual events.

montage A scene whose visual pattern and emotional effect is attained mainly through the editing of several brief shots.

multitrack medium The communication of information in film through several paths: (1) theatrical performance (live or animated), (2) words (spoken and written), (3) music, (4) sound effects (noise and silence), and (5) photographic images (moving and still).

music Refers to the score composed to establish structural patterns throughout a scene, a sequence, or the entire film and to evoke emotional reactions in the audience.

nondiegetic sound Refers to sound that clearly does not occur within the screen space such as a voiceover or additional sounds of music.

nontraditional plot See **plot.**

novella A short novel or a long short story, but whatever reference point is used, there is general agreement that its length falls somewhere in between.

objective or **dramatic point of view** See **point of view.**

omniscient narrator See **point of view.**

opening up Refers to a number of techniques developed by adapters to transpose the **story** from stage to screen **conventions,** such as filming settings, scenes, and characters only suggested or implied in the drama, visualizing symbols, and using camera work and **editing** to move the story into **cinema time** and **space.**

pan shot or **panning** See **camera movement.**

period emphasis Stress on re-creating a historical era in detail through use of such things as costumes, manners, music, and sets.

personification Consists in giving the attributes of a human being to an animal, an object, or a concept.

pitch The high or low quality of a sound. Like **loudness,** constantly being modulated during the film.

plot A structural device that enables the author and screenwriter to maintain causal links while presenting events outside the constraints of chronological order. For example, an author or adapter need not start at the beginning of the story with the first event but can begin *in medias res* (in the middle of things) and then flash back to show past events that led up to the present or flash forward to indicate future consequences. A screenwriter may also decide to rearrange events so that the source's ending becomes the film's beginning. These changes in chronological order are often made to elicit emotional reactions such as surprise or suspense or an impending sense of doom.

Plot is usually divided into three parts following Aristotle's *The Poetics:* a beginning, a middle, and an end. Some critics use Gustav Freytag's expanded definition of Aristotle's tripartite structure: **exposition, rising action, climax, falling action,** and **catastrophe.** (The last term is also called **resolution** or **denouement.**) The exposition or introduction establishes the place and time of the action, introduces the character or characters, gives any necessary background information, and establishes the mood or tone of the story. The rising action introduces a conflict, or complication, that intensifies the original situation and moves towards a major turning point or climax. The downward or falling action shows events going from bad to worse, leading to some final reversal of fortune for the protagonist.

Other forms of plot are not dominated by cause and effect. A **nontraditional plot** may present events in nonlinear sequence, use coincidence rather than causality to link events, and leave the resolution indeterminate or open-ended. Some stories consist of a series of episodes, called an **episodic plot,** that are loosely related by the presence of a hero, a specific location, a theme, or a historical event. Plots are sometimes distinguished by their mood and outcome. **Comic plots** usually end with a happy event such as marriage; **tragic plots** may end with the protagonist's isolation and death. **Subplots** are minor or subordinate actions often used to contribute interest and action to the main plot.

Some critics identify character instead of plot as the defining feature of narrative. In this view, plot is a framework of actions that focuses attention on character. The character's desires, motives, or goals lead to action. However, when someone claims a story is more character-driven than plot-driven, keep in mind that character and action are often so intertwined that it is difficult to distinguish between the two. In sophisticated narratives, action grows out of character and character grows out of action.

point-of-departure strategy An approach in which most of the narrative elements from the short story are **dropped,** except, for example, the plot premise, a character's name, or just the title, and these rudiments are used as a point of departure.

point of view The vantage point from which a narrative is presented. Discussion of point of view includes in what person and tense the narrator speaks, in what time and place the narrator speaks, and what attitudes the narrator brings to the story. Point of view can be **first person,** in which the narrator of the story refers to himself or herself as "I" and is a major or minor participant in the story or merely a witness; **objective** or **dramatic point of view,** in which the narrator uses the third person and is limited to recounting what characters say or do and does not interpret characters or actions or tell us what characters think or feel; **omniscient point of**

view, in which the narrator is all-knowing and whose knowledge of characters and events is not restricted by time, place, or character; and third-person single-character point of view, in which the narrator's knowledge is confined to what is seen, thought, felt, and remembered by a single character.

production determinants Those things that have nothing to do with the text but may be powerfully influential in changing aspects of the adaptation.

props Any objects employed on a set. These objects can be a stationary part of the set such as a table or a chair or moveable physical items like a book or a gun.

protagonist A specific character who is the main focus of a story.

rearrangement A reordering of events from a text for any number of reasons—to build suspense, to create clearer causality, or to fit the demands of a movie genre.

resolution See **plot.**

rising action See **plot.**

round character See **character.**

saturated color Intensified color.

sequence A fairly large section of a film featuring a whole action.

sequence strategy An approach designed to correlate the actual and the re-created in a **docudrama.** Here footage of actual people, places, things, and events are inserted into the film either before or after footage of actors, substituted places and things, or staged events.

sets Artificially constructed or actual places used as background for actions. They are the physical space shown by the camera in which the actors move.

setting The place, the time, and the social milieu in which the characters live and act.

shot   The basic unit of film. The shot is a single, continuous run of the camera that records an uninterrupted action that viewers see on the screen. Shots are generally divided into four types according to how much of the human figure is shown: **long shot,** a shot that shows the full human figure of a character or characters within an environment; **medium shot,** a shot that shows a character from the knee up within part of the setting; **close-up,** a shot that shows the full head and shoulders of a character or an object in detail; and extreme close-up, a shot that shows a detail of the head of a character or of an object.

shot/reverse shot   See **continuity editing.**

silence or **dead track**   The total absence of sound in a scene.

sound   The **dialogue, music, sound effects,** and **silence** heard in films.

sound effects   Noises made by people and objects situated within the scene shown on screen.

static character   See **character.**

story   Refers to the characters, settings, and happenings in a narrative.

straight-on or **eye-level**   See **camera angle.**

subjective camera   A camera that limits itself to shots of what one character sees.

subplot   See **plot.**

substitution   An element from a text that is replaced by something else in a film that is reasonably similar. A substitution counts as a **kept element.**

symbol   A representation in a text of something that is itself but also represents something else, often an idea or an attitude. Symbols refer to something in the material world but also suggest some more abstract meaning.

theme   The main idea, or the central generalization, implied or stated in a work.

tilt shot or **tilting**   See **camera movement.**

timbre   The tone of a musical score. It is often used to evoke emotion in an audience during a scene.

tracking shot   See **camera movement.**

tragic plot   See **plot.**

truncating   A strategy for shortening a scene by showing only a slice of it to suggest the whole.

voiceover narration   Dialogue or speech spoken by actors off screen.

wipe   See **editing.**

FURTHER READING on Film Adaptation

ANDREW, DUDLEY. *Concepts in Film Theory.* New York: Oxford University Press, 1984.

BEJA, MORRIS. *Film and Literature: An Introduction.* New York: Longman, 1979.

BLUESTONE, GEORGE. *Novels into Films.* Berkeley: University of California Press, 1957.

BORDWELL, DAVID. *Narration in the Fiction Film.* Madison: University of Wisconsin Press, 1989.

BORDWELL, DAVID, ET AL. *The Classical Hollywood Cinema.* New York: Columbia University Press, 1985.

BOYUM, JOY GOULD. *Double Exposure: Fiction into Film.* New York: Universe Books, 1985.

BUHLER, STEPHEN M. *Shakespeare in the Cinema: Ocular Proof.* Albany: State University of New York Press, 2002.

CARTMELL, DEBORAH, AND IMELDA WHELEHAN, EDS. *Adaptations: From Text to Screen, Screen to Text.* London: Routledge, 1999.

CHATMAN, SEYMOUR. *Coming to Terms: The Rhetoric of Narrative in Fiction and Film.* Ithaca: Cornell University Press, 1990.

————. *Story and Discourse: Narrative Structure in Fiction and Film.* Ithaca: Cornell University Press, 1978.

ELLIOTT, KAMILLA. *Rethinking the Novel/Film Debate.* Cambridge: Cambridge University Press, 2003.

FLEISCHMAN, AVROM. *Narrated Films: Storytelling Situations in Cinema History.* Baltimore: Johns Hopkins University Press, 1992.

GIDDINGS, ROBERT, AND ERICA SHEEN. *The Classic Novel: From Page to Screen.* New York: St. Martin's Press, 2000.

————, et al. *Screening the Novel: The Theory and Practice of Literary Dramatization.* New York: St. Martin's Press, 1990.

GRIFFITH, JAMES J. *Adaptations as Imitations.* Cranbury: University of Delaware Press, 1997.

HORTON, ANDREW, AND JOAN MAGRETTA. *Modern European Filmmakers and the Art of Adaptation.* New York: Frederick Ungar, 1981.

KLEIN, MICHAEL, AND GILLIAN PARKER, EDS. *The English Novel and the Movies.* New York: Frederick Ungar, 1981.

LUPACK, BARBARA TEPA, ED. *Nineteenth Century Women at the Movies: Adapting Classic Women's Fiction to Film.* Bowling Green, OH: Bowling Green State University Popular Press, 1999.

MANVELL, ROGER. *Theater and Film.* Madison, NJ: Farleigh Dickinson Press, 1979.

MARCUS, FRED H. *Film and Literature: Contrasts in Media.* Scranton, PA: Chandler, 1971.

McFARLANE, BRIAN. *Novel to Film: An Introduction to the Theory of Adaptation.* Oxford: Oxford University Press, 1996.

———. *Words and Images: Australian Novels into Film.* Victoria, Australia: Heinemann, 1983.

MORRISSETTE, BRUCE. *Novel and Film: Essays in Two Genres.* Chicago: University of Chicago Press, 1985.

NAREMORE, JAMES, ED. *Film Adaptation.* New Brunswick, NJ: Rutgers University Press, 2000.

ORR, JOHN, AND COLIN NICHOLSON, EDS. *Cinema and Fiction: New Modes of Adapting 1950–1990.* Edinburgh: Edinburgh University Press, 1992.

PELLOW, C. KENNETH. *Films as Critiques of Novels: Transformational Criticism.* Lewiston, NY: Mellen Press, 1994.

REYNOLDS, PETER, ED. *Novel Images: Literature in Performance.* London: Routledge, 1993.

SINYARD, NEIL. *Filming Literature: The Art of Screen Adaptation.* New York: St. Martin's Press, 1986.

WAGNER, GEOFFREY. *The Novel and the Cinema.* Cranbury, NJ: Associated University Presses, 1975.

Some **INTERNET SITES**

Here are a number of starting points for doing research on film adaptations on the Internet. Since Web sites are sometimes moved or discontinued, we can't always guarantee the accuracy of the addresses.

Internet Movie Database

www.imdb.com
Internet Movie Database (IMDB) is an excellent resource for information on film adaptations. It identifies the text the film is based on and the screenwriter, provides a list of cast and crew, and offers links to movie reviews.

Film Reviews

www.mrqe.com/lookup
The Movie Review Query Engine links to over 35,000 reviews from various print and Internet sources. This is the place to start when you want online reviews of older films.

www.critics.com
This is a good site if you are interested in reviews of more recent films. For every film, there are links to fifteen reviews published in various media in the United States. Through its selection of reviews, the site attempts to offer "a national critical consensus" on the success of a film.

www.metacritic.com
This site summarizes movie reviews with links to entire reviews. It assigns a score of 0–100 to each review and averages the numbers into a metascore that suggests how well the film is reviewed overall and how it compares to other films reviewed.

rogerebert.suntimes.com
This site offers all of Roger Ebert's film reviews from the *Chicago Sun Times* since 1985.

Book Reviews

www.nytimes.com/pages/books
The New York Times offers free book reviews back to 1996. Fees are charged for reviews published before 1995.

www.amazon.com
This site will help you locate a text (and its film adaptation in VHS or DVD format). For texts, it supplies publication information and gives excerpted reviews from *Library Journal* and *Publishers Weekly*.

www.nybooks.com
Offers current reviews from the *New York Review of Books* for free. Archive reviews go back to 1963.

acqweb.library.vanderbilt.edu
This is a directory that links to numerous book reviews on the Web.

Film Scripts

www.script-o-rama.com
Drew's Script-O-Rama offers film scripts and transcripts of films.

www.movie-page.com/movie_scripts.htm
Free scripts for educational purposes.

Box Office Information

www.boxofficeguru.com

www.the-numbers.com/index.php
Box Office Guru and The Numbers offer regularly updated budget and box office data.

Glossaries

www.glossarist.com
This site offers links to dictionaries and glossaries of film, video, and literary terms.

Lists and Gateway Sites

www.lib.berkeley.edu/MRC/litbib.html
A bibliography of books and articles on the subject of adaptation, lists of authors and their adapted works, and links to film reviews. One link explains how to document film sources. Sponsored by UC Berkeley.

www.gethelp.library.upenn.edu/guides/film/film.html
An extensive bibliography of resources useful for doing research on film. Sponsored by the University of Pennsylvania.

www.library.ucla.edu/librarles/arts/websltes/wwwmov.htm
Links to film sites, databases, and directories. Sponsored by UCLA.

digital-librarian.com/movies.html
An extensive list of Web sites relevant to film study.

afi.cinemedia.org
Cinemedia is a film and media directory that provides more than 25,000 links.

www.cinema-sites.com
Links to many excellent film sites.

www.mith2.umd.edu/WomensStudies/FilmReviews
A collection of film reviews as part of the University of Maryland's Women's Studies Database.

www.people.virginia.edu/~pm9k/libsci/womFilm.html
A reference guide to women in cinema. Sponsored by the University of Virginia.

www.indiana.edu/~bfca/index.html
An archive and resources for studying African-American films. Sponsored by Indiana University.

www.lavavideo.org
This archive offers a place to search for Latin American and U.S. Latino-made films and videos.

www.planetout.com/pno/popcornq
Gay and lesbian oriented film reviews.

fii.chadwyck.co.uk
Film Index International offers detailed information on international films. Registration required.

Silent Films

Edison Motion Pictures
www.memory.loc.gov/ammem/edhtml/edmvhm.html
This page is part of the Library of Congress' American Memory Project and offers information on American silent films as well as silent films for viewing.

www.silentsmajority.com
An online journal of silent films.

Screen Musicals

www.classicmoviemusicals.com
This site offers basic information on classic film musicals. It has summaries, credits, awards, songs, and information on the availability of a screen musical in various formats.

www.filmmusic.com
Information on movie soundtracks.

Animation

www.awn.com
News on animated films and links to relevant Web sites.

Other Sites

www.pbs.org/wgbh/masterpiece
Masterpiece Theatre Online offers learning resources for the study of adaptation.
For example, several scenes from Henry James's *The American* are made available
in four different versions: the novel, James's play, the script, and the film.

www.filmsite.org
Elaborately detailed summaries of landmarks in classic/Hollywood American
films.

www.allmovie.com
A film database with information similar to IMDB.

www.learner.org/exhibits/cinema
Offers a tutorial on how Hollywood films are made.

www.afi.com
The American Film Institute offers film news, information on film
preservation, and the AFI Catalog of Feature Films, which contains
information on American films produced from 1893 to 1950 and 1961 to 1970.
AFI membership is required.

www.oscars.org/awardsdatabase/index.html
Lists of Academy Award winners and nominees.

TEXT CREDITS

HAMMETT, DASHIELL. *The Maltese Falcon*. New York: Vintage, 1992. 3–10.
NOLAN, JONATHAN. "Memento Mori." *Esquire* 135 (March 2001): 186+. <http://www.esquire.com/features/articles/2001/001323_mfr_memento_1.html>.
POE, EDGAR ALLAN. "The Raven." < http://www.ibiblio.org/gutenberg/etext97/1epoe10h.htm#1>.

PHOTO CREDITS

INDEX